THE TESTAMENT OF STONE

THEMES OF

IDEALISM AND INDIGNATION

FROM THE WRITINGS OF

LOUIS SULLIVAN

THE TESTAMENT OF STONE

Edited, with an Introduction, by MAURICE ENGLISH

NORTHWESTERN UNIVERSITY PRESS · 1963

the Editor's share in this volume is dedicated to

Fanita, Brian, and Deirdre

'the opening of the eyelids of the world is what democracy is about'

ACKNOWLEDGMENTS

My thanks are due to Miss Ruth Schoneman and the staff of the Burnham Library of the Art Institute of Chicago, for making available the mass of writings by and about Sullivan there collected, from which this selection has been made. Particular thanks are due for permission to present in book form for the first time: "The Modern Phase in Architecture"; "An Unaffected School of Modern Architecture — Will It Come?"; "The *Chicago Tribune* Competition"; "Reflections on the Tokyo Disaster"; and selections from "Natural Thinking." The original form in which these pieces have been published, if at all, is specified in the headnotes.

Thanks are due also to Wayne State University Press, and to Miss Elaine Hedges, for permission to reprint passages from the volume edited by her, *Democracy: A Man-Search* by Sullivan.

The ornamental drawings in the book were ably done by Miss Elizabeth G. Stout, who adapted her designs from details of the Chicago Stock Exchange elevator grillwork, the Getty Tomb in Chicago, and the Wainwright Building in St. Louis. The University of Minnesota Press, publisher of John Szarkowski's *The Idea of Louis Sullivan* (copyright 1956 by the University of Minnesota), and the Northwestern University Department of Art were helpful in providing source material for the drawings.

CONTENTS

INTRODUCTION

Therefore the art of developing Democracy into a complete, complex yet simple working civilization is the one great art of expression confronting men today. It is the one art including all arts, all activities, individual and collective. It is in the development of the technique of such art that modern man is to concentrate his thought, bend his faculties, and exercise his superb powers as creator.

Louis Henri Sullivan (1856-1924), the Chicago architect who is generally regarded as the main source of modern architecture, composed during his lifetime a number of books, magazine articles, lectures, and poems in prose. Some of these are intimately related to his career as an architect; others are the expression of his alternative career, also abortive, as a philosopher and prophet of democracy.

These writings range from book-length manuscripts to brief talks and letters-to-the-editor, a thousand words or so in length. Some have never been printed, but remain in manuscript in the Burnham Library of the Art Institute of Chicago; others have not been put into book form, but can be found in old issues of architectural and building-trade magazines.

The reasons for now publishing a selection of these neglected works are several. There is a revival of interest in Sullivan's work and thinking, and this revival is likely to continue. But among his writings, some of the most detailed in expounding his thoughts on democracy, education, and other social and philosophical subjects, are the hardest to come by. For example, the highly characteristic "Natural Thinking: A Study In Democracy" remains — except for sections included in this volume — in manuscript. His comments on the Imperial Hotel, built in Tokyo by his former chief draftsman Frank Lloyd Wright, and on the *Chicago Tribune* architectural competition, are in 1923 and 1924 issues of an architectural journal.

These writings are of varying importance to Sullivan's career and convictions as an architect; they all, however, have much to say on the larger issues of democracy, education, man's destiny in America and in the Cosmos. This volume of selections is explicitly focussed on Sullivan the social thinker and prophet. So true is this that his finest single piece of writing, "The Tall Office Building Artistically Considered," is not included in these pages; it says little on the great themes he considered when he was not dealing with the art of building. One can read this architect as an American process philosopher, although he scorned "mere philosophers."

In assessing the value of a Sullivan anthology, it is important to bear in mind his own attitude toward his writings.

Sullivan regarded himself, and was regarded by his associates, as "essentially a poet" (in his attitude toward life, and his general style of personality, as well as in architecture); and he considered himself as having a vocation not only as an architect, but also as bard, seer, and prophet. Thus, while his first known piece of writing deals with "Characteristics and Tendencies of American Architecture" (1885), he followed it only a year later with a prose poem, a celebration of nature and an anticipation of a great American flowering of art, which relates to his view of the universe, and to the role of the individual in society, as much as it does to architecture.

Seeing himself as another Whitman, Sullivan recognized that a later counterpart of that poet needed some systematization of ideas about how democracy was to develop in the raging noondays of industrial capitalism. He tried to work out such a system from his one fruitful insight concerning form and function, applied it brilliantly to architecture, and then spent many of his years as an out-of-work architect, in passionately exploring its relevance to wide aspects of human and natural life. He fed his mind for this purpose with the works of many seminal thinkers ranging from Nietzsche through Spencer to William James, as well as with popularizations of the science and sociology of his period.

His writings on democracy hold our interest because of his ability to grasp its social and aesthetic values, and to relate these to one another; because of the intensity with which he was able to feel and express certain philosophical and Messianic convictions; because of his insistence on the value of the individual, indeed of the poet, rather than the mass, as the bearer and creator of culture in a democracy.

Sullivan's literary style ranges from the sentimentally poetic through the forcefully expository (most of all when he focuses on architecture) to the jarringly crude and gauche. He has considerable power of invective, but it often degenerates into sheer nagging and scolding. In his middle and later years rage at his own frustrations, and a sense of the degeneration of American democracy, had an obsessive effect on Sullivan; page after waste page of jeering or snarling rhetoric benumb or alienate the most sympathetic of readers.

But at their purest and most disinterested, his indignation and idealism are valuable, never more so than today. It is necessary to rescue Sullivan from himself, in order to appreciate him as a writer and thinker. Once this is done, a very specific, though incomplete, portrait of a man emerges from his pages; the poignant figure of the American artist at death-grips with the society in which he lived.

The fate of the artist in this country was never more dramatically illustrated than in Sullivan's career. Unlike others who led lives of equal or greater pathos — Poe or Hart Crane for instance — his tragedy was the result not of sheer alienation, but of a head-on confrontation with industrial capitalism in its most rampant and voracious form. This confrontation, in which his success and failure were both almost total, is a live issue in almost all of Sullivan's writings, and gives them all an extra dimension and meaning.

A man of fixed conviction, Sullivan did not yield to the hostility and indifference of his environment, to its wastage of his genius as a builder, without trying to take its measure as a searching social critic, and without opposing its murk and violence with his vision of an ideal democracy to come. He rejected both the materialism of his day and the bleak prospects for man summarized in the doctrine of the survival of the fittest: he wrote as someone fighting for a more humane future for the race.

This Reader has been selected, then, not to illustrate Sullivan the architect, or the prophet of modern architecture, but Sullivan as Jeremiah, and also as the herald of a time when New York and Chicago might be rebuilt in the image of the City of Man. In this latter role, he attempted as a writer (no less than he had as an architect) to be the catalyst from which the Western traditions of the classic and the romantic would be merged into a new "organic" synthesis: the art — and social order — of democracy.

II

The word "romantic" occurs frequently in the writings of Sullivan, always with the conventional implications of rich and exalted feeling, exotic beauty, magic, and mystery. Taking the word with these connotations, Sullivan used it purposefully, and not in a loose, sentimental way. "Romantic" was a value for Sullivan, and fitted into a hierarchy of values, in architecture and in his general philosophy.

He was perhaps unaware of another way of using the word "romantic," which can shed light on his life and work, and his unfulfilled careers as architect and thinker—and also on the environment in which he worked and from which he struggled to draw and demonstrate an order, both aesthetic and social.

The textbooks tell us that classicism involves ideals of proportion, control, objectivity. Scholars who have examined the concept with a sense of history, are able to add something to our understanding by locating it in a social context. The classic work of art, they tell us, is the product of a culture with a high degree of unity: a culture where state and religion are identified with each other in a way which expresses, and does not suffocate, the aspirations of the individual; where the individual feels himself a citizen not in any abstract or partial way, but intimately, unselfconsciously, daily: being a citizen involves his attitude toward his gods, his economic role as a guildsman or merchant or priest, his performance as an athlete in the sacred festivals, his going to the theater, all his actions, in fact, throughout his life. Assume such a community to have the wealth and security, plus the stimulus from outside and in, which foster curiosity and an ardent approach toward the understanding and celebration of life, and you have — we are told — Athens and Florence and lesser metropolises whose art has briefly approximated that equilibrium called the classic.

This equilibrium is not only brief, but imperfect, because life is imperfect, and because, too, art is equally a repudiation of the static, the balanced, the temperate in life — as well as an attempt to recreate these elements on some ideal level of being. It is a plausible guess that the classic has never been able to achieve expression without an impulse of revolt, of hostility toward archon, syndic and priest, of flight and quest: without the romantic impulse.

Until modern times, men have had no choice except to maintain social equilibrium as best they could, and when it broke down, to reconstitute it, over laborious centuries if need was, with brutal speed whenever possible. Men fled to cities from nature as from an enemy, from their own instincts as from other enemies: until a few centuries ago, some sources of the "romantic" were too disturbing, too suspect, to be distinguished and identified — much less juxtaposed against the concept "classic" as implying a different but defensible set of values.

It is an accepted aspect of the uniqueness of our society, that the past order of civilization broke down, and in considerable measure disappeared, so irrecoverably that no one now can seriously expect to achieve the "classic" in art or in social order, as that term has been understood in past centuries. "Whirl is king, having driven out Zeus" and the task is to replace the old, external orders of society with a new one drawn from man's knowledge of the external universe, and of himself.

Where this knowledge exists only partially or not at all — in the realm of art — the romantic attitude is an almost necessary one for the individual beginner as well as for the community which is setting out — that common task in our time — to fashion its culture anew. Assume a society in which consensus, dogma, and unwritten constitutions not only guided men in all their acts, but did so in a way that gave meaning and order to their lives (or at a minimum, provided a point of departure for the revision of accepted meanings and values) : in such a society, that intense expression of human aspiration which we call classic art could recur at favored intervals. Assume a world from which these are banished, and artist and thinker alike must undertake not a struggle but a hunt, or rather a quest. The student of physical sciences may be exempted from this rule, but not — up to this point in the modern centuries — the student of human behavior, the artist, the poet, and that significant figure of recent epochs, the speculative prophet, the unaffiliated Messiah.

From this point of view, Goethe's statement: "classicism is health, romanticism is disease" is not necessarily wrong, but it is not illuminating. Dante in his time could control the romantic impulse which animated his travels through the afterlife, by subordinating it to the dominant myth of his age; Shakespeare could perform the feat of combining the classic confrontation — the duel, the face-to-face combat — with the romantic theme of the chase or search, each expressed with a maximum of intensity, yet neither overwhelming the other; but with Milton the balance is already upset: a romantic hero pursues God in that quest for power which is the poem's secret obsession. It had become increasingly difficult for the classic not to emerge as frigid or artificial, a mask; or not to break into romantic or realistic modes of seeing life.

The fate of the man who persists in seeing life romantically, as Shaw said, is despair. The artist who necessarily starts from his position as an isolate in the city, the state, the universe — therefore, from the recognition of his isolation from himself — must attempt to reconcile his position with some possibility of order in society and in the universe. He cannot really change his position as an isolate, given the nature of our society and what we think we know of our universe; therefore he cannot fully mature into any parallel to a "classic" artist. But unless he is willing to settle down in the half-way house of realism, or in that polishing of techniques and fragments called aestheticism, he can live and die trying.

III

Although Louis Sullivan said he valued only universal truths — "generalizations so broad as to admit of no exception whatever" — we may defiantly suspect that the spirit is often most alive in those crucial exceptions that invariably rise to demolish even the broadest generalizations, and thereby goad us on toward some more complex grasp of reality. It has been fruitful to consider here the dichotomy scholars have established between the classic and romantic; but one cannot do so for very long, without being struck by the massive exception that architecture offers.

To an extent unique among the arts, architecture is married to its social functions, and cannot come into being apart from them. A poem, a play, a piece of music, can be created in solitude and left to find an audience or not: but buildings are built exclusively in relation to people and in order to fulfill functions which society, and not the artist, stipulates. And these functions are utilitarian.

Architecture is the fine art which is firmly grounded in the routines of daily life; which depends, to exist, on needs which have nothing to do with aesthetic or spiritual values in the first instance. For this reason, the architect is the only artist who is not in control of the materials of his art. He creates not with paper and pencil, or in just space enough to dance or declaim, or with a fistful of clay or metal, but with substantial quantities of expensive materials, for which he is beholden to others.

The extent to which a romantic architect like Gaudi is an isolate in his own art is illuminating. Not more revolutionary or original than Whitman or Gauguin, he yet stands companionless and without progeny in the history of architecture, as they do not in the history of poetry and painting. Society's demands are strong enough to make the romantic architect a rarity because they make him almost a contradiction in terms.

Taken in reverse, this thesis is a pregnant one: architecture is permanently allied to those aspects of culture which are most social and most susceptible of objective measure and control. It is, therefore, the closest of the arts to the conditions which, in the past, have proved to be essential to the creation of "the classic." In modern times, its wedding to science and technology has proven, on the whole, easy and intimate after a hesistant courtship. For decades, architecture has been able to live without the clumsy seductions and quarrelsome concubinage through which music, painting, and poetry have sought to come to terms with the primary forces of modern culture.

In principle, therefore, architecture would seem to have been in possession of those prerequisites needed to lead the other arts, in this century, toward a new articulation of human experience, a new celebration of our common humanity. The movement from romantic quest toward some organic form which would be the contemporary re-creation of the classic seemed an almost inevitable one for architecture to take, even before this century began.

It was with superb endowments to demonstrate this, and with full consciousness of his inaugural role in American culture, that Sullivan lived out his life in Chicago—for fifteen years an acknowledged master-builder; for another twenty-five, still acknowledged but rarely employed, he survived as an impoverished scold, a flawed Messiah whom his fellow-citizens maddeningly ignored. His life, in its success and failure, was a test of the basic premises of American democracy in this century; his writings, an attempt to state where that democracy had failed, but also to see beyond that failure and assert the conditions under which its potential might yet be realized.

It is fashionable to emphasize the crudity of Chicago when Sullivan first came to the city. Since that crudity, while taking new forms, has only slightly abated, the theme can easily be rephrased, with new and old illustrations. But the poignancy of Sullivan's destiny in Chicago is most keenly felt if one sees not only the mud, the slaughterhouses, the plutocracy, the brutality and graft, but the fact that concurrently with all these, the city for a brief decade or two offered some of its choicest spirits a superb illusion, that of having established the conditions needed to revive the civic unity of belief and enterprise from which a classic symmetry had formerly come.

Does this seem too preposterous a fantasy? It did at the time, to many intellectuals in the city, as its does today. Nevertheless, it is impossible to read the writings of Sullivan's youth, and those of some of his contemporaries, without being struck by their common expectation not only of the emergence of a new style of building, but of a style which would be a reflection of a new country, of a new democratic spirit, and which would meet the utilitarian needs of the community in a way which would somehow celebrate also its ideals and triumphs.

Sullivan's own writings begin with a confident, lyrical assertion that this would surely happen: a prediction of that organic architecture which would be, literally, one expressive organ of a happy and fecund democracy. These writings go on then to brilliant demonstrations of how, and in what forms, that architecture would manifest itself. They continue with an urgent demand that the new buildings, now long overdue, should in fact arise. But the tone darkens and becomes exasperated; the awaited birth becomes the occasion first of a search, then of an autopsy; stridently, insistently, the writings pass into a decades-long examination of why the birth was aborted, why the phoenix never rose in flame from the shore of Lake Michigan.

What, Sullivan went on asking, would be needed to make the metamorphosis possible? — and the question led him, following his inspired original intuition about form and function, to locate architecture and all the arts in the center of a religious view of democracy: (That religious view of democracy, in turn, Sullivan set in a holistic view of the universe, a universe which he felt as alive, and as a unity — "the Universe and all therein may be expressed by the word Ego"—). Few men have felt and expressed that religious sense of democracy with Sullivan's naked directness — and fewer yet have had the courage and passion to test the daily comings and goings of all of us, by the standards of that faith. Sullivan does this, in his writings, with an urgency and insistence that is immeasurably presumptuous and admirable.

These convictions of Sullivan's in fact have roots in an intellectual event of long duration and momentous importance in the history of Western man. To understand the nature of that event, it is necessary to take an even bolder view of the concept "romantic" than that expressed earlier in these pages: to see it, in fact, first as part of the animating spirit in Christianity, the hope which inspired the marvellous quest of the Christian centuries for an ideal life in a supernatural city, and to see it, thereafter, as the impulse which in modern times has worked toward the secularization of that quest, its transformation into the conviction that the ideal city could be built here and now, in Chicago, where the onion swamp had been, and the cattle-runs were crowded. Sullivan was explicit about this: "If these elements are to be robbed of their divinity," he wrote, "let them at least become truly human." But he was rashly insistent that this must happen soon.

IV

Unhappily for this intransigent man, the role which history assigned the United States in the development of democracy, during the last century and so far in this one, has proved not to be the role which he (in the tradition of Jefferson, Emerson, and Whitman) assumed it was in his youth and insisted it ought to be in his later years: that of creating an ideal community, the democracy of the highest common denominator, a forcing-house where the uniqueness of the individual — happily responsive to his fellows — might be refined into such a burst of creativity as Athens and Florence never knew.

How immeasurably naive this dream appears, especially as dreamed in the murk of that Chicago of half a century ago, now that we see it in the decades which shape a pause between the Second World War and its sequels. But this, in itself, is reason enough for reading Sullivan: his world-view, unquenchably optimistic in the teeth of his personal failure and his society's betrayal of itself, is eager, fresh, and bracing. No one speaks like him today.

The function of American democracy, we know now, has been to demonstrate that a large segment of the human race could, in the new world born out of the Renaissance and the Age of Reason, achieve material well-being and, however imperfectly, govern itself: a feat never accomplished in the past by any nation at all, for all its citizens, and still being imperfectly achieved on this continent.

And if one large segment of the human race, then — why not? — all of it.

But this demonstration has meant the sacrifice, on what a stupendous scale!, of every form of excellence to any form of abundance:

it has not been essential, during the run of the experiment, that the cloth be of the finest weave or cut, the buildings very commodious or durable; it has been enough that the son of the peasant, the grandson of the serf, the immigrants from the Rain Forest and the Stone Age, should have some prospect of possessing, themselves, clothes and homes of their own. More than a prospect: the immediate function of America has been to glut us, the multitude, with material goods. In the first place, to assuage an immemorial hunger; in the second, to let us discover the limits of appetite.

Experiments of this sort change their own conditions and the nature of all the participants: those most removed from the hungers of the multitudes in America have been affected by their participation in the assuaging of those hungers. The bleak fascination of Chicago as a city, for anyone who feels it at all, is partly the fact that it was a major laboratory of this experiment, the democracy of the lowest common denominator. By the time of the Chicago fire, (Sullivan moved to the city a year later), of its 334,270 inhabitants, more than 249,536 were immigrants, 62% of whom spoke a foreign language. While a few men like Sullivan envisaged a future American society in terms of Pericles' speech to the Athenians, the dispossessed of all Europe, newly enfranchised, bankrupt, hungry, and unlettered, were arrived by the hundreds of thousands. They were uttering those cries for bread and circuses which have been one voice of democracy in our time, while Sullivan was conceiving of architecture as an expression of the religious aspect of democracy, and insisting: "I call it a senseless social crime that out of our natural fecundities we produce so few great men." ("Natural Thinking," p. 89.)

Taking their history through Sullivan's lifetime to our own, cities like Chicago might well be seen simply as the belly's answer to Jefferson. But the experiment of introducing mankind to self-mastery by first glutting his elementary appetites will come to an end, a wasteful success, not long after our decades. Its success in this country has convinced Europe, and will ultimately convince Russia and Asia. Before or after the firestorms, a new phase of the democratic experience will begin: a competition for excellence. Sullivan, then, will emerge even more as a prophet and a portent.

But those who turn toward his writings will encounter swamps and deserts. This man, who set out to discern and describe the conditions under which an organic art might flourish in the new age of humanity, was one of the most ambitious and self-confident of writers. He was also one of the most uneven, with frequent jarring lapses of taste and tone. Torrents of bad prose flowed from Sullivan's pen, interrupted occasionally by even worse poetry. It is all too easy to become discouraged, even repelled, before finding any nuggets in these turgid waters. But the nuggets are there, even in abundance.

Sullivan's faults as a writer are of a peculiar kind: his talent was certainly that of a poet, but a poet who was not really at ease using words. Time and again, he attempts passages of deeply felt logic, the equivalent of which, in stone and steel, he could bring off superbly; in his writings, these passages offer occasional felicities, but disastrous ultimate effects. And while he had advanced as an architect from the romanticism so marked in his earliest buildings, like the Troescher, and even the Ryerson tomb with its pyramid top, to a full sense of the necessary "organic" character of modern architecture, he was incapable of a comparable advance as a writer. As a subject, his own art of building sometimes steadied him: his best writing is that devoted to the exposition of its themes. But even his attacks on the crudity, confusion, and hifalutin in American building are often couched in language which is crude, confused, and hifalutin.

There is another, more disturbing defect in Sullivan's writing. The frustration of his genius, the bitterness engendered by addressing passionate exhorations to ears that were not listening — these corroded his spirit, and his habits of writing. The architect, we have remarked, has to accomplish his tasks, unlike other artists, strictly on society's own terms. When Gauguin went to Tahiti, and James to London, each found some reward for alientation and deracination. But Sullivan, with a sensibility as vulnerable as theirs, had to stand and fight on Prairie Avenue, on Michigan Boulevard, and in the Loop; otherwise his defeat would have been decisive, and his name would now be forgotten.

The price of all this is recorded in passages where we are sometimes startled to hear the deep voice of Lear raging at the spoiling of his kingdom; but more often, in shrill gusts of recrimination. These are often directed at us, and naturally enough, they often seem boring, presumptuous, and alienating. They provide the editor's major justification for his counter-presumption in offering selections from his author, instead of the integral text. In the case of some writings, most notably *Democracy: A Man-Search*, the integral text is all but unreadable: embarrassment as much as fatigued resentment arrest the attention.

Even here, however, before giving up, the reader may grow aware of one source of his embarrassment: he is being made the witness of an amazing marriage. A part of Sullivan's achievement came from his coupling of Nietzsche and Whitman; it is not surprising that the bedding together of two such androgynous spirits should have resulted in strange births. But the audacious attempt to state Nietzschean themes in terms of the New World vistas of the American poet is by no means unsuccessful. It is the pernicious in those themes which is moderated and humanized in Sullivan's vision, while the windily expansive rhetoric of the poet is sobered by a sense of history and of society. The best of Sullivan's pages prompt us to consider again the basic premisses of our lives as inhabitants of this nation (and this universe). They offer a vision of the whole as a living organism, transcendent and imminent in our lives. Yes, that vision deserves a more coherent expression than this ravaged visionary was able to give: but such expression as he could find, deserves to find its readers.

Finally, Sullivan in all his writings outside the field of his art, grossly oversimplified the insights which his intuition and native generosity of spirit offered for the riddles of life. Man, he kept naively insisting, was "at bottom, simply unselfish," and nature was ultimately benignant. The ability to perceive that these statements and their opposites are *both* true, was beyond Sullivan. It is not only that he was intellectually blind to certain intransigent realities: he refused to face the evidence of his own life. His very refusal makes many of his pages read like a scream.

At this point, the reader will ask: What is the justification for commending to me such a writer, some of whose more ambitious works lay in the files of a museum, almost untouched, for fifty years, and at whom such drastic criticisms can be levelled?

V

Sullivan realized early that history had brought man to a point where he was in principle able to take his further development into his own hands; and therefore could only avoid doing so at peril; that man had become, in some sense, his own creator. This fact, he was sure, gave enormous urgency to the inner meaning of democracy. Sullivan's insistence on this fact, and all its implications, is what gives his writings a measure of prophetic value.

He indicts man for ignorance and waste. Not ignorance of facts or theories or systems, but ignorance of his own nature, and of the beneficent power latent in what he variously calls "instinct" and "imagination" and "ego." This power makes it possible for his puny possessor, if he does not waste it, to remake himself, his world, who knows? perhaps his universe.

But conscious imagination, true ego, is rare. Sullivan feels that man has put himself at the mercy of rulers, creeds, and systems because he is unaware of the power of imagination, of its existence in himself; he feels that all forms of society have been shaped by unconscious projections of the mass imagination. Few who read it will be unimpressed by his description of the birth of all human phenomena — gods and demons, good and evil, the vilest massacres and the smallest meanness, the omnipotence of kings, the flamboyance of wealth, art and science and learning, prostitution, suffering and heroism — from the fecund abnegation of the poor.

As man becomes more conscious of his imagination, and as conscious intelligence comes under its sway, man will acquire greater control over himself and his environment. If not — Sullivan had a true sense of the bleak alternatives — "The day of the fanatic is approaching," he wrote early in this century, " — it is in the air . . . We are approaching in these many ways an hour of gross passion."

In his writings, Sullivan believed, he was giving us fundamental answers. What he really gives is testimony: "I was the man, I suffered, I was there," — testimony to the ultimate poignancy of each life, the aimlessness of modern man, the waste of talent in a dollar democracy. He was a visionary, and sometimes a clairvoyant, not a wise man; a seer, not a sage. He does not, as he thinks, supply us with a philosophy, but he makes the search for one more urgent, and more a matter of everyone's responsibility.

He does this by a naked directness, plus his few but enduring insights. Though he concealed much from himself as well as from his readers, in another sense he is touchingly frank — his outrage, grief and hope are as fresh as a child's. This frankness reaches down to something fundamental in the reader, too, if he is willing to listen, and not be put off when the rhapsody turns for a while to rant.

It is common to say, of some good writer: "You feel his presence in what he writes." In Sullivan's case, even at his worst, you feel his breath on your neck, his finger plucking at your sleeve. He hooks and baits and stabs the reader with questions, reproaches, taunts. Everything is in the present, everything is drama. At times you can hear him weep, see him bleed.

We are not accustomed to the passion which makes the urgent

speaker, who however has nothing to sell but a vision of the New Jerusalem, grasp us by the arm — all us consumers and employees — as we move up the escalator in a State Street department store, or purchase a pack of cigarettes in Times Square, to demand with exasperating irrelevance and pertinacity: "Do you remember when you were also a citizen? When you lived in a community? Do you know what Democracy means? Is Chicago, multiplied from Odessa to Calcutta, what Democracy means? Do you know that we could tear it down and rebuild it in a generation? What of the City of Man?"

Today, this insistent, scolding eccentric is still jabbing his tobacco-stained finger at us, against a dust-filled background in which Chicago is rebuilding itself indeed — and his Garrick building, that jet of elegance fountaining out of the boorish Loop, has gone down under the wreckers' ball to make room for a parking garage. The Auditorium continues to moulder, and Sullivan's own home remains a fire-gutted slum-house, while the promoters erect more and more warehouses and filing cabinets for people-as-functions. And he has not even the relevance that comes from offering the really right answers.

But he goes on asking, tauntingly, the right questions. And if the story of his country is to be read, eventually, as the poem Emerson envisaged and not as a mountain of computer tapes, those questions have to be asked until answers are found.

On the Head of a Pin

The following passage is from *The Autobiography Of An Idea,* an account of his work and thought which Sullivan wrote in 1922 and 1923, for publication in the *Journal* of the American Institute of Architects. (He died in a cheap hotel room, on the South Side of Chicago, in 1924.) In five or six hundred words, these two paragraphs remarkably encapsulate the basic idea that animated Sullivan as an artist and thinker, and with equal felicity capture the emotional tone of his life in these two modes. It is placed here as a kind of keystone to his work, and an illustration of his prose at its finest.

Throughout all the activities of professional life, Louis never ceased in steady contemplation of the nature of man and his powers, of the mystery of that great life which enfolds and permeates us all; the marvel of nature's processes which the scientists call laws; and the imperturbable enigma of good and evil. He was too young to grasp the truth that the fair-appearing civilization within which he lived was but a huge invisible man-trap, man-made. Of politics he knew nothing and suspected nothing, all seemed fair on the surface. Of man's betrayal by man on a colossal scale he knew nothing and suspected nothing. He had heard of the State and had read something about the State, but had not a glimmering of the meaning of the State. He had dutifully read some books on political economy because he thought he had to, and had accepted their statements as fact. He had also heard vaguely something about finance and what a mystery it was. In other words, Louis was absurdly, grotesquely credulous. How could it be otherwise with him? He believed that most people were honest and intelligent. How could he suspect the eminent? So Louis saw the real world upside down. He was grossly ignorant. He prospered, so the world was fair. Later he sent forth his soul into the world and by and by his soul returned to him with an appalling message.

For long Louis had lived in a fool's paradise; it was well he so lived in illusion. For had the hideous truth come to him of a sudden, it would have "dashed him to pieces like a potter's vessel." So he kept on with his innocent studies, becoming more and more enamoured of the sciences, particularly those dealing with forms of life and the aspects of life's urging, called functions. And amid the immense number and variety of living forms, he noted that invariably the form expressed the function, as, for instance, the oak tree expressed the function oak, the pine tree the function pine, and so on through the amazing series. And, inquiring more deeply, he discovered that in truth it was not simply a matter of form expressing function, but the vital idea was this: That the function *created* or organized its form. Discernment of this idea threw a vast light upon all things within the universe, and condensed with astounding impressiveness upon mankind, upon all civilizations, all institutions, every form and aspect of society, every mass-thought and mass-result, every individual thought and individual result. Hence, Louis began to regard all functions in nature as powers, manifestations of the all-power of Life, and thus man's power came into direct relationship with all other powers. The application of the idea to the Architectural art was manifest enough, namely, that the function of a building must predetermine and organize its form. But it was the application to man's thought and deeds; to his inherent powers and the results of the application of these powers, mental, moral, physical, that thrilled Louis to the depths as he realized that, as one stumbling upon a treasure, he has found that of which he had dreamed in Paris, and had promised himself to discover—a universal law admitting of no exception in any phase or application whatsoever.

PART ONE

ARCHITECTURE AND DEMOCRACY

CHARACTERISTICS AND TENDENCIES OF
AMERICAN ARCHITECTURE

In 1885, Sullivan was 29 years old; he had behind him a New England boyhood; brief periods of study for the career of architect in Cambridge, Massachusetts, and Paris; brief apprenticeships in Philadelphia and New York. Having also worked as a draughtsman in various architectural firms in Chicago, he was now a full partner in the firm of Adler and Sullivan, and was consciously exploring the preconditions, social and esthetic, of an American art of building. The task of designing the Auditorium Building (now Roosevelt University), which first made him nationally prominent, was two years in the future, when he delivered the following talk, in St. Louis, to the Western Association of Architects.

Many who have commented upon the practice of architecture in this country have regarded the absence of a style, distinctively American, as both strange and deplorable; and with a view to betterment they have advanced theories as to the nature, and immediate realization, of such a style that evidence a lack of insight equally strange and deplorable. These theories have been for the greater part suggested by the feelings awakened in contemplating the matured beauty of Old World art, and imply a grafting or transplanting process. They have been proved empirical by the sufficient logic of time; their advocates having ignored the complex fact, that, like a new species of any class, a national style must be a growth, that slow and gradual assimilation of nutriment and a struggle against obstacles are necessary adjuncts to the purblind processes of growth, and that the resultant structure can bear only a chemical or metaphysical resemblance to the materials on which it has been nurtured.

We will, therefore, for the purposes of this paper disregard these dreams of a Minerva-like architectural splendor springing full-formed into being, and look rather for the early signs of a spontaneous architectural feeling arising in sympathy with the emotions latent or conspicuous in our people.

It is reasonable to believe than an unconquered country, peopled by colonization and natural increase, may bear in its younger and its coming generations a race whose birthright, implying freedom to receive and assimilate impressions, shall nurture emotions of rare quality and of a fruitfulness commensurate with the energy in an unexhausted soil.

It would be erroneous to assume that there will be no evidence of the activity of such emotions until as a large accumulation they break all bonds asunder. The individual is from day to day seeking expedients by means of which to shape his immediate surroundings into a realization of his desires, and we may assume it to be quite probable that the initial impelling force, operating through the individual, has already in many cases produced significant and valuable results. These results, if not thoroughly typical, must have in them much that is eminently characteristic, and that bear the stamp of internal origin.

To test this hypothesis we have therefore but to look into the daily life of our architecture, and, in the complexion of its many fleeting phases, seek here and there for instances, some perhaps almost trivial, in which the existence of spontaneous and characteristic emotional feeling may be detected. Sometimes we shall find this impulse appearing as an element of warmth tingeing scholastic formalism; sometimes as a seemingly paradoxical inspiration in the works of the uncultivated. We may certainly expect to meet with it in the efforts of those upon whose imagination the chromatic eloquence of words and of music have taken strong holds; and above all, we are to look for it in the creations of the gifted ones whose souls are finely attuned to the touching beauty of nature and of humanity. To an apprehension of this subtle element, we may be happily guided by the suggestions of analogy. Our recent American literature comes aptly to this use. Glancing through its focusing substance, as through the lens of a camera, we may perceive an image of the abstraction we seek, and, by an extension of the process, we may fix an impression of its form and texture, to be developed at will.

Our literature is the only phase of our national art that has been accorded serious recognition, at home and abroad. The noticeable qualities of its present phases seem to be: excessive regard for minute detail, painful self-consciousness of finish, timidity and embarrassment in the delineation of all but the well-behaved and docile emotions, and a tacit fiction as to the passions: all beautifully executed with much patient, earnest labor, and diplomatically tempered to the understanding.

Exquisite, but not virile, our latter-day literature illustrates quite emphatically the quality of our tentative and provisional culture, which must ere long throw off these seedling leaves, when a higher temperature shall infuse glowing vitality into root and stem, and exuberant foliation give more certain assurance of the coming flower of our soil. Our literature, and in fact all that which we Americans complacently call our art, is too much a matter of heart and fingers, and too little an offspring of brain and soul. One must indeed have faith in the processes of nature to prophesy order eventuating upon so strange a chaos of luxuries. But to this end, transmitted knowledge must gradually be supplemented by the fresh impressions of the senses and the sensibilities, the fund so accumulated yielding richly of its own increase. This supplemental acquisition must of necessity be of slow growth, for we have all been educated to a dependence upon our artistic inheritance.

Our art is for the day, is suited to the day, and will also change as the day changes. The law of variation is an ever present force, and coordination is its goal. The first step toward a new order of things is accomplished when there appear minds receiving and assimilating fresh impressions, reaching new conclusions, and acting upon them. By this sign, we may know that such a movement is already upon us, and by the aid of the indicated literary analogy we may follow its erratic tendencies, and note its increase in strength and individuality: we may see the germ of poetry which each man has within him, slowly awakening into life, and may feel the presence of an American romanticism.

This romanticism is, in the main, also exquisite but not virile. It seeks to touch all things with softened hand. Under the influence of its warmth of feeling, hard lines flow into graceful curves, angularities disappear in a mystical blending of surfaces.

One by one the completed styles of foreign climes are passing under this hand, each in turn being quietly divested of its local charm, and clothed in a sentiment and mannerism unmistakably our own. Power laments, meanwhile, at the feet of a modern Omphale, his voice attuned to the domestic hum of the times.

Appreciation of the beauties of this romanticism is to some extent dependent upon the verbal explanation and comment of its exponents. A knowledge of their vocabulary is often of assistance in disclosing softness and refinement in many primitive expedients, and revealing beauty in barren places. Familiarity with the current phraseology of the allied arts is also useful in assisting the student to a comprehension of many things apparently incomprehensible. Metaphor and simile are rampant in this connection, a well-chosen word often serving to justify an architectural absurdity.

But overloaded as is this fabric of impulse with florid and complicated intertwinings of affection, when we examine the material thereof, we find it excellent and valuable.

Searching critically among the works executed in this feeling, we note in the varying examples, and indeed in parts of the same structure, a curious *mélange* of super-sentimentalisms. Conspicuous at first glance, in some an offensive simplicity, in others a highly wrought charlatanism; further, we perceive ingenuity in device, or superb flow of spirits—all more or less leavened with stubborn common sense. After such an investigation, we may gladly become convinced that behind a somewhat uncertain vision resides a marvelous instinct.

National sensitiveness and pride, conjoined with fertility of resource, will aid as active stimuli in the development of this instinct toward a more rational and organic mode of expression, leading through many reactions to a higher sphere of artistic development.

We are now in the primary department, vaguely endeavoring to form a plastic alphabet by means of which to identify our beliefs. Progress in this respect has been very slow and results meagre: for our beliefs have still within them too much of uncertainty and diffidence to take rank as convictions. Without these latter a sufficient creating power is lacking. The formation of an alphabet, and the simplest combinations of its terms, are matters of much importance; and easy progress in this respect is seriously impeded by complications of thought. To look at things simply and clearly is quite easy, until counter influences are set at work; then comes a struggle for survival, which now and then is successful—the result being an addition, however small, to our stock of elementary forms.

The ability to develop elementary ideas organically is not conspicuous in our profession. In this respect, the architect is inferior to the business man and financier, whose capacity to expand a simple congenial idea, once fixed, into subtle, manifold, and consistent ramifications is admirable, and a shining example which we have often ignored, creating thereby an undesirable impression.

This view leads us on to a consideration of the element of power. Until this element is widely introduced into our work, giving it the impress of brilliancy, intuition, and great depth of feeling, that work, exhaustively considered, will remain but little more than a temporary expedient.

The presence of power, as a mental characteristic in one class of our people, augurs well for the belief that it may pervade our ranks. The beginnings of power are usually so crude and harsh as to be revolting to a refined taste, and hence it is instinctively shunned; but once subtilized, flushed with emotion and guided by clear insight, it is a worker of miracles; responsive to its ardent wooings, nature yields up her poetic secrets.

We surely have in us the germ of artistic greatness—no people on earth possessing more of innate poetic feeling, more of ideality, greater capacity to adore the beautiful, than our own people; but architects as a professional class have held it more expedient to maintain the traditions of their culture than to promulgate vitalizing thought. Here then we are weak, and should sentiment gain a pronounced ascendency, we may remain weak.

On us rests partially the responsibility, and partially on the public. We have at times individually sought to lead the public, when we more wisely should have followed it; and have, as a body, often followed, when, with beneficent results we could have led. While we may compromise for a time, through a process of local adaptation, no architectural style can become a finality, that runs counter to popular feeling. The desire at once to follow and to lead the public should be the initial attitude of our profession toward the formation of a national style. For while we conduct the technical operations, the shaping and controlling process is mainly in the hands of the public who are constantly keeping us within bounds. We cannot wholly escape this control, while we are without a national architecture fully representing the wishes of the public, and ministering to its conceptions of the beautiful and the useful. This can evidently not come to pass forthwith, for the public itself can only partially and imperfectly state its wants. Responding readily, however, to the intuition of those who anticipate its desires, it accepts provisionally year by year all the satisfaction it can get; so that while one recognized style after another shall pass through our hands to be tried and finally rejected in the search for permanent satisfaction, a modified residuum from each will doubtless be added to a fund representing our growth in emotional and spiritual wealth. The progress of this growth toward consummation in a national style, involves the lives of many generations, and need be of but little practical concern to us of today. We work at short range and for immediate results. Perhaps, however, there would be infused into our profession an abiding *esprit de corps*, should consideration of this subject and its associated themes lead to a substantial agreement upon our status, our tendencies, and our policy.

If the conclusions set forth in this paper be accepted as correct, it becomes clearly evident, however, that the formative beginnings of this national style, now in progress, are of the utmost immediate interest to us, in part through feelings of patriotism, in part because of a surmise that those who approach most nearly in the substance of their work and administration to the qualities inherent to our race and potential to a national style, will come nearest to the hearts of our people.

Harassed though the architect may be, by the cares and responsibilities of his daily life, there exists nevertheless within him, in the midst of this turmoil, an insuppressible yearning toward ideals. These delicate promptings should be both protected and nourished, that, like the flowering plants springing by the sun's gentle persuasion from little seeds buried in the coarser elements of the soil, they also, because of the warmth of human feeling, may bloom at times by the wayside, yielding refreshing odors and the joy of color to the plodding wayfarer.

The soft beams of the full-orbed moon fall with pathetic caress upon the slumbering life of the world; paling with the dawn, her tender vigil ended, she melts into the infinite depths when the ruddy herald of day proudly summons the workers. So does the soul watch over its greater ideals until the thrilling radiance of power shall awaken them to action.

Ideal thought and effective action should so compose the vital substance of our works that they may live, with us and after us, as a record of our fitness, and a memorial of the good we may have done. Then, in the affluence of time, when a rich burden of aspiring verdure may flourish in the undulating fields of thought, wrought into fertility through the bounty of nature and the energy of the race, the mellowed spontaneity of a national style reaching its full and perfect fruition shall have come from out the very treasury of nature.

EMOTIONAL ARCHITECTURE AS COMPARED WITH INTELLECTUAL

The architect's next basic statement of his themes was made almost a decade later, in an address to the annual convention of the American Institute of Architects, New York City, 1894. Nothing Sullivan ever wrote is more characteristic of him than this ambitious discourse, with its urgent concern for the role of education, its insistence on seeing architecture not only in a social role but in grandiose philosophical and historical perspective, and its rhetorical marriage of esthetic and messianic passions. In it are expressed or suggested all the recurrent themes he developed in later writings. The masterful tone in which they are stated here reflects the mood of a man who had, in the four or five years prior to this date, set modern architecture on its course by designing many of his master works, among them the Wainwright Building in St. Louis and the Guaranty Building (now the Prudential) in Buffalo, the first skyscrapers conceived and executed in terms of the new esthetic principles he was enunciating. There is no premonition, here, that his long years of nearly total inactivity as an architect were drawing near, with the dissolution, in 1895, of his partnership with Dankmar Adler.

How strange it seems that education, in practice, so often means suppression; that instead of leading the mind outward to the light of day it crowds things in upon it that darken and weary it. Yet evidently the true object of education, now as ever, is to develop the capabilities of the head and of the heart. He therefore who possesses a sound head and a responsive heart is worthy of enlightened guidance, is amenable to educational influence.

Let us now imagine a simple youth so equipped, so gifted, I am almost forced to say, an inborn poet, untaught, unschooled, and living an outdoor life. So familiarly has he fared with sunshine and air, and the living things, that they seem, as indeed they are, everyday and common to him. Yet the mere community of their lives, the similarity in the experiences of the boy, the plants and the animals in that native, simple, naif, unsullied state that we who are perhaps unduly artificial call by contrast natural—this state has drawn him very near to them all.

Breathing the same air as they, maturing in the same glowing sunshine, sustained by the same satisfying moisture, he and they expand side by side, defining themselves intimately to each other; and the boy, growing always, after a while feels himself to be not only with them but of them. His is a brotherhood with the trees; a wistful eye he softens to the flowers; he has a comely friendship for them all.

He knows that the young leaves love the dew; that the tendril reaches quietly for the twig it may cling to. He has seen the fern unfolding its brown spiral to become anon green and regular. He has splashed knee-deep in the marsh; he knows the dank fragrance very well; he parts his friends the rushes to make a way for his eyes that seek what they may devour—his eyes with a keen and endless appetite. His hands touch the warmish water—sniffing the active air, he lives as only a boy can live—his lively sensibilities always in physical touch with his surroundings, in the full and irrepressible enjoyment of his five senses.

These five senses, and they only, stand between him and nature. It is they that interpret her affection; and the ready language that they deal in keeps him in such a natural sympathy, so well in touch, so intimately at ease, that he does not for a moment realize that he is then and there doing that which education, so-called, once having made inoperative in him, he will in after years, poet though he be, reacquire only with the utmost difficulty the power to do.

This something that he is doing, and the physical and psychic state that it implies we call *Touch*: Meaning not the touch of the painter, not the touch of the sculptor, not the mechanical and technical touch of the fingers only, nor quite their negligent contact with things, but the exquisite touch of the sensibilities, the warm physical touch of the body, the touch of a sound head and a responsive heart, the touch of the native one, the poet, out of doors, in spontaneous communion with nature.

So has our youngster started easily and naturally, all alone without premeditation or guidance, upon the road to knowledge, to leadership and power. For this sensibility, this healthfulness, this touch, that is his is the first essential prerequisite in the early analytical strivings of the mind: It is that perfect concrete analysis by the senses and the sympathies which serves as a basis for the abstract analysis of the intellect.

Let us not forget our little man, for he is to companion me in spirit through this discourse. I believe he exists somewhere, has in his breast the true architectural afflatus, and will some day come forth the Messiah of our art. For he has that early and sure understanding by the eyes that will survive the future uncertainties of the brain. He has that exalted animal sense which alone can discern the pathway to hidden knowledge, that acute and instant scent in matters objective leading to matters subjective that we call *Intuition*.

This physical endowment, this sense of touch is, decidedly, wherever found, a generous gift of nature; but it is potent for results in so far only as it is urged into sustained and decisive action by a certain appetite or desire.

This desire, this insistence, this urgency which will not be denied; this uncomfortable hunger, this uneasy searching, this profound discontent, oh! so deep; this cry for more, this appetite, this yearning, ever unsatisfied, is not of the body alone but of the soul, and, always and everywhere, in all times and in all places, high or low, wherever found, it is the dominant characteristic of man's eminence in nature—it is the justification of the eminence of a few men among their fellows.

For appetite, in a state of nature, implies not only a keen desire and a search for the food wanted, but, as well, a rejection of all else, thus insuring a wonderful singleness of purpose, a concentration of action, a definiteness of end in the selection of that nourishment of the faculties which, when assimilated, is to become in turn thought and expression through the agency of a second desire equally great, equally intense, equally insistent, namely, the desire to act. This desire to act we call *Imagination*.

These two great desires, which are in essence the desire to absorb and the desire to emit, the desire to know and the desire to test, the desire to hear and the desire to utter, are the basis not only of a true and effective education, not only are they the wholesome body and the enchanting voice of art, but they are greater than these, for they are the animating quality of that higher purpose and significance of art that we call poetry.

Now, the desire to act that in due time follows upon nutrition can assert itself tangibly and fully only by means of three agencies, the which, by virtue of its life-giving qualities, this nutritive power has called into being. All three of them must coöperate in turn in order to produce a fully rounded result. They are first, the *Imagination,* which is the very beginning of action because it is a sympathy that lives both in our senses and our intellect—the flash between the past and the future, the middle link in that living chain or sequence leading from nature unto art, and that lies deep down in the emotions and the will. It is this divine faculty which, in an illumined instant, in that supreme moment when ideas are born, reveals the end with the beginning, and liberates, as an offspring of man, that which before had rested, perhaps for untold centuries, dormant but potential in the inmost heart of nature. This is the supreme crisis. This is the summit of the soul, the fertile touch of the spirit, the smile of nature's bounty—the moment of *Inspiration!* All else is from this moment on, a foregone conclusion, an absolute certainty to the mastermind: a task surely but not a doubt.

Second in this trinity comes *Thought,* the faculty that doubts and inquires, that recognizes time and space and the material limitations, that slowly systemizes, that works by small increments and cumulations, that formulates, that concentrates, works, reworks and reviews; that goes slowly, deliberately; that makes very firm and sure, and that eventually arrives at a science of logical statement that shall shape and define the scheme and structure that is to underlie, penetrate and support the form of an art work. It is the hard, the bony structure, it is the tough, tendinous fiber; it may be at times, perhaps, as limber as the lips that move, yet it is never the need of smiling—never the smile.

Third, last, and the winsome one, exuberant in life and movement, copious in speech comes *Expression,* open-armed and free, supple, active, dramatic, changeable, beautifully pensive, persuasive and wonderful. Hers it is to clothe the structure of art with a form of beauty; for she is the perfection of the physical, she is the physical itself, and the uttermost attainment of emotionality. Hers is an infinite tenderness, an adorable and sweet fascination. In her companionship imaginative Thought, long searching, has found its own, and lives anew, immortal, filled with sensibility graciousness and the warm blood of a fully rounded maturity.

Thus Art comes into Life! Thus Life comes into Art!

And thus, by reason of a process of elaboration and growth, through the natural storage and upbuilding of the products of nutrition, lifting themselves higher and higher into organization, the physical and spiritual experiences of our lives, seeking reproduction, shall find imaginative utterance, in their own image, in *a harmonious system of thinking and an equally harmonious method of expressing the thought.*

And so it shall come that when our nourishment shall be natural, our imagination therefore fervid, intense and vision-like; when our thinking and our speech shall have become as processes of nature; when, in consequence, from its mysterious abode in visible things, the invisible and infinitely fluent spirit of the universe passing to us shall have made our tongues eloquent, our utterance serene, then, and not till then, shall we posses, individually and as a people, the necessary elements of a great *Style.*

For otherwise and without this unitary impulse our expression, though delicate as a flower, our thinking as abstract as the winds that blow, our imagination as luminous as the dawn, are useless and unavailing to create; they may set forth, they cannot create.

Man, by means of his physical power, his mechanical resources, his mental ingenuity, may set things side by side. A composition, literally so called, will result but not a great art work, not at all an art work, in fact, but merely a more or less refined exhibition of brute force exercised upon helpless materials. It may be as a noise in lessening degrees of offensiveness, it can never become a musical tone. Though it shall have ceased to be vulgar in becoming sophistical, it will remain to the end what it was in the beginning: impotent to inspire, dead, absolutely dead.

It cannot for a moment be doubted that an art work to be alive, to awaken us to its life, to inspire us sooner or later with its purpose, must indeed be animate with a soul, must have been breathed upon by the spirit and must breathe in turn that spirit. It must stand for the actual, vital first-hand experiences of the one who made it and must represent his deep-down impression not only of physical nature but more especially and necessarily his understanding of the out-working of that *Great Spirit* which makes nature so intelligible to us that it ceases to be a phantasm and becomes a sweet, a superb, a convincing *Reality.*

It absolutely must be the determination and the capacity of the artist that his work shall be as real and convincing as is his own life; as suggestive as his own eyesight makes all things to him; and yet as unreal, as fugitive, as inscrutable, as subjective, as the why and wherefore of the simplest flower that blows.

It is the presence of this unreality that makes the art work real: it is by virtue of this silent subjectivity that the objective voice of an art song becomes sonorous and thrilling.

Unless, therefore, subjectivity permeate an art work, that work cannot aspire to greatness; for whatever of imagination, of thought and of expression it may possess, these as such will remain three separate things—not three phases of one thing.

An artist must necessarily, therefore, remain a more or less educated handworker, a more or less clever sophisticator, a more or less successful framer of compromises, unless, when he was born, there was born with him a hunger for the spiritual; for all other craving avails as naught. Unless, as a child, with that marvelous instinct given only to children he has heard the voice of Nature murmuring in the woodland or afield or seaward, no after hearing can avail to catch this revelation.

And thus it is that subjectivity and objectivity, not as two separate elements but as two complementary and harmonious phases of one impulse, have always constituted and will always constitute the embodied spirit of art.

No phase of human nature can contain greater interest for the student of psychology than the history—natural, political, religious and artistic—of the successive phases for good and for ill of Objectivity and Subjectivity. *They are the two controlling elements in human endeavor.* They have caused in their internecine warfare misery and perturbation. They are ordinarily known and spoken of as the intellectual and the emotional, but they lie deeper, much deeper, than these: they lie in the very heart of nature. Coming into man's being they have been antagonistic because of the fanaticism and one-sidedness of human nature, because of its immobility. Because from the beginning man has been beset by beautiful, by despicable illusions. Because one set of men have believed in what they could not see. Because it has too often happened that the man who could see with the outer eye could not see with the inner eye; because the other man, rhapsodizing with the clear insight of faith, had no thought for the things of this world. Neither has believed in the virtue of the other. Neither has inferred from the presence of the other, the necessary existence of a balancing but hidden power. Now and then through the ages they have come twin-born in the bosom of an individual man, upon whose brow the generations have placed the wreath of immortality.

So vast, so overwhelming is the power of a great, a properly balanced subjectivity, so enormously does it draw on the spiritual nutrition and stored up vitality of the world, that, soon sapping this up, and still craving, the man possessed of it, urged by it, goes straight to the unfailing bounty of nature, and there, by virtue of his passionate adoration, passing the portals of the objective, he enters that extraordinary communion that the sacred writers called to "walk with God."

There can be doubt that the most profound desire that fills the human soul, the most heartfelt hope, is the wish to be at peace with Nature and the Inscrutable Spirit; nor can there be a doubt that the greatest Art Work is that which most nearly typifies a realization of this ardent, patient longing. All efforts of the body, all undertakings of the mind, tend, consciously or unconsciously, toward this consummation, tend toward this final peace: the peace of perfect equilibrium, the repose of absolute unity, the serenity of a complete identification.

When, therefore, turning from this our contemplation we compare the outworking of the vital processes of nature with the so-called creative activity of the average man of education and culture, we wonder at the disparity, we seek its cause.

When, after having with joy observed the quality of identity and singleness that nature imparts to her offspring, when with aroused expectancy, with a glowing sense of the richness, fullness and variety that might and should come from the man's brain with the impulse of nature's fecundity flowing through it, we seek—we are amazed to find in this man's work no such thing.

When we, in place of a fertile unity which we had hoped for, come suddenly upon miscellany and barrenness, we are deeply mortified, we are rudely shocked.

We are dismayed at this: That man, nature's highest product, should alone have gone awry, that with remarkable perversity he should have strayed; that for the simple and obvious he should substitute the factitious, the artificial.

The cause needs not a long searching, it is near at hand. It lies precisely in that much-glorified, much-abused word, "education."

To my view no word in the entire vocabulary of the English language contains so much of pathos, so much of tragedy, as this one pitiful word, "education," for it typifies a fundamental perversity of the human soul, a willful blindness of the mind, a poverty of the heart.

For one brain that education has stimulated and strengthened, it has malformed, stupefied and discouraged thousands. Only the strongest, only the masterful can dominate it, and return to the ownership of their souls.

For it is education's crime that it has removed us from nature. As tender children it took us harshly away with stern words, and the sweet face of our natural mother has faded in the unspeakable past, whence it regards us at times, dimly and flittingly, causing in us uneasy and disturbing emotion.

And thus it is through a brutish and mean system of guidance, through the density of atmosphere that we have breathed that we are not what our successors may easily become, a race filled with spiritual riches in addition to the vast material wealth.

That in place of a happy people, open-eyed children of nature teeming with beautiful impulses, we are a people lost in darkness, groping under a sooty and lurid sky sinister with clouds that shut out the sunshine and the clear blue heavens.

Yet the murky materialism—the fierce objectivity, the fanatical selfishness—of this dark age of ours, in this sense the darkest of all dark ages, is so prodigious, so grotesque, so monstrous, that in its very self it contains the elements of change; from its own intensity, its own excess, its complex striving, it predetermines the golden age of the world.

The human mind in all countries having gone to the uttermost limit of its own capacity, flushed with its conquests, haughty after its self-assertion upon emerging from the prior dark age, is now nearing a new phase, a phase inherent in the nature and destiny of things.

The human mind, like the silk-worm oppressed with the fullness of its own accumulation, has spun about itself gradually and slowly a cocoon that at last has shut out the light of the world from which it drew the substance of its thread. But this darkness has produced the chrysalis, and we within the darkness feel the beginning of our throes. The inevitable change, after centuries of preparation, is about to begin.

Human development, through a series of vast attractions and perturbations, has now arrived at a materialism so profound, so exalted, as to prove the fittest basis for a coming era of spiritual splendor.

To foresee this necessity, consider but a moment the richness of our heritage from the past, its orderly sequence, its uplifting wave of power, its conservation of force.

Think of the Hindoo, with folded hands, soaring in contemplation, thousands of years ago—think of what he has left to us. Think of the Hebrew man coming out of Ur, of the Chaldees, to find for us the One Great Spirit. Think of the somber Egyptians, those giants who struggled so grimly with fate—think of the stability they have given to us. Think of the stars of Israel singing in the morning's dawn. Think of the lonely man of Nazareth breathing a spirit of gentleness of which the world had never heard before. Think of the delicately objective Greeks, lovers of the physical, accurate thinkers, the worshippers of beauty. Think that in them the Orient, sleeping, was born anew. Think of the Goth, and with him the birth of emotion as we know it. Think of modern Music, arising in glory as the heart took wings—*a new thing under the sun.* Think deeply of the French Revolution and Democracy—the utterance of freedom, the beginning of the Individual Man. Think now of our own age with its machinery, its steam power, its means of communication, its annihilation of distance. Think of the humanitarianism of our day. Think, as we stand here, now, in a new land, a Promised Land that at last is ours, think how passionately latent, how marvelous to contemplate is America, our country. *Think that here destiny has decreed there shall be enacted the final part in the drama of man's emancipation: the redemption of his soul!*

Think of these things, think of what they signify, of what they promise for us, and think then that as architects it peculiarly behooves us to review our own special past, to forecast our future, to realize somewhat our present status.

Summoned to answer before an enlightened judgement seat, how shall we now give other, alas, than a wretched accounting of our stewardship? How shall we excuse our sterility? We surely need to inquire, for we must need explain the emaciation of our art in the midst of plenty; its weakness in the midst of strength, its beggarly poverty in the midst of abundance.

By what glamour or speciousness of words shall we persuade a wrathful judgment toward kindness? How can our vapid record be made to plead for us?

Shall we summon the clear-eyed intellectual Greek or the emotional and introspective Goth to bear witness that we stand as ambassadors in their names—we would surely be repudiated.

Shall we call to the fateful Egyptian or the dashing, polished Assyrian— one would scorn us, the other would flout us.

Who are we then, and how shall we explain our sinister condition, our mere existence?

Shall we claim we are second cousins to Europe, or must we, before we can ourselves behold the truth, so far abase our heads in the ashes as to acknowledge that we of the great and glorious ending of the nineteenth century are the direct lineal descendants of the original bastards and indiscretions of architecture?

Or, still seeking excuses in our fin-de-siècle pocket, shall we plead in the language of myth that our art, like Brünhilde, lies sleeping; that she awaits a son of nature, one without fear, to penetrate the wall of flame, to lift her helmet's visor?

Dreading the storm, shall we seek shelter under the spreading plea that poets are born, not made; that, if Nature for all these centuries has not brought forth a great master spirit in the architectural art, it must be for very good reasons of her own—for reasons definitely interwrought with the beneficence of her own rhythmical movements. That, with her endless fecundity, there must be a profoundly significant reason for this barrenness.

Or, perhaps, shall we simply say that men have now turned to other gods, that they have forgotten the ancient deities?

That there has arisen in our land a new king who knows not Joseph; that he has set o'er us taskmasters to afflict us with burthens?

All these pleadings may be true, yet after all they do not explain why we make easy things very difficult, why we employ artificial instead of natural processes, why we walk backward instead of forward, why we see cross-eyed instead of straight-eyed, why we turn our minds inside out instead of letting them alone; they do not explain why we are so vulgarly self-conscious, so pitifully bashful, so awkward in our art, so explanatory, so uncertain that we know anything at all or are anybody in particular, so characterless, so insipid, so utterly without savor. They do not explain why the intellectual and emotional phases of the architectural mind do precisely the wrong thing when the right thing is quite attainable.

No! I pretend to advocate the real, the true cause of my generation, of my art. I do not wish to abase them except in so far as he who loveth chasteneth. I know that the secret of our weakness lies not only in our plethoric dyspepsia, in our lack of desire, in our deficiency in gumption and moral courage, but that it lies primarily in the utterly purposeless education we have received.

I know that the architectural schools teach a certain art or method of study in which one is made partly familiar with the objective aspects and forms of architecture. I know that this, as far as it goes, is conscientiously and thoroughly done. But I also know that it is doubtful, in my mind, if one student in a thousand emerges from his school possessed of a fine conception of what architecture really is, in form, in spirit, and in truth; and I say this is not primarily the student's fault. I know that before entering his architectural school he has passed through other schools, and that they began the mischief; that they had told him grammar was a book, algebra was a book, geometry another book, geography, chemistry, physics, still others; they never told him, never permitted him to guess for himself, how these things were actualy intense symbols, complex ratios, representing man's relation to nature and his fellow man; they never told him that his mathematics, etc., etc., came into being in response to a *desire* in the human breast to come nearer to nature; that the full moon looked round to the human eye ages before the circle was dreamed of.

Our student knows, to be sure, as a result of his teaching, that the Greeks built certain-shaped buildings, that the Goths built certain-shaped buildings, and that other peoples built other buildings of still other shapes. He knows, moreover, if he has been a conscientious hewer of wood and drawer of water, a thousand and one specific facts concerning the shapes and measurements and ratios of the whole and the parts of said buildings, and can neatly and deftly draw and color them to scale. He moreover has read in the philosophies, or heard at lectures, that the architecture of a given time gives one an excellent idea of the civilization of that time.

This, roughly speaking, is the sum total of his education; and he takes his architectural instruction literally, just as he has taken every other form of instruction literally from the time he was a child; because he has been told to do so, because he has been told that architecture is a fixed, a real, a specific, a definite thing; that it's all done, that it's all known, arranged, tabulated and put away neatly in handy packages called books. He is allowed to believe, though perhaps not distinctly so taught, that, to all intents and purposes, when his turn comes, if he wishes to make some architecture for Americans, or for this generation at large, he can dip it out of his books with the same facility that dubs a grocer dipping beans out of a bin. He is taught by the logic of events that architecture in practice is a commercial article, like a patent medicine, unknown in its mixture, and sold to the public exclusively on the brand.

He has seriously been told at the school, and has been encouraged in this belief by the indorsement of people of culture, that he can learn all about architecture if he but possess the attributes of scholarship and industry. That architecture is the name of a system of accredited, historical facts as useful, as available and as susceptible to inspection as the books of a mercantile house.

Everything literal, formal and smart in his nature has been encouraged, the early and plastic glow of emotion and sensibility has been ignored.

He has been taught many cold and dead things, but the one warm living thing that he has not been taught and apparently never will be taught is the stately and all-comprehending truth that architecture, wherever it has appeared and reached a spontaneous culmination is not at all what we so stupidly call a reality, but, on the contrary, it is a most complex, a glowing and gloriously wrought metaphor, embodying as no other form of language under the sun can do, the pure, clean and deep inspiration of the race flowing as a stream of living water from its well-spring to the sea.

He has not been taught that an architect, to be a true exponent of his time, must possess first, last and always the sympathy, the intuition of a poet; that this is the one real, vital principle that survives through all places and all times.

This seeking for a natural expression of our lives, of our thoughts, our meditations, our feelings, is the architectural art as I understand it; and it is because I so understand it, that ignoring the viciousness of the past, I gladly make an appeal to the good that is in human nature; that goodness of heart and soundness of head, that ready and natural response of the soul in which I have always trusted and shall always trust. It is to this sane and wholesome quality that I plead for the abiding sincerity and nobility of our art. It is to this *manliness* that I call to come before the judgment seat and make an answer for us.

I know very well that our country will in due time possess a most interesting, varied, characteristic and beautiful architecture; that the time will begin whenever we take as our point of the departure the few and simple elements of architecture and not its complex forms. That this time will come just so soon as the young are relieved of the depressing weight of a factitious education, the benumbing influence of an instruction that insulates them from the vitalizing currents of nature. Just so soon as those having them in charge, coming to the full sense of the fact, realizing how truly dangerous a thing is a little knowledge, a partial knowledge, dreading to assume the responsibility for stunted, for imperfectly developed natures, feeling how deeply necessary it is that a technical or intellectual training be supplemented by a full, a rich, a chaste development of the emotions, shall say to the young that they are free, that from the musty school they may fly to the open air, to the sunshine, to the birds, the flowers, and wanton and joyous in their own fancies, face to face with the integrity of nature, they shall substitute for the arbitrary discipline of the school the natural, the easy self-control of a dignified manhood, to the end that not books but personal feeling, personal character and personal responsibility shall form the true foundation of their art.

It has, alas, for centuries been taught that the intellect and the emotions were two separate and antagonistic things. This teaching has been firmly believed, cruelly lived up to.

How depressing it is to realize that it might have been taught that they are two beautifully congenial and harmonious phases of that single and integral essence that we call the soul. That no nature in which the development of either is wanting can be called a completely rounded nature.

That, therefore, classical architecture, so called (meaning the Greek), was one-sided and incomplete because it was almost exclusively intellectual. That the emotional architecture (meaning especially the Gothic) was likewise one-sided and incomplete, however great and beautiful its development of feeling, because of the almost total absence of mentality. That no complete architecture has yet appeared in the history of the world because men, in this form of art alone, have obstinately sought to express themselves solely in terms either of the head or of the heart.

I hold that architectural art, thus far, has failed to reach its highest development, its fullest capability of imagination, of thought and expression because it has not yet found a way to become truly plastic; it does not yet respond to the poet's touch. That it is today the only art for which the multitudinous rhythms of outward nature, the manifold fluctuations of man's inner being have no significance, no place.

That the Greek architecture, unerring as far as it went—and it went very far indeed in one direction—was but one radius within the field of a possible circle of expression. That, though perfect in its eyesight, definite in its desires, clear in its purpose, it was not resourceful in forms; that it lacked the flexibility and the humanity to respond to the varied and constantly shifting desires of the heart.

It was a pure, it was a noble art, wherefore we call it classic; but after all it was an apologetic art, for while possessing serenity it lacked the divinely human element of mobility. The Greek never caught the secret of the changing of the seasons, the orderly and complete sequence of their rhythm within the calmly moving year. Nor did this self-same Greek know what we now know of nature's bounty, for music in those days had not been born; this lovely friend, approaching man to man, had not yet begun to bloom as a rose, to exhale its wondrous perfume.

That the Gothic architecture, with somber, ecstatic eye, with its thought far above with Christ in the heavens, seeing but little here below, feverish and overwrought, taking comfort in gardening and plant life, sympathizing deeply with nature's visible forms, evolved a copious and rich variety of incidental expressions, but lacked the unitary comprehension, the absolute consciousness and mastery of pure form that can come alone of unclouded and serene contemplation, of perfect repose and peace of mind.

I believe, in other words, that the Greek knew the statics, the Goth the dynamics of the art, but that neither of them suspected the mobile equilibrium of it—neither of them divined the movement and stability of nature. Failing in this, both have forever fallen short, and must pass away when the true, the *Poetic Architecture* shall arise; that architecture which shall speak with clearness, with eloquence and with warmth of the fullness, the completeness of man's intercourse with nature and with his fellow men.

Moreover, we know, or should by this time know, that human nature has now become too rich in possessions, too well equipped, too magnificently endowed that any hitherto architecture can be said to have hinted at its resources, much less to have exhausted them by anticipation.

It is this consciousness, his pride, that shall be our motive, our friend, philosopher and guide in the beautiful country that stretches so invitingly before us.

In that land, the schools, having found the object of their long, blind searching, shall teach directness, simplicity, naturalness; they shall protect the young against palpable illusion. They shall teach that, while man once invented a process called composition, nature has forever brought forth organisms. They shall encourage the love of nature that wells up in every childish heart, and shall not suppress, shall not stifle the teeming imagination of the young.

They shall teach, as the result of their own bitter experience, that conscious mental effort, that conscious emotionality, are poor mates to breed from, and that true parturition comes of a deep, instinctive, subconscious desire. That true art, springing fresh from nature, must have in it, to live, much of the glance of an eye, much of the sound of a voice, much of the life of a life.

That nature is strong, generous, comprehensive, fecund, subtile; that in growth and decadence she continually sets forth the drama of man's life.

That, thro' the rotating seasons, thro' the procession of the years, thro' the march of the centuries, permeating all, sustaining all, there murmurs the still, small voice of a power that holds us in the hollow of its hand.

THE MODERN PHASE IN ARCHITECTURE

In practice as head of his own office, Sullivan waited for commissions which came less frequently, although among them was his last major one; what is now the Carson, Pirie, Scott & Co. department store on State Street, Chicago. Meanwhile his sense of the urgency of his mission remained constant; and so did his need to express it to the young practitioners of his art. Both are clear in the following letter, dated May 30, 1899 and addressed to Max Dunning, secretary of the Chicago Architectural Club at the time it was written. Presumably read by Dunning to a convention of architects in Cleveland in 1899, it was published in the *Inland Architect and News-Record* in June of that year.

The Cleveland meeting of the Architectural Clubs of the country will mark, I believe, the auspicious opening of a new era in the growth of architectural thought.

It should, in the nature of things, be of serious import to us, of the present and active generation, to know what the generation to follow thinks and feels.

Its thoughts may be immature, its feelings vague and formless; yet, nevertheless, in them the future life of our art is surely working out its destiny: and the sincerity of them is not to be denied.

Youth is the most ambitious, the most beautiful, but the most helpless stage of life.

It has that immediate and charming idealism which leads in the end toward greatness.

Youth is ineffable.

I have said good bye to mine—with solicitude I welcome yours.

Perceiving, as I do, the momentous sway and drift of modern life, knowing as I do that the curtain has arisen on a drama the most intense and passionate in all history, I urge that you cast away as worthless the shopworn and empirical notion that an architect is an artist—whatever that funny word may mean, and accept my assurance that he is and imperatively shall be a poet—and an interpreter of the national life of his time.

Do you fully realize how despicable a man is who betrays a trust?

Do you know, or can you foresee, or instinctively judge how acutely delicate will become, in your time, the element of confidence and dependence between man and man and between society and the individual?

If you realize this, you will realize at once and forever, that you, by birth, and by the beneficence of the form of government under which you live—that you are called upon, not to betray, but to express the life of your own day and generation. That society will have just cause to hold you to account for your uses of the liberty that it has given to you, and the confidence it has reposed in you.

You will realize, in due time, as your lives develop and expand, and you become richer in experience, that a fraudulent and surreptitious use of historical documents, however suavely presented, however cleverly plagiarized, however neatly re-packaged, however shrewdly intrigued, will constitute and will be held to be a betrayal of a trust.

You know very well what I mean. You know in your own hearts that you are to be fakirs or you are to be honest men.

It is futile to quibble, or to protest, or to plead ignorance or innocence, or to asseverate and urge the force of circumstance.

Society is, in the main, honest—for why should it not be—and it will not ask and will not expect you to be liars. It will give to you every reasonable and every legitimate backing, if you can prove to it, by your acts, that artistic pretention is not a synonym for moral irresponsibility.

If you take the pains truly to understand your country, your people, your day, your generation; the time, the place in which you live—if you seek to understand, absorb and sympathize with the life around you, you will be understood and sympathetically received in return. Have no fear as to this.

Society soon will have no use for people who have no use for it. The clairvoyance of the age is steadily unfolding—and it will result therefrom, that the greatest poet will be he who shall grasp and deify the commonplaces of our life: those simple, normal feelings which the people of his day will be helpless, otherwise, to express—And here you have the key, with which, individually, you may unlock, in time, the portal of your art.

I truly believe that your coming together will result in great things. You have my sympathy.

I am with you in spirit—for, in you, resides the only hope, the only sign of dawn that I can see—making for a day that shall regenerate an art that should be, may be and must be the noblest, the most intimate, the most expressive, the most eloquent of all.

Your youth is your most precious heritage from the past—I am with you.

AN UNAFFECTED SCHOOL OF MODERN ARCHITECTURE — WILL IT COME?

Also in 1899, a magazine called *The Artist* reprinted the following essay, from the catalog of an exhibition of the T Square Club of Philadelphia, where it had been published as one of various replies to the title-question, solicited from leading architects and professors of architecture. The editor noted that Sullivan had re-phrased the question before answering it.

Sir——In reply to your inquiry, 'Do you as yet see any sings tending to indicate the development of an indigenous architecture in America?' I say that in my judgment there are such signs and indications, but they are not as clearly defined as I should wish to see them. The opportunities for developing an indigenous art are so abundant, so vital, so convincing, that I must confess to a sincere surprise that progress toward that end has not been more spontaneous and more significant.

It is not, for my mind, a thinkable proposition that from a people democratic and free, self-reliant, resourceful, possessed of their own bodies, possessed of their own souls, self-centered, deep of aspiration, there shall not some day suspire as an exhalation an architectural art germane to those gifts, responsive to that throb, eloquently voicing every form, every aspect of what is genuine in our national life.

On the other hand, it is clear to me that architecture, as now generally practiced, is feudal or monarchical; an architecture of the governed for the governing. Against this set the thought that self-government is the highest form of government; and is it not toward this that we aspire as a nation and as individuals?

Is it, therefore, reasonable to suppose that the art forms of a not free people can really express the life of a free people? Yet that is the popular supposition.

American architects as a class must become American in thought and sympathy before we can have any widespread manifestation of an indigenous art. That this will come about in due time I have not a doubt, for we certainly have an abundance of talent, and there is certainly an undercurrent of dissatisfaction with prevailing methods. Restlessness and discontent are always the heralds of great movements.

To emphasize the thought: Before we can have an indigenous architecture, the American architect must himself become indigenous. How this is to be done is very easy to explain, but rather difficult of performance; for it is equivalent to asking him to become a poet, in the sense that he must absorb into his heart and brain his own country and his own people.

The rest is difficult also, but certain as the rising of tomorrow's sun is certain; for the power of imagination and the science of expression become limitless when we open our hearts to nature and to our people as the source of inspiration. It is practically in this active, vital faculty of reciprocity that we are now paralytics.

THE YOUNG MAN IN ARCHITECTURE

The turn of the century brought with it a note of strain and rancor in Sullivan's writing: he had for some years previous endured a series of personal and professional humiliations and defeats; and meanwhile he considered that the forces blighting American democracy and its culture were growing, not weakening, in their virulence. It was characteristic of Sullivan's temper that in the face of this, his own conviction and insistence grew, instead of weakening. But for the first time we encounter passages of arrogant hectoring; the exasperation of the prophet in the wilderness begins to be heard in this paper, read before the Architectural League of America, June, 1900.

It is my premise that the Architectural League of America has its being in a sense of discontent with conditions now prevailing in the American malpractice of the architectural art; in a deep and wide sense of conviction that no aid is to be expected from the generation now representing that malpractice; and in the instinctive feeling that, through banding together, force, discretion and coherence may be given to the output of these feelings which are, in themselves, for the time being, vague and miscellaneous, however intensely they may be felt.

Did I not believe that this statement substantially represents the facts, I should be the last to take an interest in your welfare—I would be indifferent concerning what you did or what you did not.

That you have abundant reason for discontent needs no proof; let him read who runs through the streets.

That you have cause for discontent is evident. That you should feel discontent gives one a delightfully cynical sense of shock, and a new-born desire to believe in the good, the true, the beautiful and the young.

American architecture is composed, in the hundred, of ninety parts aberration, eight parts indifference, one part poverty and one part Little Lord Fauntleroy. You can have the prescription filled at any architectural department-store, or select architectural millinery establishment.

As it is my desire to speak from the viewpoint that architecture should be practiced as an art and not strictly as a commercial pursuit, and as I am assuming that you agree with me in this respect, we may now pertinently inquire wherein does this American architecture differ from the architecture of the past.

It differs in little, if in anything, provided we except the few great epochs. Human nature has changed but little since the time Man was slaughterer or the slaughtered of the great white bear.

Seldom, in the past, has Man thought of aught but war, which menaced his life; religion, which menaced his soul; hunger, which menaced his stomach; or love, which concerned his progeny. From time to time this tempestuous sky has calmed, for a divine moment, and the glory of man has shone forth upon a fertile land. Then came the angry elements—and the sun departed. This, in brief, is the recurrent history of man from the beginning. You change the values in the formula to suit the epoch, the century or the generation.

Ninety-nine years of the hundred the thoughts of nine hundred and ninety-nine people of the thousand are sordid. This always has been true. Why should we expect a change. Of one hundred so-called thoughts that the average man thinks (and thus he has ever thought), ninety-nine are illusions, the remaining one a caprice.

From time to time in the past, these illusions have changed their focus and become realities, and the one caprice has become an overwhelming desire.

These changes were epoch making.

And the times were called golden.

In such times came the white-winged angel of sanity.

And the great styles arose in greeting.

Then soon the clear eye dimmed.

The sense of reality was lost.

Then followed architectures, to all intents and purposes quite like this American architecture of today:

Wherein the blind sought much discourse of color.

The deaf to discuss harmonics.

The dry of heart twaddled about the divinity of man.

The mentally crippled wrought fierce combats in the arena of logic.

And so it has come about that the white-winged angel has been on a far journey these six hundred years.

Now, insisting for the moment, in spite of the hierarchy, that this white-winged absence is of gentle sex, I entreat your close attention:

Let radiant and persuasive Youth lure her back again to earth!

For that she hovers in the visible blue of your firmament I can prove to you beyond a gossamer of doubt.

That she awaits with eager ear the spring-enthralling voice of adolescence, the clear, sweet morning-call of a pure heart, the spontaneity and jocund fervor of a bright and winning mind, the glance of a modest and adoring eye!

That she awaits.

That she has so long awaited.

That she cannot make herself first known to you.

Alas, 'tis of her enchantment that she is invisible and dumb!

Perhaps this is enough of poesy.

Let us say, enough likewise of the prevailing cacaphony; of

The howling of the vast and general horde of Bedlamites.

The purring of the select company of Ruskinites.

The gasping of the Emersonites.

The rasping of the Spencerites.

The moaning of the Tennysonites.

The whimper of the aesthetes.

The yowling of reformers.

The yapping of strenuous livers.

The rustle of the rustlers.

The hustle of the hustlers.

The howl of the taxpayers.

And the clang of the trolley car:

All, signs, omens and predictions of our civilization.

We are commanded to know that there is much of mystery, much of the esoteric, in the so-called architectural styles. That there is a holiness in so-called pure art which the hand of the Modern may not profane.

So be it.

Let us be the Cat.

And let the pure art be the King.

We will look at him.

And we will also look at the good king's good children, the great styles.

And at his retinue of bastards, the so-called other styles.

There is, or at least there is said to be, a certain faculty of the mind, whereby the mind or the faculty, as you choose, is on the one hand enabled to dissolve a thing into its elements, and, on the other hand, to build up these or similar elements into the same or a similar thing. This process is, I believe, called Logic; the first operation going by the name, analysis, and the second, synthesis. Some men possess the half-faculty of separating; others the half-faculty of upbuilding. When the whole faculty exists in one man, in a moderate degree, he is said to be gifted. When he has it in a high degree, he is said to be highly gifted; and when in the highest degree he is called a genius or a mastermind. When a man has neither the one half-faculty nor the other half-faculty he is mentally sterile.

I fear lest the modern architect be placed in this category, by reason of his devious ways.

Let us suppose ourselves nevertheless, moderately gifted and apply our analysis to the great styles:

Presto, dissolve!

We have as residuum, two uprights, and a horizontal connecting them.

We have two bulky masses and an arch connecting them.

Revolve your arches and you have a dome.

Do the trick a few times more with a few other styles and you have the Elements of Architecture.

We approach in the same way a master mind, and all speedily disappears leaving insoluble Desire.

The architectural elements, in their baldest form, the desire of the heart in its most primitive, animal form, are the foundation of architecture.

They are the dust and the breathing spirit.

All the splendor is but a gorgeous synthesis of these.

The logic of the books, is, at best, dry reading; and, moreover, it is nearly or quite dead, because it comes at second hand.

The human mind, in operation, is the original document.

Try to read it.

If you find this for the moment too difficult and obscure, try to study a plant as it grows from its tiny seed and expands toward its full fruition. Here is a process, a spectacle, a poem, or whatever you may wish to call it, not only absolutely logical in essence, because exhibiting in its highest form the unity and duality of analysis and synthesis, but, which is of vastly greater import, vital and inevitable: and it is specifically to this phenomenon that I wish to draw your earnest attention, if it be true, and I sincerely hope that such is the fact, that you wish to become real architects—not the imitation brand. For I wish to show to you, or at least to intimate to you, how naturally and smoothly and inevitably the human mind will operate if it be not harassed or thwarted in its normal and instinctive workings.

Some day, watch the sun as he rises, courses through the sky, and sets. Note what your part of the earth does meanwhile.

Ponder the complex results of this simple, single cause.

Some year, observe how rhythmically the seasons follow the sun. Note their unfailing, spontaneous logic; their exquisite analyses and synthesis—their vital, inevitable balance.

When you have time or opportunity, spare a moment to note a wild bird, flying; a wave, breaking on the shore. Try to grasp the point that, while these things are common they are by no means commonplace.

Note any simple thing or act whatsoever provided only, it be natural not artificial—the nearer undisturbed nature the better; if in the wilderness better still, because wholly away from the perverting influence of man.

Whenever you have done these things attentively and without mental bias or preoccupation, wholly receptive in your humor, there will come to your intelligence a luminous idea of a resultant organic complexity, which together, will constitute the first significant step in your architectural education, because they are the basis of rhythm.

There will gently dawn in your mind an awakening of something vital, something organic, something elemental, that is urging things about you through their beautiful, characteristic rhythms, and that is holding them in most exquisite balance.

A little later you will become aware with amazement that this same impulse is working on your own minds, and that never before had you suspected it. This will be the second step in your architectural education.

Later you will perceive, with great pleasure, that there is a notable similarity, an increasing sympathy between the practical workings of your own minds and the workings of nature about you.

When this perception shall have grown into a definite, clear-cut consciousness, it will constitute the closing of the first chapter and the opening of all the remaining chapters in your architectural education, for you will have arrived at the basis of organized thinking.

You will have observed doubtless that, thus far, while endeavoring to lead you toward a sane and wholesome conception of the basis of the architectural art, I have said not a word about books, photographs or plates. I have done this advisedly, for I am convinced beyond the shadow of a doubt that never can you acquire from books, or the like, alone, even a remote conception of what constitutes the real, the living architectural art. It has been tried for generations upon generations with one unvarying result: dreary, miserable failure.

To appreciate a book at its just value, you must first know what words signify, what men signify and what nature signifies.

Books, taken in their totality, have one ostensible object, one just function—namely, to make a record of Man's relation to his fellowmen and to Nature, and the relation of both of these to an all-pervading, Inscrutable Spirit.

To these relations, Mankind, in its prodigious effort to define its own status, has given thousands upon thousands of names.

These names are called words.

Each word has a natural history.

Each word is not the simple thing it appears, but, on the contrary, it is a highly complex organism, carrying in its heart more smiles, more tears, more victories, more downfalls, more bloody sweats, more racial agonies than you can ever dream of.

Some of these words are very old.

They still cry with the infancy of the race.

Therefore, should I begin by putting into your hands a book, or its equivalent, I would, according to my philosophy, be guilty of an intellectual crime.

I would be as far from the true path, as I now most heartily regard most teachers of the architectural art to be.

I would be as reckless and brutal as my predecessors. But I would not be as unconscious of it as they appear to be. Therefore, I say with emphasis, begin by observing.

Seek to saturate your minds by direct personal contact with things that are natural, not sophisticated.

Strive to form your own judgments, at first in very small things, gradually in larger and larger things. Do not lean upon the judgment of others if it is reasonably within your power to form your own.

Thus, though you may often stumble and wander, such experiences will be valuable because personal; it is far better that they occur in youth than in maturer years. Gradually, by virtue of this very contact with things, you will acquire that sure sense of physical reality which is the necessary first step in a career of independent thinking.

But strive not, I caution you, after what is called originality. If you do you will be starting in exactly the wrong way. I wish distinctly to impress upon you, that what I am advocating and what I am in turn striving to point out to you is the normal development of your minds. That if the mind is properly nurtured, properly trained, and left free to act with spontaneity, individuality of expression will come to you as naturally as the flower comes to the plant, for it is nature's law.

When you begin to feel the flow and stimulation of mind which are first fruits of wholesome exercise of the faculties, you may begin to read the books. Read them carefully and cautiously, not superciliously.

Bear in mind that books, generaly speaking, are composed mainly of sophistries, assumptions, borrowings, stealings, inadequate representations or positive perversions of truth. The author, too frequently, is posing, masquerading or ambuscading. His idea is to impress you. He himself well knows how little he has to say that can, in strictness, be classed as truth in his possession only. You will soon have no trouble in discerning the exception, and the exceptions, by their value, will conclusively prove the rule.

Later you may turn from the documents called books to the documents called buildings and you will find that what I have said of books applies with equal force to buildings and to their authors. Soon you will be enabled to separate the wheat from the chaff.

Thus, one after the other, you may pass in review the documents called Music, Painting, Sculpture, Agriculture, Commerce, Manufactures, Government, etc. You will find them, for your purposes, much alike. You will, ere long, acquire an inkling of the fullness and the emptiness of these documents, if, as I advise, you keep closely in touch with nature.

When you know something more of the working of the human mind than you now know (and the day will not be long in coming if you follow the program I am indicating), you will not be greatly surprised, when taking a backward glance, that those in high places today seemingly believe or profess to believe that the fruit need bear no relation to the tree.

You will be no more amused than I am at the psychological irony presented by the author of a callously illogical building declaring in solemn tones that it is the product of a logical mind.

You will smile with wonderment when you recall that it is now taught, or appears now to be taught, that like does not beget like; whereas you will know that nature has, for unnumbered ages and at every instant, proclaimed that like can beget nothing but its like:

That logical mind will beget a logical building.

That an illogical mind will beget an illogical building.

That perversity will bring forth perversity.

That the children of the mind will reveal the parent.

You will smile again when you reflect that it was held in your youth that there was no necessary relationship between function and form. That function was one thing, form another thing.

True, it might have seemed queer to some if a pine tree had taken on the form of a rattlesnake, and, standing vertically on its tail, had brought forth pine cones; or that a rattlesnake, vice versa, should take on the form of a pine tree and wiggle along the ground biting the heel of the passer-by.

Yet, this suggestion is not a whit queerer than are some of the queer things now filling the architectural view, as, for instance, a steel frame function in a masonry form.

Imagine, for instance:

Horse-eagles:

Pumpkin-bearing frogs:

Frog-bearing pea vines;

Tarantula-potatoes;

Sparrows in the form of whales, picking up crumbs in the streets.

If these combinations seem incongruous and weird, I assure you in all seriousness that they are not a whit more so than the curiosities encountered with such frequency by the student of what nowadays passes for architecture.

With this difference, only, that, inasmuch as the similarity is chiefly mental, it can produce no adequate impression on those who have never felt the sensitizing effect of thought.

You will remember that it was held that a national style must be generations in forming and that the inference you were to draw from this was that the individual should take no thought for his own natural development because it would be futile so to do, because, as it were, it would be an impertient presumption.

I tell you exactly the contrary: Give all your thought to individual development, which it is entirely within your province and power to control; and let the nationality come in due time as a consequence of the inevitable convergence of thought.

If anyone tells you that it is impossible, within a lifetime, to develop and perfect a complete individuality of expression, a well-ripened and perfected personal style, tell him that you know better and that you will prove it by your lives. Tell him with little ceremony, whoever he may be, that he is grossly ignorant of first principles, that he lives in the dark.

It is claimed that the great styles of the past are the sources of inspiration for this architecture of the present. This fact is the vehement assertion of those who 'worship' them.

Would you believe it? Really would you believe it!

So it appears that like can beget its unlike after all. That a noble style may beget, through the agency of an ignoble mind, an ignoble building.

It may be true that a blooded male may beget, through a mongrel female, a cur progeny. But the application of this truth to the above instance wherein occurs the great word Inspiration, implies a brutal perversion of meaning and a pathetic depravity in those who use that word for their sinister ends.

For inspiration, as I conceive it, is the intermediary between God and man, the pure fruition of the soul at one with immaculate nature, the greeting of noble minds.

To use this word in a tricky endeavor to establish a connection legitimizing the architecture of the present as the progeny of the noblest thought in the past, is, to my mind, a blasphemy, and so it should appear to yours.

In truth the American architecture of today is the offspring of an illegitimate commerce with the mongrel styles of the past.

Do not deceive yourselves for a moment as to this.

It is a harsh indictment.

But it is warranted by the facts.

Yet, let us not be too severe. Let us remember and make what allowance we may for the depressing, stultifying, paralyzing influence of an unfortunate education. After all, every American man has had to go to school. And everything that he has been taught over and above the three R's has been in essence for his mental undoing.

I cannot possibly emphasize this lamentable fact too strongly. And the reason, alas, is so clear, so forcible, so ever-present, as you will see.

We live under a form of Government called Democracy. And we, the people of the United States of America, constitute the most colossal instance known in history of a people seeking to verify the fundamental truth that self-government is Nature's law for Man.

It is of the essence of Democracy that the individual man is free in his body and free in his soul.

It is a corollary therefrom, that he must govern or restrain himself, both as to bodily acts and mental acts; that, in short, he must set up a responsible government within his own individual person.

It implies that highest form of emancipation, of liberty—physical, mental and spiritual—by virtue whereof man calls the gods to the judgment, while he heeds the divinity of his own soul.

It is the ideal of Democracy that the individual man should stand self-centered, self-governing—an individual sovereign, an individual god.

Now, who will assert, specifically, that our present system of higher architectural education is in accord with this aspiration? That the form, Education, bears any essential relation other than that of antagonism to the function, Democracy?

It is our misfortune that it does not.

We, as a people, are too youthful. We are too new among the world forces. We are too young. We have not yet had time to discover precisely the trouble, though we feel in our hearts that something is amiss. We have been too busy. And so comes about the incongruous spectacle of the infant Democracy taking its mental nourishment at the withered breast of despotism.

To understand it from our point of view, examine! These are the essential points:

We are to revere authority.

We are to take everything at second-hand.

We are to believe measurements are superior to thought.

We are advised not to think.

We are cautioned that by no possibility can we think as well as did our predecessors.

We are not to examine; *not* to test, *not* to prove.

We are to regard ourselves as the elect, because, forsooth, we have been instructed by the elect.

We must conform.

We are not to go behind the scenes.

We are to do as we are told and ask not foolish questions.

We are taught that there is a royal road to our art.

We are taught hero worship: we are not taught what the hero worshipped.

We are taught that nature is one thing, man another thing.

We are taught that God is one thing, man another thing.

Does this conform to the ideal of Democracy?

Is this a fitting overture to the world's greatest drama?

Is it not extraordinary that we survive it even in part?

Is it a wonder that our representative architecture is vapid, foolish, priggish, insolent, and pessimistic?

Manifestly you cannot become truly educated in the schools.

Ergo, you must educate yourselves.

There is no other course, no other hope.

For the schools have not changed much in my generation; they will, I fear, not change much in your generation, and soon it will be too late for you.

Strive, strive therefore while you are young and eager, to apply to your mental development the rules of physical development!

Put yourselves in training, so to speak.

Strive to develop in your minds the agility, flexibility, precision, poise, endurance, and judgment of the athlete.

Seek simple, wholesome, nourishing food for the mind.

You will be surprised and charmed with the results.

The human mind in its natural state, not drowsed and stupefied by a reactionary education, is the most marvelously active agency in all nature.

You may trust implicitly in the results of this activity if its surroundings are wholesome.

The mind will inevitably reproduce what it feeds upon.

If it feeds upon filth, it will reproduce filth.

If it feeds upon nature, it will reproduce nature.

If it feeds upon man, it will reproduce man.

If it feeds upon all of these, it will reproduce all of these.

It will reproduce infallibly whatever it is fed upon.

It is a wonderful machine; its activity cannot wholly be quenched except by death. It may be slowed down or accelerated, it cannot be stopped.

It may be abused in every conceivable way, but it will not stop, even in insanity, even in sleep.

So beware how you tamper with this marvelous mechanism, for it will record inevitably, in all its output, whatever you do to it.

The human mind is the summation of all the ages. It holds in trust the wisdom and the folly of all the past.

Beware what you do to it, for it will give you bad for your bad, good for your good. It is a mechanism of such inconceivable delicacy and complexity.

Man through his physical infancy is most carefully nurtured. His delicate and fragile helpless little body is tenderly watched with all the solicitude of parental affection. Indeed, under the law he is still a child until the age of twenty-one.

But his mind! Who cares for his mind?

After he has passed from the simple, beautiful ministrations at his mother's knee, who guards this ineffably delicate impressionable organism?

Oh, the horror of it!

Oh, ye gods, where is justice, where is mercy, where is love!

To think that the so-called science of political economy is so futile, so drugged with feudalism that it has not noted this frightful waste, this illogical interruption of the happiness of the human family, this stark, staring incongruity in our education!

That it does not perceive, in its search for the sources of wealth, the latent richness of the human mind, its immense wealth of practical possibilities, the clearly marked indications of enormous productiveness—a productiveness sane and of vital consequence to the public welfare!

So much for a science which regards man as a mechanical unit. It is typical, in a measure, of the learning we have donned as a misfit garment.

You have every reason to congratulate yourselves that you are young, for you have so much the less to unlearn, and so much the greater fund of enthusiasm. A great opportunity is yours. The occasion confronts you. The future is in your hands—will you accept the responsibility or will you evade it?

That is the only vital question I have come here to put to you.

I do not ask an answer now.

I am content with putting the question.

For it is the first time that the question ever has been put squarely to you.

I ask only that you consider this:

Do you intend, or do you not intend; do you wish or do you not wish to become architects in whose care an unfolding Democracy may entrust the interpretation of its material wants, its psychic aspirations?

In due time doubtless you will answer in your own way.

But I warn you the time left for an answer in the right way is acutely brief.

For you as you are, you are not as young as you were yesterday— And tomorrow?

Tomorrow!

WHAT IS ARCHITECTURE: A STUDY IN THE AMERICAN PEOPLE OF TODAY

During the early years of the century Sullivan endured increasing solitude and professional inactivity. But he thereby gained an opportunity, which he seized hungrily, to bring his intellectual prowess, tested in working out a theory of architecture, to the study of human history. A less comprehensive and systematic thinker than he may have supposed himself to be, Sullivan nevertheless had the advantage of a man who organizes all his thoughts around a few consistent, and highly fecund, insights, applying them to the conditions of his own life and work. The following piece, first published in *The American Contractor*, January, 1906, states all its author's central themes, with a view of architecture less as an art than as an index and expression of social health or disease — and with an increase in the disturbing tendency to deliver his message in a style which sometimes is jarringly reminiscent of the hot gospellers of the period.

The intellectual trend of the hour is toward simplification. The full powers of the modern scientific mind are now directed, with a common consent, toward searching out the few and simple principles that are believed to underlie the complexity of Nature, and such investigation is steadily revealing a unitary impulse underlying all men and all things.

This method of analysis reveals a curious aspect of Man, namely: that as he thinks, so he acts; and, conversely, one may read in his acts what he thinks—his real thoughts, be it understood, not what he avows he he thinks. For all men think, all men act. To term a man unthinking is a misuse of words; what really is meant is that he does not think with accuracy, fitness and power. If, then, it be true that as a man thinks so must he act in inevitable accordance with his thought, so is it true that society, which is but a summation of individuals, acts precisely as it thinks. Thus are the thoughts of a people to be read in the acts of a people, as clearly as words are read upon the printed page.

If, in like manner, we apply this method of analysis to the complex spread of historical and contemporaneous architecture, we perceive, clearly revealed in their simplicity, its three elementary forms, namely, the pier, the lintel, and the arch. These are the three, the only three letters, from which has expanded the Architectural Art as a great and superb language wherewith Man has expressed, through the generations, the changing drift of his thoughts. Thus, throughout the past and the present, each building stands as a social act. In such act we read that which cannot escape our analysis, for it is indelibly fixed in the building namely, the nature of the thoughts of the individual and the people whose image the building is or was.

Perhaps I should not leave the three elements, pier, lintel, and arch, thus baldly set forth. It may not appear to the reader that the truth concerning them is as clear and simple as I state it. He may think, for example, that there was a marked difference between the Egyptian and the Greek Architectures, even though both were based on pier and lintel only. There was a marked difference. The difference that existed between the Egyptian and the Greek minds. The Egyptian animated pier and lintel with his thought—he could not do otherwise; and the Egyptian temple took form as an Egyptian act—it could not be otherwise. So Greek thought, clearly defined, took form in the Greek temple, clearly defined, and the Greek temple stood clearly forth as a Greek act. Yet both were as simply pier-and-lintel as I, in setting one brick upon two separated other bricks, simply expose the principles of pier and lintel.

Similarly the Roman aqueduct and the medival cathedral were both in the pier-and-arch form. But what a far cry from Roman thought to medieval thought! And how clearly is that difference in thought shown in the differences in form taken on in each case by pier and arch, as each structure in its time stood forth as an act of the people. How eloquently these structures speak to us of the militant and simple power of Roman thought, of the mystic yearning of medieval thought.

But, you may say, these structures were not acts of the people, rather, in one case the act of an emperor, in the other case an act of the church. Very well; but what really was the emperor but an act of the people—expressing the thought of the people; and what was the church but simiilarly the thought of the people in action? When the thought of the Roman people changed, the vast Roman fabric disintegrated; when the thought of the medieval people changed, the vitality of the church subsided exactly in proportion as the supporting thought of the people was withdrawn. Thus every form of government, every social institution, every undertaking, however great, however small, every symbol of enlightenment or degradation, each and all have sprung and are still springing from the life of the people, and have ever formed and are now as surely forming images of their thought. Slowly by centuries, generations, years, days, hours, the thought of the people has changed; so with precision have their acts responsively changed; thus thoughts and acts have flowed and are flowing ever onward, unceasingly onward, involved within the impelling power of Life. Throughout this stream of human life, and thought, and activity, men have ever felt the need to build; and from the need arose the power to build. So, as they thought, they built; for, strange as it may seem, they could build in no other way. As they built, they made, used and left behind them records of their thinking. Then, as through the years new men came with changed thoughts, so arose new buildings in consonance with the change of thought—the building always the expression of the thinking. Whatever the character of the thinking, just so was the character of the building. Pier, lintel, and arch changed in form, purpose and expression, following, with the fidelity of Life, Man's changing thoughts as he moved in the flow of his destiny—as he was moved ever onward by a drift unseen and unknown—and which is now flowing and is still unseen and unknown.

This flow of building we call Historical Architecture. At no time and in no instance has it been other than an index of the flow of the thought of the people—an emanation from the inmost life of the people.

Perhaps you think this is not so; perhaps you think the feudal lord built the fortified castle. So he did, ostensibly. But where did his need and power so to build come from? From his retainers. And whence came the power of his retainers? From the people. As the people thought, so they acted. And thus the power of the feudal lord rested upon the thought, the belief of the people; upon their need and upon their power. Thus all power rests upon the consent of the people, that is, upon their thought. The instant their thought begins to change, that instant the power, resting upon it and sanctioned by it, begins its waning. Thus the decay of the old and the formation of the new are synchronous effects of one cause. That single cause is: Thought. Thus we perceive that the simplest aspect of all human activity is change.

To analyze the influences that cause thought to change would take me, now, too far afield. Suffice it to say that thought, once having undergone change, does not again become the same—however great the lapse in time. Thus is there ever new birth, never rebirth.

It may now become clear to my reader that we ought, in viewing historic Architecture, to cease to regard it under the artificial classification of
styles, as is now the accepted way, and to consider (as is more natural
and more logical) each building of the past and the present as a product
and index of the thought of the people of the time and place. In this way we
shall develop in our minds a much broader, clearer panorama of the actual
living flow of Architecture through the ages; and grasp the clear, simple,
accurate notion, that Architecture always has been, and still is, a simple
impulse of which the manifestation in varied form is continuously changing.

I should add, perhaps, that in speaking of the people, I do not use the
word in the unhappy sense of the lower classes, so-called. I mean all the
people; and I look upon all the people as constituting a social organism.

I am quite aware that these are views not generally held among architects. Indeed you will not find a thesis of this kind set forth in books
or taught in schools. For the prevailing view concerning Architecture is
strangely artificial and fruitless, as indeed are the current American
ideas concerning almost any phase of the welfare of all the people. That
is to say; our democratic land, ideas, thoughts, are weirdly, indeed des-
tructively, undemocratic—an aspect of our current civilization which later,
I shall consider.

I therefore ask my reader, for the time being at least, to repose sufficient
confidence in my statements, that he may lay aside his existing notions
concerning Architecture, which are of necessity traditional, and, as such,
acquired habits of thinking, unanalyzed by him; and thus lay his mind
open to receive and consider the simple and more natural views which
make up my paper, to the end that he may perceive how far astray we
are from an Architecture natural, truthful, and wholesome, such as should
characterize a truly democratic people. I ask this because the welfare of
democracy is my chief concern in life; and because I have always regarded Architecture, and still so regard it, as merely one of the activities
of a people, and, as such, necessarily in harmony with all the others. For
as a people thinks concerning Architecture, so it thinks concerning everything else; and as it thinks concerning any other thing, so it thinks concerning Architecture; for the thought of a people, however complicated
it may appear, is all of-a-piece, and represents the balance of heredity and
environment at the time.

I trust, further, that a long disquisition is not necessary in order to
show that the attempt at imitation, by us of this day, of the by-gone forms

of building, is a procedure unworthy of a free people; and that the dictum of schools, that Architecture is finished and done, is a suggestion humiliating to every active brain, and, therefore, in fact, a puerility and a falsehood when weighed in the scales of truly democratic thought. Such dictum gives the lie, in arrogant fashion, to healthful human experience. It says, in a word: The American people are not fit for democracy. Perhaps they are not. If so, we shall see how and why. We shall see if this alleged unfitness is really normal and natural, or if it is a feudal condition imposed upon the people by a traditional system of inverted thinking. We shall see if those whom we have entrusted with leadership in our matters educational have or have not misled us. We shall see, in a larger sense, if we, as a people, not only have betrayed each other, but have failed in that trust which the world-spirit of democracy placed in our hands, as we, a new people, emerged to fill a new and spacious land.

All of this we shall presently read in our current Architecture, and we shall test the accuracy of that reading by a brief analysis of the thought and activities of the American people as they are expressed in other ways. For, be sure, what we shall find in our Architecture, we shall as surely find elsewhere and everywhere.

If it is assumed that the art of reading is confined to the printed page, we cannot go far. But if we broaden and quicken our sense of reading until it appears to us, in its more vital aspect, as a science, an art of interpretation, we shall go very far indeed. In truth, there will be no ending of our journey; for the broad field of nature, of human thought and endeavor, will open to us as a book of life, wherein the greatest and the smallest, the most steadfast and the most fleeting, will appear in their true value. Then will our minds have escaped slavery to WORDS and be at liberty, in the open air of reality, freely and fully to deal with THINGS.

Indeed, most of us have, in less or greater measure, this gift of reading things. We come into it naturally; but, curiously enough, many are ashamed because it does not bear the sanction of authority, because it does not bear the official stamp of that much misunderstood word scholarship, a stamp, by the way, which gives currency to most of the notions antagonistic to the development of our common thinking powers. It is this same scholastic fetichism, too, that has caused an illogical gap between the theoretical and the practical. In right thinking such gap cannot exist. A true method of education, therefore, should consist in a careful and complete development of our common and natural powers of thinking, which, in reality, are vastly greater, infinitely more susceptible to development than is generally assumed. Indeed, the contumacy in which we habitually underrate the latent powers of the average human mind is greatly to our discredit. It constitutes, in fact, a superstition. A superstition whose origin is readily traceable to the scholasticism of past centuries, and to the tenacious notion of social caste. It is definitely the opposite of the modern and enlightened view now steadily gaining ground, that the true spirit of democratic education consists in searching out, liberating and developing the splendid but obscured powers of the average man, and particularly those of his children.

It is disquieting to note that the system of education on which we lavish funds with such generous, even prodigal, hand, falls short of fulfilling its true democratic function; and that particularly in the so-called higher branches its tendency appears daily more reactionary, more feudal.

It is not an agreeable reflection that so many of our university graduates lack the trained ability to see clearly, and to think simply, concisely, constructively; that there is perhaps more showing of cynicism than good faith, seemingly more distrust of men than confidence in them, and, withal, no consummate ability to interpret things.

In contrast, we have the active-minded but 'uneducated' man, he who has so large a share in our activities. He reads well those things that he believes concern him closely. His mind is active, practical, superficial; and, whether he deals with small things or large, its quality is nearly the same in all cases. His thoughts almost always are concerned with the immediate. His powers of reflection are undeveloped, and thus he ignores those simple, vital things which grow up beside him, and with which, as a destiny, he will some day have to reckon, and will then find himself unprepared. The constructive thinking power of such men, the imaginative reach, the incisive intuition, the forceful will, sometimes amaze us. But when we examine closely we find that all this is but a brilliant superstructure, that the hidden foundation is weak because the foundation-thought was not sought to be placed broad, deep and secure in the humanities. Thus we have at the poles of our thinking two classes of men, each of which believes it is dealing with realities, but both in fact dealing with phantoms; for between them they have studied everything but the real thoughts and the real hearts of the people. They have not sufficiently reckoned with the true and only source both of social stability and of social charge. If, in time, such divergence of thought, as it grows in acuteness, shall lead to painful readjustments, such will be but the result, natural and inexorable, of a fatal misunderstanding, the outgrowth of that fatal defect in our system of thinking which is leading us away from our fellows.

If I say that these aspects of our thought are readable in our current Architecture, I am not saying too much, for acts point surely to the parent thoughts, and in everything that men do they leave an indelible imprint of their minds. If this suggestion be followed out, it will become surprisingly clear how each and every building reveals itself naked to the eye; how its every aspect, to the smallest detail, to the lightest move of the hand, reveals the workings of the mind of the man who made it, and who is responsible to us for it. Everything is there for us to read, to interpret; and this we may do at our leisure. The building has not means of locomotion, it cannot hide itself, it cannot get away. There it is, and there it will stay—telling more truths about him who made it, who thought it, than he in his fatuity imagines; revealing his mind and his heart exactly for what they are worth, not a whit more, not a whit less; telling, plainly, the lies he thinks; telling with almost cruel truthfulness of his bad faith, his feeble, wabbly mind, his impudence, his selfish egoism, his mental irresponsibility, his apathy, his disdain for real things. Is it cruelty to analyze thus clearly? Is it vivisection thus to pursue, step by step, to uncover nerve after nerve, dispassionately to probe and test and weigh act after act, thought after thought, to follow every twist and turn of the mind that made the building, sifting and judging it until at last the building says to us: 'I am no more a real building than the thing that made me is a real man!'

If so, then it must, correspondingly, be a pleasure and a genuine beneficence to recognize and note, in some other building, the honest effort of an honest man, the kindly willingness and frankness of a sincere mind to give expression to simple, direct, natural thinking, to produce a building as real as the man who made it.

And is it not, as naturally, helpful to recognize and note in still another building a mind perhaps not too well trained, perhaps not very sure of itself, but still courageously seeking a way; the building showing where the mind stumbles and tries again, showing just where the thought is not immanent, not clear, not self-centered?

It is not the part of wisdom to cheer, to encourage such a mind, rather than to dishearten it with ridicule? To say to it: Learn that the mind works best when allowed to work naturally; learn to do what your problem suggests when you have reduced it to its simplest terms; you will thus find all problems, however complex, taking on a simplicity you had not dreamed of; accept this simplicity, boldly, and with confidence, do not lose your nerve and run away from it, or you are lost, for you are here at the point men so heeedlessly call genius—as though it were necessarily rare; for you are here at the point no living brain can surpass in essence, the point all truly great minds seek—the point of vital simplicity—the point of view which so illuminates the mind that the art of expression becomes spontaneous, powerful and unerring, and achievement a certainty; so, if you would seek and express the best that is in yourself, you must search out the best that is in your people; for they are your problem, and you are indissolubly a part of them; it is for you to affirm that which they really wish to affirm, namely, the best that is in them, and they as truly wish you to express the best that is in yourself; if the people seem to have but little faith it is because they have been tricked so long; they are weary of dishonesty, much more weary than you know, and in their hearts they seek honest and fearless men, men simple and clear of mind, loyal to their own manhood and to the people. The American people are now in a stupor; be on hand at the awakening. The lion is now in the net, or the larva in the cocoon—take the simile you prefer.

But to simplify the mind is, in fact, not so easy. Everything is against you. You are surrounded by a mist of tradition which you, alone, must dispel. The schools will not help you, for they too, are in a mist. So, you must develop your mind as best you can. The only safe method is to take nothing for granted, but to analyze, test and examine all things, for yourself, and determine their true values; to sift the wheat from the chaff, and to reduce all thoughts, all activities, to the simple test of honesty. You will be surprised, perhaps, to see how matters that you once deemed solid, fall apart; and, how things that you once deemed inconsequential, take on a new and momentous significance. But in time your mind will clarify and strengthen, and you will have moved into that domain of intellectual power wherein thought discriminates, with justice and clarity, between those things which make for the health, and those which make for the illness of a people. When you have done this, your mind will have reached its balance; you will have something to say, and you will say it with candor.

In the light of the preceding statements, the current mannerisms of architectural criticism must often seem trivial. For of what avail is it to say that this too small, that too large, this too thick, that too thin, or to quote this, that or the other precedent, when the real question may be: Is not the entire design a mean evasion, a parasitic growth? Why magnify this, that or the other little thing, if the entire scheme of thinking, that the building stands for, is false, and puts a mask upon the people, who want true buildings, but do not know how to get them so long as architects betray them with architectural phrases?

Why have we not more of vital architectural criticism? Is it because our professional critics lack penetration? Because they lack courage? Is it because they, who should be free, are not free? Is it because they, who should know, do not know? Do they not see, or will they not? Do they know such buildings to be lies, and refrain from saying so? Or are they, too, inert of mind? Are their minds, too, benumbed with culture, and their hearts, thus, made faint?

How is a people to know what, for them, a real and fitting Architecture may mean, if it is not first made clear to them that the current and accepted Architecture with which their minds are rapidly being distorted—is false to them! To whom are we to look if not to our trusted critics? And if these fail us, what then?

But—the cynic may observe—what if they do fail us! They write merely in the fashion. For everybody else betrays everybody else. We are all false; and why should a false people expect other than a false Architecture? A people always gets what it deserves, neither more or less. It's up to the people, anyway. If they want a real Architecture, let them become real, themselves. If they do not wish to be betrayed, let them quit betraying. If they really wish loyalty, let them be loyal. If they really wish thinkers, let them so think. If they really do not wish humbug Architecture, let them cease being humbugs themselves. There is so much of truth in this discouraging view, that I shall later clarify it.

For the moment, however, it is significant in passing to note, concerning our architectural periodicals. They float along, aimlessly enough, drifting in the tide of heedless commercialism—their pages filled with views of buildings, buildings, like words, words, words. Building in this 'style,' that and the other; false always, except now and then and here and there in spots, where the 'style' has been dropped in spots, and where, in consequence, the real building appears in spots; or where the architect, under "compulsion," has had to let the style go—and do something sensible; or, rarely, where the architect, of his own free will, has chosen to be clean, and has expressed himself with feeling and simple, direct eloquence. The publishers may well say: Make the Architecture and we will publish it; we are but mirrors of the times: If our pages are filled with pretentious trash, it is because architects make it. We publish what our critics write, such as it is, and what architects write, such as it is. We give our readers, who are mostly architects, what they give us. If they want better, they will let us know. We are willing.

And a word concerning 'Handbooks on Architecture.' All that need be said of them is that they are the blind leading the blind.

Concerning more ambitious works: while they contain certain, or rather uncertain, attempts at philosophy, such discussion is left in the air as a vapor; it is not condensed into terms of vital, present use.

Thus, it happens that the would-be searcher after architectural reality finds no air, no comfort. He is led into a jungle within whose depths his guides are lost, and he is left without compass and without a star. And why is this so? The answer is at hand: Because it has long and tacitly been assumed, by our would-be mentors, that the Architectural Art is a closed book, that the word FINIS was written centuries ago, and that all, obviously, that is left for us moderns is the humble privilege to select, copy, and adapt. Because it has not been assumed that ALL buildings have arisen, have stood, and stand as physical symbols of the psychic state of the people. Because no distinction has been made between WAS and IS. And—what is most dispiriting—this lunacy continues its erratic parade in plain open view of the towering fact that modern science, with devoted patience of research, has evolved, is perfecting and has placed freely at our service the most comprehensive, accurate and high-powered system of organic reasoning that the world has known. These methods and powers, the breadth and fertility of this supreme search for the all-life-process, this most fruitful function of democracy, is by those connected with the Architectural Art and its teaching, today regarded vacantly. Strangely they undervalue that which for us all, in all truth, in the serenity of human hope, heralds a sunrise for the race. Truly, procreant modern thought, clothed in all its radiance of good will, is a poet, a teacher and a prophet not known in the land of these.

Confronting this ignoble apathy of those we have trusted, let us assume, if it be but in fancy, a normal student of Nature and of Man. Let us asume a virile critic, human and humane, sensitive to all, and aware of this modern daybreak. He will have been a life-seeker of realities. His compass pointing ever to the central fact that all is life; his drinkwater, the knowledge that act and thought are fatefully the same; his nourishing food, the conviction that pure democracy is the deepest-down, the most persistent, while the most obscured desire within the consciousness of man—so equipped, he will have traversed the high seas and the lands, from poles to equator. All latitudes and longitudes of the prolific world of repressed but aspiring humanity. He will hold history, as a staff, in his hand. He will weigh the Modern Man in a just balance, wherein he will set against that man his accountability to all the people. He, as dispassionately, will weigh the people, collectively, against their manifest responsibility and accountability to the child and to the man.

Let us suppose him, now, in his wandering, to have come into Our Land. That he views our Architecture, weighs it, evaluates it; then, turning in thought, looks out upon us, as a people, analyzes us, weighs us, takes our measure, appraises us; that he then places People and Architecture in the great balance of History, and thoughtfully weighs, carefully appraises; then places the people, with all their activities, in the new balance of Democracy, again to weigh, again to appraise; and then puts us with our self-called Common Sense into the serene balance of Nature; and, at the last, weighs Us and Our All, in the fateful balance of All-Encompassing Life—and makes the last appraisement! What, think you, will be his revaluing of our valuations of things, of thoughts, of men? What, in the sifting, would prove wheat, what, in the weighing, would have substance, what in this refiner's fire would be the dross? After his reflections, what will he say? What will he say, after weighing us against our broad, fertile land, with its many waters, its superb and stimulating air, its sumptuous and placid beauty? How will he define us when he shall have searched our minds and hearts? For we cannot hide! What will he say when he shall come to hold us in a close accounting of our stewardship of the talent, Liberty, the treasure that the world has paid so dear in sorrow to transmit to us?

What he might say, would prove a new and most dramatic story.

But surely he might, in part, speak thus:

As you are, so are your buildings; and, as are your buildings, so are you. You and your Architecture are the same. Each is the faithful portrait of the other. To read the one is to read the other. To interpret the one is to interpret the other. Arising from both, as a miasma: What falsity! What betrayal of the present and the past! Arising from both, as the most thrilling, the more heart-piercing of refrains, as the murmur of a crowd, I hear the cry: 'What is the use?' that cry begun in frivolity, passing into cynicism, and now, deepening into pessimism. That cry which in all time and in all peoples became the cry of death or of revolution, when from frivolity it had merged through pessimism—into an utterance of despair! Your buildings, good, bad and indifferent, arise as warning hands in the faces of all—for they are what you are. Take heed! Did you think Architecture a thing of books—of the past? No! Never! IT WAS, ALWAYS, OF ITS PRESENT AND ITS PEOPLE! IT, NOW, IS OF THE PRESENT, AND OF YOU! This Architecture is ashamed to be natural, but is not ashamed to lie; so, you, as a people, are ashamed to be natural but are not ashamed to lie. This Architecture is ashamed to be honest, but it is not ashamed to steal; so, then, by the unanswerable logic of Life, you are ashamed to be honest but are not ashamed to steal. This Architecture is filled with hypocrisy and cant. So, likewise, are you, but say you are not. This Architecture is neurasthenic; so have you burned the candle at both ends. Is then this Democracy? This Architecture shows, ah, so plainly, the decline of Democracy, and a rank new growth of Feudalism—sure sign of a people in peril! This Architecture has no serenity—sure symbol of a people out of balance. This Architecture reveals no lucid guiding principle—nor have you yet evolved a lucid guiding principle, sorely though you now need it! This Architecture shows no love of Nature—you despise Nature. In it is no joy of living—you know not what the fullness of life signifies—you are unhappy, fevered and perturbed. In these buildings the Dollar is vulgarly exalted—and the Dollar you place above Man. You adore it twenty-four hours each day: it is your God! These buildings show lack of great thinkers, real men, among your architects; and, as a people, you are poor in great thinkers, real men—though you now, in your extremity, are in dire need of great thinkers, real men. These buildings show no love of country, no affection for the people. So have you no affection for each other, but secretly will ruin each and any, so much do you love gold, so wantonly will you betray not only your neighbor but yourselves and your own children, for it!

Yet, here and there, a building bespeaks integrity—so have you that much of integrity. All is not false—so are you not wholly false. What leaven is found in your buildings—such leaven is found in you. Weight for weight, measure for measure, sign for sign—as are your buildings, so are you!

A colossal energy is in your buildings, but not true power—so is found in you a frenzied energy, but not the true power of equipoise. Is this an indictment? Not unless you yourselves are an indictment of yourselves. There stand the buildings, they have their unchanging physiognomy. Look! See! Thus, this is a reading, an interpretation.

Here and there are buildings, modest, truthful and sincere: products of a genuine feeling existing in you. They are not truly ashamed where you

are not ashamed; they are natural where you are natural; they are democratic where you are democratic. Side by side they stand against the false
and feudal—all intermixed. So are your thoughts and acts intermixed,
democratic and feudal, in a strange and sinister drift.

Your buildings show no philosophy. So have you no philosophy. You
pretend a philosophy of common sense. Weighed in the balance of your
acts, your common sense is light as folly: a patent-medicine folly; an
adulterated-food folly, a dyspeptic folly, the folly of filth and smoke in
your cities, and innumerable every-day follies quite the reverse of that
common sense which you assume to mean clear-cut and sturdy thinking
in the affairs of daily life. You boast a philosophy of Success. It has long
been your daily harangue. But, weighed in the balance of Democracy,
your successes are but too clearly, in the main, feudal. They are pessi-
misms, not optimisms. You did not think to count the cost; but are beginning now to catch a corner of its masked visage. The sight of the true
full cost will stagger you—when the mask is fully drawn aside, and it
stands clearly revealed! You would not foresee a crisis, BUT CRISIS FORE-
SAW YOU, AND NOW IS UPON YOU.

You tacitly asumed philosophy to be an empty word, not a vital need;
you did not inquire; and in so blindfolding your minds, you have walked
straight to the edge of an abyss.

For a Sound Philosophy is the Saving Grace of Democratic People! It
means, very simply, a balanced system of thinking, concerning the vital
relations of a people. It is intensely practical. Nothing can be more so.
For it saves waste. It looks far behind and far ahead. It forestalls Crisis. It
nurtures, economizes and directs the vitality of a people. It has for its
sole and abiding objective, their equilibrium, hence their happiness.

Thus, foibles and follies have usurped in your minds the vacant seat of
Wisdom. Thus, has your Dollar betrayed you, as it must. And thus, has
NOT been given to the World that which was and still remains your highest
office, and your noblest privilege to give, in return for that Liberty which
was once yours, and which the world gave to you: A sane and pure accounting of Democracy; a philosophy founded upon Man—thereby setting
forth, in clear and human terms, the integrity, the responsibility and the
accountability of the individual—in short, a new, a real Philosophy of the
People.

It is not yet too late.

Let such philosophy be the spiritual first-fruit of your fair and far-flung
land. For you must now think quickly, and with a penetration, concen-

tration, simplicity, accuracy and nerve, the necessity of which you have hitherto belittled and denied. Your one splendid power and reserve lies in your resourceful intelligence when forced by your distress into a crisis. Your Architecture hints at this in its many-sided practicalities. Your history in this land has proved it. Use this power at once!

Again, this Architecture, in the large sense, is barren of poetry; yet, strangely enough it faintly contains in its physiognomy a latent suggestion, which bespeaks dramatic, lyric, eloquent and appealing possibilities, In fine, it expresses obscurely the most human qualities you as a people possess, and which, such is your awkward mental bashfulness, you are ashamed to acknowledge, much less to proclaim. One longs to wash from this dirty face its overlay of timidity and abasement; to strip from its form the rags of neglect and contumely, and to see if indeed there be not beneath its forlorn and pitiful aspect, the real face and form of unsuspected Cinderella.

I surmise—or is it a hope born of visible possibilities? A sense of not negligible probabilities? For, truly, what in all the world is more sweet, in the last analysis, however fickle and at times childishly cruel, than is the American heart!

On this foundation, deeper and stronger than you suspect, I would, if I were you, build a new superstructure, really truer to yourselves, and more enduring, than that which now is crumbling upon its weak support of over-smartness and fundamental untruth.

Fortunate, indeed, are you, that your corruption has been so crude; for you can still survive the surgery of its eradication.

It is on this sound heart, and that still better part of it as yet unmatured and unrevealed to your own consciousness, that I would build anew and aright.

For he who knows even a genuinely little of Mankind knows this truth: The heart is greater than the head. For, in the heart, is Desire; and, from it, comes forth Courage and Magnanimity.

To be sure, you had assumed that poetry meant verses; and that reading such was an unworthy weakness for men of brains and hard-headed business. You have held to a fiction, patterned upon your farcical common sense, that sentiment has no place in affairs. Again you did not inquire; you assumed, took for granted—as is your heedless way. You have not looked into your own hearts. You have looked only at the vacancy of convention from which realities have long since departed. Only the husks remain there, like the shells of beetles upon the bark of a living tree.

You have not thought deeply enough to know that the heart in you is the woman in man. You have derided your femininity, where you have suspected it; whereas, you should have known its power, cherished and utilized it, for it is the hidden well-spring of Intuition and Imagination. What can the brain accomplish without these two! They are the man's two inner eyes; without them, he is stone blind. For the mind sends forth their powers both together. One carries the light, the other searches; and between them they find treasures. These they bring to the brain, which first elaborates them, then says to the will, 'Do'—and Action follows.

Poetically considered, as far as the huge, disordered resultant mass of your Architecture is concerned, Intuition and Imagination have not gone forth to illuminate and search the hearts of the people. Thus are its works stone blind. If such works be called masculine, this term will prove but a misuse of neuter. For they are empty of procreant powers. They do not inspire the thoughtful mind, but much do they depress it; they are choked with inarticulate cries which evoke pathos in the hearer.

Consider, now, that poetry is not verse—although some verse may be poetic. Consider, now, poetry as apart from words and as resident in things, in thoughts, in acts. For if you persist in regarding print or language as the only readable or hearable things—you must, indeed, remain dull interpreters of the voices of Nature, and of the acts and thoughts of men of the present and the past, in their varied, but fundamentally alike activities. No; poetry, rightly considered, stands for the highest form of intellectual scope and activity. Indeed, it were truer to say psychic activity, if it be known what realities lie behind the mask of that word.

And, be it said in passing, most words are masks. Habit has accustomed you to this company of masks, beautiful some of them, repellent others, but you seldom draw aside a word-mask to see, for yourselves, the countenance of reality which it may both reveal and conceal. For, as I have said, you do not inquire, you are prone to take things for granted. You have seen masks since childhood, and have assumed and still assume them to be real, because, since childhood, you have been told they were, and are, real, by those to whose selfish interest it was, and is, that you cherish the illusion. Latterly, however, you have sufficiently awakened to draw aside the mask-word 'Respectability.'

You dearly love the mask-word, Brains, which means physical action; and sniff at the word Intellect, which stands for clear, powerful constructive reflection. Therefore, as this is your thought, naturally enough, you are the victims of your impulsive acts, and of your apathy toward far-reaching, inevitable, yes inexorable, consequences.

It is vitally with realities that poetry deals. But you say it does not; so that settles the matter as far as you are concerned—at least you think it does—in reality it settles you—it keeps you self-bound.

You say that poetry deals only with metaphor and figures of speech. What is your daily talk but metaphor and figures of speech! Every word, genuinely used, is a picture; whether used in conversation or in literary production. Mental life, indeed physical life, is almost entirely a matter of eyesight.

Now poetry, properly understood, means the most highly efficient form of mental eyesight. That is to say, it is that power of seeing and doing which reveals to Man's inner self the fullness and the subtle power of Life.

Poetry, as a living thing, therefore, stands for the most telling quality that man can impart to his thoughts and his acts. Judged by this test, your buildings are dreary, empty places.

Further, these buildings reveal no genuine art of expression—and neither have you as a people genuinely expressed yourselves. You have sniffed at this, too; for you are very cynical, and very pert, and very cocksure. The leer is not long absent from your eyes. You have said in substance: What do we want of an art of expression? We cannot sell it! Perhaps not. But you can and have sold yourselves.

You have assumed that an art of expression is a fiction, something apart from yourselves; as you have assumed almost all things, of genuinely preservative value, to be fictions, apart from yourselves—things negligible, to be put on or off like a coat.

Therefore look at your body of laws—complicated, grotesque and inefficient, spiked with jokers, as guns are spiked. Look at your Constitution. Does that now really express the sound life in you, or is there a joker in that, too, that is surely strangling you? Look at your business. What is it become but a war of extermination among cannibals? Does it express Democracy? Are you, as a People, now really a Democracy? Do you still possess the power of self-government of a people, by a people, for a people? Or is it now perished, as your Abraham Lincoln, on the field of Gettysburg, hoped it might not, and as hoped a weary and heartsick people at the close of an awful struggle to preserve Democracy in its integrity, to preserve that fundamental art of expression whereby a people may, unhampered, give voice and form to the aspiration of their lives, their hopes, as they press onward toward the enjoyment of their birthright, the birthright of every man—the right to happiness!

Do you realize with what caustic accuracy this stupor is shown in your buildings? They, too, stand for the spiked laws of an art of expression. For what is there to express but the true life of a people? What is there, in a Democracy, but All the People? By what right does any man say: I am! I own! I am therefore a law unto myself! How quickly among you has I LEAD! BECOME—I POSSESS! I BETRAY! How glibly have you acquiesced! With what awful folly have you assumed selfish egotism to be the basis of Democracy!

How significant is it, that, now, a few rough hands are shaking you, a few sharp shrill voices calling: Awake before it is too late!

But, I hear you say, testily, we are too young to consider these accomplishments. We have been so busy with our material development that we have not found the time to consider them.

Know then, that, to begin with, they are not accomplishments but necessaries. And, to end with, you are old enough, and have found the time to succeed in nearly making a fine art of—Betrayal, and a science of—Graft!

Know, that you are as old as the race. That each man among you has in him the accumulated power of the race, ready at hand for use, in the right way, when he shall conclude it better to think straight and hence act straight, rather than, as now, to act crooked and pretend to be straight.

Know, that the test, plain, simple HONESTY (and you all know, every man of you knows, exactly what that means), is always at your hand.

Know, that as all complex manifestations have a simple basis of origin, so the vast complexity of your national unrest, ill health, inability to think clearly and accurately concerning simple things, really vital things, is easily and swiftly traceable to the single, actual, active cause—Dishonesty; and that this points with unescapable logic and in just measure to each INDIVIDUAL MAN!

The Remedy: INDIVIDUAL HONESTY. . .

A conclusion as logical and as just!

But, you may say, how absurdly simple.

Doubtless it is absurd, if you think it is, and will so remain, as far as you are concerned, just so long as you think it is—and no longer. But just so long will your social pains and aches and unrest continue; and these you do not consider absurd.

When Newton saw the apple fall, he saw what you might likewise call an absurdly simple thing. Yet with this simple thing he connected up the Universe.

Moreover, this simple thing, Honesty, stands in the Universe of Human Thought and Action, as its very Center of Gravity, and is our human mask-word behind which abides all the power of Nature's Integrity, the profoundest FACT which modern thinking has persuaded Life to reveal.

What folly, then, for Man to buck against the stupendous FLOW of LIFE; instead of voluntarily and gladly placing himself in harmony with it, and thus transferring to himself Nature's own creative energy and equipoise.

But, you say, All this is above our heads.

No it is not! IT IS CLOSE BESIDE YOUR HAND! And therein lies its power.

Again you say: How can honesty be enforced?

It cannot be enforced.

Then how will the remedy go into effect?

It cannot go into effect. It can only COME into effect.

Then how can it come?

Ask Nature.

And what will Nature say?

Nature is always saying: "I center at each man, woman and child. I knock at the door of each heart, and I wait. I wait in patience—ready to enter with my gifts."

And is that all that Nature says?

That is all.

Then how are we to receive Nature?

By opening wide the door of your minds! For your greatest crime against yourselves is that you have locked the door in Her face, and have thrown away the key! Now you say! There is no key!

Then how shall we make a new key?

First: Care scrupulously for your individual and collective physical health. Beware of those who are undermining it; they are your deadliest danger. Beware of yourselves if you are undermining it, for you are then your own deadliest enemy. Thus will you achieve the first vital preliminary—a quiet, strong and resilient nervous system. Thus will your five senses become accurate interpreters of your physical surroundings; and thus, quite naturally, will the brain resume, in you, its normal power to act and react.

Second: Begin at once the establishment of a truly democratic system of education. The basis of this must be CHARACTER; and the mind must be so trained in the sense of reality that it may reach the fullness of its power to weigh all things, and to realize that the origin and sustenance of its power comes from without, and is Nature's bounteous, unstinted gift to all men.

Such system of education will result in equilibrium of body, mind and heart. It will therefore develop real men and women—as is Nature's desire.

It will produce social equilibrium in every aspect of human affairs. It will so clearly reveal the follies that have cursed you, that you will abandon them forever. For you will then recognize and gladly accept the simple, central truth that the individual grows in power only as he grows in integrity, and that the unfailing source of that integrity lies in the eternal integrity of Nature and of that Infinite Serenity of which Nature is but a symbol.

Thus will you make Democracy a religion—the only one the world will have developed—befitting freemen—free in the integrity of their bodies, free in the integrity of their thought.

So doing, all aspects of your activities will change, because your thoughts will have changed. All of your activities will then take on organic and balanced coherence, because all of your thoughts will have a common center of gravity in the integrity of individual Man.

And, as the oak tree is ever true to the acorn from which it sprang, and propagates true acorns in its turn, so will you then give true expression and form to the seed of Democracy that was planted in your soil, and so spread in turn the seeds of true Democracy.

Thus, as your thoughts change, will your civilization change. And thus, as Democracy takes living and integral shape within your thought, will the Feudalism, now tainting you, disappear. For its present power rests wholly upon your acquiescent and supporting thought. Its strength lies wholly in you, not in itself. So, inevitably, as the sustaining power of your thought is withdrawn, this Feudalism will crumble and vanish!

So have you no need of Force, for force is a crude and inefficient instrument. THOUGHT is the fine and powerful instrument. Therefore, HAVE THOUGHT FOR THE INTEGRITY OF YOUR OWN THOUGHT. For all social power, for good, or for ill, rests upon the thought of the People. THIS IS THE SINGLE LESSON IN THE HISTORY OF MANKIND THAT IS REALLY WORTH THE WHILE.

Naturally, then, as your thoughts thus change, your growing Architecture will change. Its falsity will depart; its reality will gradually appear, For the integrity of your thought, as a People, will then have penetrated the minds of your architects.

THEN, TOO, AS YOUR BASIC THOUGHT CHANGES WILL EMERGE A PHILOS-
OPHY, A POETRY, AND AN ART OF EXPRESSION IN ALL THINGS: FOR YOU WILL
HAVE LEARNED THAT A CHARACTERISTIC PHILOSOPHY, POETRY AND ART OF
EXPRESSION ARE VITAL TO THE HEALTHFUL GROWTH AND DEVELOPMENT
OF A DEMOCRATIC PEOPLE.

As a People you have enormous latent, unused power.

Awaken it.

Use it.

Use it for the common good.

Begin now!

For it is as true today as when one of your wise men said it:—THE WAY
TO RESUME IS TO RESUME!

THE CHICAGO TRIBUNE *COMPETITION*

An event of both real and symbolic importance in the history of American architecture occurred in 1923: the *Chicago Tribune* invited architects from all over the world to enter a competition for the best design for its new skyscraper building, to be built on Michigan boulevard, just north of the Chicago River. Given the newspaper's explicit assurance that the winning design would be chosen exclusively on the ground of aesthetic excellence, this competition seemed likely to speed acceptance of the new architecture. Dismay was correspondingly great when the *Tribune's* management reversed a preliminary decision to award the prize to a widely-admired entry by Eliel Saarinen, and awarded it instead to a local architect whose "Gothic" design was carried out in the building which occupies the site today. This event, to Sullivan a repetition on a smaller scale of the betrayal of American culture in the World's Fair thirty years earlier, provoked from him a scornful, impassioned protest which is here reprinted for the first time from the February, 1923 issue of *The Architectural Record*.

Some seventy years ago, a philosopher, in the course of his studies of the Ego, separated men into two classes, distinct, yet reciprocally related, to wit: Masters of Ideas, and those governed by ideas. It was upon ideas as powers for good or ill that he laid the heavy hand; upon ideas as a living force obedient to the mastery of vision, springing forth from imagination's depths, from the inexhaustible reservoir of instinct.

Ego, considered solely as free spirit, stands out visibly as Master of Ideas. Ego, examined as a spirit benumbed through lack of action, hence inert and unfree, becomes dim of vision and renounces its will. It thus becomes the slave of imposed ideas whose validity it assumes it has not the strength to test, even were the idea of testing to arise. Hence in timidity, it evokes the negative idea of Authority as a welcome substitute for its declining volition.

Masters of ideas are masters of courage; the free will of adventure is in them. They stride where others creep. The pride of action is in them. They explore, they test, they seek realities to meet them face to face—knowing well that realities and illusions exist commingled within and without, but also knowing well that Ego is its own. Hence they walk erect and fearless in the open, with that certitude which vision brings—while slaves are slaves by choice. They seek shelter in the *shadows* of ideas.

Ever such were the great free spirits of the past, and such are those of our own day.

Masters of ideas of the past and now, frequently have sought and seek dominion, and have reached it because the idea of dominion coincides precisely with the idea of submission. Other masters of ideas then and now, mostly those of immense compassion, have been and still are crucified by those so long in the dark that the idea of spiritual freedom is abhorrent.

A consciousness is now growing and widely spreading in our modern world of thought, among masters, of truly great ideas, that unless we become free spirits casting off the cruel, and awakening to the constructive power of beneficence, we shall vanish in decay and self destruction.

The simple world idea, now in process of becoming, in the hearts of men, is the idea of freedom from the domination of feudal ideas. Is there a power that can stop this becoming? There is not.

The eyelids of the world are slowly, surely lifting. The vision of the world of men is slowly, surely clearing. A world-idea is sprouting from its seed in the rich soil of world-sorrow. Beneath the surface of things as they are, everywhere it is germinating, unconsciously with the many, consciously with the few.

The old idea that man must ever remain the victim of Fate, will fade as fear fades. The new idea that man may shape his destiny will appear in its place, in a dissolving scene of the world-drama, as Democracy arises through the humus of the age-long feudal idea. For Democracy would remain, as now it is, a senseless word, a vacant shell, a futile sentimentalism, a mere fetish, did it not carry in its heart the loftiest of optimistic aspirations, wholly warranted, spite of all appearance to the contrary, and grasp the mastery of ideas wholly beneficent in power to create a world of joy devoid of fear.

The world is growing more compact every day, and every day the day is shortening, while the fleeting hour becomes thereby so much the fuller. The cold rigidity of frontiers is melting away, unnoted by the blind—

every day the world becomes increasingly mobile, every day there is a silent interchange, every day communication is more fleet, and humanity, in response, more fluent. Slowly day by day, with enormous and gathering momentum, the hearts of the world draw together. The process is silent and gentle as the dew fall. There are those who see this; there are those who do not. There are those who see in the lightnings and the raging storms of the feudal idea, reaching now the climacteric of its supreme mania for dominion, the symbol of self-destruction of a race gone wholly mad. But that is not so. The masters of the feudal idea alone have gone mad with hate; the multitudes are sound. They have lost a pathetic faith in the feudal concept of self-preservation which has wooed and betrayed them. They are moving somnambulistically now, upwards towards a faith that is new and real, a constructive idea, common to all, because springing from the hearts of all, of which all shall be masters, and about which shall form for the first time beneath the sun, a sane hope and faith in Life, a faith in Man—an idea which shall banish fear and exalt courage to its seat of power.

This idea will become the luminous, the central idea of all mankind because it is the offspring of that which is deepest down in all. It is and will continue as long as life lasts in the race, the shining symbol of man's resurrection from the dead past, of man's faith in himself and his power to create anew.

There are those who will decry this hope as they view in despair a world writhing in the depths of pessimism, of mendacity and intrigue. Yet are they those who are without faith in mankind, in themselves. For this is the modern affirmation: Man is not born in sin, but in glory.

All of this has sharply to do with the TRIBUNE Competition, for in that showing was brought into clearest light the deadline that lies between a Master of Ideas and one governed by ideas. There they came, squarely face to face: the second prize and the first. All the others may be grouped aside, for what is involved here is not a series of distinctions in composition or in detail, but the leading forth into the light of day of the profoundest aspiration that animates the hearts of men. This aspiration has remained inarticulate too long; its utterance at large has been choked by varied emotions of fear; the splendor of its singleness of purpose has been obscured by the host of shadows generated in bewilderment of thought, in a world that has lost its bearings and submits in distress to the government of dying ideas.

In its preliminary advertising, the TRIBUNE broadcasted the inspiring idea of a new and great adventure, in which pride, magnanimity and its honor were to be inseparably unified and voiced in "the most beautiful office building in the world," to be created for it by any man sufficiently imaginative and solid in competence in whatever spot on the surface of the earth such a man might dwell.

Specifically, on the third page of its formal and official program, these statements are made:

"To erect the most beautiful and distinctive office building in the world is the desire of the TRIBUNE, and in order to obtain the design for such an edifice, this competition has been instituted."

These words are high-minded; they stir imagination.

At the beginning of the paragraph immediately succeeding are found these words:

"The competition will be of international scope, qualified architects of established reputation in all parts of the world being eligible."

These words are magnanimous; they stir not only the world of architectural activity, but as well that of enlightened laity. Never perhaps, in our day, has such interest in architecture been aroused.

Not yet content in its eagerness, and purposing to make assurance of good faith and loyalty to an ideal triply sure, there is to be found on page 13, the final page of the program, the following statement:

"It cannot be reiterated too emphatically that the primary objective of The CHICAGO TRIBUNE in instituting this Competition is to secure the design for a structure distinctive and imposing—the most beautiful office building in the world."

The intensive use of the word *primary* gives to the full clause the imposing promise of a token, of a covenant with the Earth. With that one word, *primary*, the TRIBUNE set its bow in the cloud.

The craving for beauty, thus set forth by the TRIBUNE, is imbued with romance; with that high Romance which is the essence, the vital impulse, that inheres in all the great works of man in all places and all times, that vibrates in his loftiest thoughts, his heroic deeds, his otherwise inexplicable sacrifices, and which forms the halo of his great compassions, and of the tragedy within the depths of his sorrows. So deeply seated, so persistent, so perennial in the heart of humanity is this ineffable presence, that, suppressed in us, we decay and die. For man is not born to trouble, as the sparks fly upward; he is born to hope and to achieve.

If a critique of architecture, or any other art, or any activity whatsoever, is to be valid, it must be based upon a reasoned process. It must enter with intelligence into the object or subject at hand, there to seek what signifies, and yet maintain such detachment as to render judgment unconstrained and free. A true critique is not satisfied with the surface of things, it must penetrate that surface to search the animus, the thought; it must go deeply to the roots, it must go to origins, it must seek the elemental, the primitive; it must go to the depths and gauge the status of the work thereby. A true critique must likewise derive of the humanities. It is not its function to deal with cold truths but with living truths.

Viewed in this light, the second and the first prize stand before us side by side. One glance of the trained eye, and instant judgment comes; that judgment which flashes from inner experience, in recognition of a masterpiece. The verdict of the Jury of Award is at once reversed, and the second prize is placed first, where it belongs by virtue of its beautifully controlled and virile power. The first prize is demoted to the level of those works evolved of dying ideas, even as it sends forth a frantic cry to escape from the common bondage of those governed by ideas. The apposition is intensely dramatic to the sensitive mind. Yet it is in this very apposition that we find a key wherewith to unlock and swing open wide a door, and reveal to all the vast and unused power resident in the great architectural art when inspired into motion by a Master of Ideas. The Finnish master-edifice is not a lonely cry in the wilderness, it is a voice, resonant and rich, ringing amidst the wealth and joy of life. In utterance sublime and melodious, it prophesies a time to come, and not so far away, when the wretched and the yearning, the sordid and the fierce, shall escape the bondage and the mania of fixed ideas.

It is wretched psychology to assume that man is by nature selfish. The clear eye of sympathy sees beyond a doubt that this is not so; that on the contrary, man by nature is a giver; and it is precisely this one discerns in this beauteous edifice; the native quality of manhood giving freely of inherent wealth of power, with hands that overflow, as to say: There is more and more and more in me to give, as also is there in yourselves— if but ye knew—ye of little faith.

Qualifying as it does in every technical regard, and conforming to the mandatory items of the official program of instructions, it goes freely in advance, and, with the steel frame as a thesis, displays a high science of design such as the world up to this day had neither known nor surmised. In its single solidarity of concentrated intention, there is revealed a logic of a new order, the logic of living things; and this inexorable logic of life is most graciously accepted and set forth in fluency of form. Rising from the earth in suspiration as of the earth and as of the universal genius of man, it ascends and ascends in beauty lofty and serene to the full height limit of the Chicago building ordinance, until its lovely crest seems at one with the sky.

This is not all; there remain, for some, two surprises; first, that a Finlander who, in his prior experience, had not occasion to design a soaring office building, should, as one to the manner born, grasped the intricate problem of the lofty steel-framed structure, the significance of its origins, and held the solution unwaveringly in mind, in such wise as no American architect has as yet shown the required depth of thought and steadfastness of purpose to achieve.

Philosophy has been defined by a modern philosopher as the science of substantial grounds. It is the notable absence of substantial grounds, in the ambitious works of our American architects, that so largely invalidates such works, and groups them as ephemera. But the design of the Finlander, Master of Ideas, is *based* upon substantial grounds, and therefore it lives within the domain of the enduring.

Second surprise: That a foreigner should possess the insight required to penetrate to the depths of the sound, strong, kindly and aspiring idealism which lies at the core of the American people: one day to make them truly great sons of Earth; and that he should possess the poet's power to interpret and to proclaim in deep sympathy and understanding, incarnate in an edifice rising from Earth in response to this faith, an inspiring symbol to endure.

Why did the men behind the Tribune throw this priceless pearl away?

Would that one might say words of similar nature, if less fervent, for the unfortunate first prize; but it is the business of this review to make a searching psychological analysis and summary of the two designs, as *types*, in order that the heavy of eye may see revealed the architectural art as a vast beneficent power, lying now in continental sleep, ready, ever ready, to be awakened by Masters of Ideas, who shall affirm its reality in eloquence of form.

Then shall we become articulate as a people; for to reveal one art is to reveal all arts, all aspirations, all hopes; and the substantial ground of it all shall arise from out our timid faith in man—a faith patient and long suffering under the superstitious tyranny of insane ideas. But once let the beckoning finger of the Free Spirit be seen in the open, and a voice heard that saith: Arise; come unto me. for I am Life—then will that timorous faith come forth inquiringly, and in the glow of the Free Spirit grow strong. The Ego of our Land shall thus find its own; for Man shall find Man. Why, therefore, deal in trivialities? Why inquire, with spectacles on nose, why this or that doodad should be thus or so?

Confronted by the limpid eye of analysis, the first prize trembles and falls, self-confessed, crumbling to the ground. Visibly it is not architecture in the sense herein expounded. Its formula is literary: words, words, words. It is an imaginary structure—not imaginative. Starting with false premise, it was doomed to false conclusion, and it is clear enough, moreover, that the conclusion was the real premise, the mental process in reverse of appearance. The predetermination of a huge mass of imaginary masonry at the top very naturally required the appearance of huge imaginary masonry piers reaching up from the ground to give imaginary support. Such weird process of reasoning is curious. It savors of the nursery where children bet imaginary millions. Is it possible that its author in his heart of hearts, or his head of heads, really believed that bathos and power are synonyms? It looks that way. It also looks like the output of a mind untrained in the mastery of ideas, in the long discipline of realities and the test of substantial grounds. It looks also like the wandering of a mind unaccustomed to distinguish between architecture and scene painting. This design, this imaginary building, this simulacrum, is so helpless, so defenseless when brought face to face with mastery of ideas and validity of grounds, that it is cruel to go on, for analysis is now becoming vivisection, unless we recognize the palpable effect of self-hypnotism. This is not to say that the individual who made the first-prize design did not *believe* he had a great idea. Certainly he believed it, otherwise he would not have taken himself so seriously. Such seriousness prevented him from seeing the humor of it, from seeing something funny and confiding. If the monster on top with its great long legs reaching far below to the ground could be gently pried loose, the real building would reveal itself as a rather amiable and delicate affair with a certain grace of fancy. And even so, it could be but as a foundling at the doorstep of the Finn— for it seems they breed *strong* men in Finland.

So much, for the present, concerning the second and the first prize.

Our attention now shall concentrate upon the TRIBUNE. By "The Tribune" is here meant, not alone printed white paper, but incisively the men behind its screen, who stand for ownership and control. These men made a solemn promise to the world. Why did they renege? Individually and jointly they made a triple promise—as set forth above—as members of the Jury of Award. A design setting forth the most beautiful conception of a lofty office building that has been evolved by the fertile mind of man, was presented squarely to them at the last moment. Were they frightened? Why did they welch? Did it come upon them as a ghost, an apparition— a revelation most unwelcome at a time when everything seemed nicely settled? Was this vision as trebly disconcerting as the remembered triple-promise, arising now also as a confronting ghost—the two ghosts standing side by side—likewise the two designs, in material form, standing side by side?

For no choice can exist without motive. Men are both revealed and betrayed by their acts. For men's acts show forth their inmost thoughts— no matter what their speech may be. Man can create solely in the image of his thought; for thoughts are living things—words may dissemble. In men's acts alone is the reality of their thought to be sought and found— there is no hiding place secure against the tracking searcher. In the same sense the two competing drawings are acts. Each clearly reveals the thought of its responsible author. Each sets forth in the materials of a drawing, presented as a symbol of an edifice to be, the power or the frailty of the thought within.

No manipulation of words or felicity of phrasing can screen from view the act of the Jury of Award, or the dominating will of one or more of its personnel. The final choice is most obviously an act of dominion—of brutal will. For, to cast aside, with the sop of a money prize, the surpassing work of a foreigner of high distinction and thorough discipline in executed works, was an act of savagery in private, regardless of how neatly, how sweetly, thereafter, the man may have been shown the door, as a parting and an honored guest, as one whose presence in the house had indeed triply honored his host.

Thus vanished from sight the TRIBUNE'S bow in the cloud.

Its act has deprived the world of a shining mark, denied it a monument to beauty, to faith, to courage and to hope. Deprived an expectant world of that Romance for which it hungers, and had hoped to receive. "It cannot be reiterated too emphatically that the primary objective of the *Chicago Tribune* in instituting this Competition is to secure the design for a structure distinctive and imposing—the most beautiful office building in the world."

REFLECTIONS ON THE TOKYO DISASTER

Sullivan's indignation over the outcome of the *Tribune* competition was partly assuaged by the renewal, after years of estrangement, of his friendship with Frank Lloyd Wright, which had begun when Wright was his chief draughtsman in the offices of Adler and Sullivan. The commission given Wright, to design the Imperial Hotel in Tokyo, seemed to Sullivan a favorable portent for the acceptance of the new architecture. He expressed his admiration in an article which appeared in the April, 1923 issue of *The Architectural Record*, and included a long technical description of the design, of considerable interest to architects, but not to the student of Sullivan's general esthetic and social philosophy. When the hotel famously withstood an earthquake that levelled the city of Tokyo around it, Sullivan took occasion, in *The Architectural Record* of February, 1924, to restate his conviction that great art requires a great ability to grasp reality in order to transcend it. Reprinted here for the first time, this piece appeared originally only a few months before its author's death.

In the course of my article in the February, 1923, Record concerning the *Chicago Tribune* Competition and its baseness, I took occasion to utilize the saying of a philosopher that men are self-divided into two classes: *Masters of ideas and those dominated by ideas.* And my comment on the Imperial Hotel in Tokyo, in the April, 1923, Record I prefaced by saying: On the vast stage of the world drama, two ideas, both of them immense in power, confront each other in spectacular appeal to the fears and the courage of mankind.

The casual reader, as a rule, is not accustomed to those generalizations which go under the—to him—somewhat repellent name of philosophy, and in so far as philosophy has dealt and deals solely with abstractions and nonentities, he is right in his disdain—which I share. Such philosophies as have gone by the names Platonic, Neo-Platonic, and German

Transcendentalism, have done their huge share to fill the world with sorrow, for they and their kind are the intellectual basis of tyranny. And this same casual reader is as casually apt to be unaware that day by day he lives under the tyranny of abstract dehumanized ideas; that he is under the dominion of ideas he had no share in making, ideas so diaphanous and all-pervading that they are as the air he breathes. His disdain of philosophy therefore is but disdain of a *word*. Of the saturnine content of that word he is as unsuspecting as a kitten. If he is a university man, an aspirant in philosophy, he has been taught to revere that word and its content; and in innocence he reveres them both—and so another kitten, not in the least comprehending the utter heartlessness of it all; not in the least perceiving in the world about him the corruption and dislocation that have followed in its train.

To be sure there are readers and readers. One reads industriously, and learns nothing—he is credulous. Another reads industriously and learns nothing—he is cynical. Another reads even more industriously and widely and learns nothing—he is pessimistic. But of all three, and their varieties, the credulous one is in the most pitiful plight. He may read the philosophies of abstraction and find them ennobling, he may believe himself to be lifted up and to have entered the highest attainable domain of pure thought—the realm of the ideal, the perfect, the absolute, in which the intellect reigns supreme—regarding itself in its own supernatural mirror, its gaze fatefully turned away from man and from his world. And of such belief in the unreal is the basis for all credulity—especially in evidence in the wool-gathering highbrow. Yet there is another class of reader—he who regards not authority, eminence, nor prestige, as finalities, but who seeks that which nourishes and enlarges his comprehension of life, and who, therefore, as by instinct of self-preservation, rejects that which sterilizes life—that is to say the abstract. To him therefore Life becomes an ever broadening, deepening, sublimating and impressive flow, within which he finds himself moving—his own life unfolding, and with the passing years thus arises, within, a deep religious and moral sympathy with the vast spectacle of immediate life, enfolding mankind, which he envisages as participant and spectator. In sympathy there arises within, a new pity allied to a new faith in man.

With spontaneous gesture the newly-arising philosophy, with the voice of which I speak, sweeps aside the spooks and phantasms which have tyrannized the credulous and made slaves of high and low, even in our own day of so-called enlightment, and with mind thus cleared for action and merging with the flow of life, seeks therein a comprehension of man-kind, in order to arrive at an outline of conservation, which, in its direct-ness of purpose, may supersede the abominable wastage of humanity due to the prevailing confusion of ideas.

In one aspect the eye views an incredibly frantic industry, with no objective but to *sell*, and in another aspect—an inexorable reaction of the first—a steady decline in thought beyond the immediate frenzy, a terrify-ing inability to foresee the consequences of a thought or an act; or worse, a wanton and brutal disregard.

And while it is a fact that the thoughts here above set down arise im-mediately out of contemplation of the helplessness, the shabbiness, the ruthless debauchery of commercialized American architecture—which means death—the same thought reaches out over the world and crossing the wide waters arrives at Japan with its city of Tokyo, in which has been staged, as but yesterday, a startling tragedy of ideas, wherein the abstract has crumbled in universal ruin, while one *living* thought and living thing survives. This is what is involved in the significance of the statement that on the vast stage of the world-drama two ideas, both of them immense in power, confront each other in spectacular appeal to the fears and the courage of mankind.

The emergence, unharmed, of the Imperial Hotel, from the heartrend-ing horrors of the Tokyo disaster, takes on, at once, momentous im-portance in the world of modern thought, as a triumph of the living and the real over the credulous, the fantastic, and the insane.

It emerges moreover before our gaze as an imposing upreared monu-ment to the power of common sense; to that consummate common sense which perceives, comprehends, and grasps the so-called commonplace, the real, as distinct from the abstract; to that common sense which founds its logic upon the power inhering in nature's processes, when interpreted in terms of action, as affecting results; soundly scientific in foreseeing re-sults; and which towards this end employs an accurate imagination. For it requires unusual imagination to see stone as stone, brick as brick, wood as wood, steel as steel, the earth as the earth and human beings as human beings.

We may call this power Inspiration if we please, and if we think the word sounds pleasanter than Philosophy. But it is well to bear in mind that Inspiration is philosophy in its highest estate, and that true philosophy is systemized common sense in its finest human reach.

In planning the erection of a structure in a terrain habitually given to earthquake it would seem to be natural to regard earthquake—otherwise seismic disturbance—as a fundamental. For earthquakes are not imaginary or abstract or illusory; they are real—and at times calamitous. It would seem, therefore, to be but the part of common sense *not to invite destruction.* Yet such is the pervading American credulity, such its inability to think straight; such its impulsive acceptance of go-gettism and pep and progress and enterprise as substitutes for reflection and sound thought, and social responsibility, that it succeeded by sales-methods in imposing upon the Japanese, structures so childish, so absurd, so uncomprehending, as verily to invite destruction. When came the fateful hour they danced their dance of death. To be sure the Japanese themselves were credulous enough to take the bait of boosted land values, and multiplied areas; and in their cupidity were induced to hold the bag. When the time came they found the bag filled not with purring kittens, but with terrifying wildcats.

Prior to the American invasion, there had been an English invasion; and prior to the English, a German invasion, both invasions carrying with them the sophisticated credulity of European culture. Both of these alien cultures erected solid masonry buildings upon earthquake land. When the time came, these structures groaned, and buried their dead.

Now, further, Japanese society being heaviest at the top, it would seem but in keeping that its indigenous structures, designed in the native idiom, built on narrow and tortuous lanes, should also be topheavy. When the time came the flying heavy roof tiles did their share in the general slaughter, and as well the flimsy bridges and the flimsiness in general. Thus ruined Tokyo became the prey of conflagration. Thus death arose out of the temblor and spread forth its arms over Tokyo, doomed by a false premise.

It may seem quite easy to draw conclusions after the fact. If you really think so, try your hand on the European war. Or, make a diagnosis of contemporary American architecture. Or attempt an analysis of the American mind, tracing its activities back to their common source. These are, all of them, matters after the fact.

We are now to deal with the reverse aspect of the problem. That is to say, with the primary assumption of earthquake and disaster, and how to forefend. Some five years prior to the now historic temblor a young man of fifty was called to Tokyo to consult as architect regarding the planning and construction of a great hotel to be called the Imperial. This man, a poet, who had reduced thinking to simples, began his solution with the fixed fact of earthquakes as a basis and made an emotional study of their nature and movements. The second move was the resolve never to relax his grip on the basic fact of earthquake as a menace, and to devise a system of construction such as should absorb and dispose of the powerful shocks, waves and violent tremors, and yet maintain its integrity as a fabricated structure. It may be remarked in passing, that the quality and power of emotion dramatizes the power of thought; that the poet is he whose thought, thus enriched, imparts telling power to the simple and the obvious, bringing them into the field of vivid consciousness.

It is precisely this power of the poet to bring earthquake vividly into consciousness and hold it there, that distinguishes him, in this instance, from the uninspired engineer. The latter is an extremely useful person, wherever and whenever his formulas, his slide-rule, his tables and his precedents—to which he is a slave—apply. Within the limits of routine he may successfully vary his processes in application; and there his social value ends. The same, in substance, may be said of the uninspired practicing architect, except that the latter, in addition, is invertebrate. Wherever he thinks with reasonable clearness, he approaches the engineer; but he is not a Yea-Sayer—he prefers to trim. Yet the great creative engineer—and there have been such—by virtue of clear eyesight, material realization, and the power to dream, is again the poet if he fail not in the human sense of beauty, even though he may not think so, and out of prudence may not say so. Yet he is essentially of the Yea-Sayers—and the Yea-Sayers are the great modern poets.

For many years I have contemplated man in his folly, and in his marvelous powers. But I never expected to live to read about a man who had attained to the dainty quintessence of asininity, by driving huge timber piles through sixty feet of Tokyo mud, to reach the solid underlying hard pan, and to set upon this system of piling, tightly bound to it, a high, extra-rigid, steel frame to serve as the supporting skeleton of a habitable building. Or was it not asininity at all but merely betting on a long chance? In any event the long chance became suddenly a short one. *The invitation to disaster was instantaneously accepted.* And if the asininity was real, it merged into the degenerate in its disregard of the human being. It was an even bet that the quake might obligingly come at night while the tall buildings were empty and asleep. Their shattered remains now tell a weird story, many chapters long, for the quake came at noon.

The architect of the Imperial Hotel, whose name by the way is Frank Lloyd Wright, a fact I should in all honor have mentioned earlier, had I

not been so engrossed in an attempt to clothe in words the basic idea of
my thesis—the most dangerous and destructive of all ideas—the idea of
Credulity; this architect I say, whom I have known since his eighteenth
year, and the workings of whose fine mind I believe I fairly follow, is
possessed of a rare sense of the human, and an equally rare sense of
Mother Earth, coupled with an apprehension of the material, so delicate
as to border on the mystic, and yet remain coördinate with those facts we
call real life. Such mind, sufficiently enriched by inner experiences as to
become mellow in power, and reinforced by a strong tenacious will, is
precisely the primary type of mind that resolves a problem into its simples,
and out of these simples projects in thought a masterful solution, and in
the process of transmuting thought into actual material fact, displays a
virtuosity in the manipulation of the simples of technique.

I admit it is difficult for a mind academically trained and hence in large
measure deprived of its freedom and its natural susceptibility, to grasp an
idea so foreign to its heritage of tradition as is, necessarily so, the idea
of *simples*. I go further and assert that such idea may be repugnant to
such minds—may even alarm such minds—it is too disturbing in its
ominous suggestion that thoughts may be living things—Now!—Here!
The intrusion of Life upon such minds may indeed be disheartening. And
the same statements may apply with equal force to the mind technically
trained exclusively—the world of life shut out; and as well to the business
mind, with its airy system of phantasies, its curious rules of the game, its
pontifical utterances of the higher wisdom of mendacity, and its one, solid,
credulous faith in the abstract notion, deeply cherished, that human life is
and must ever be a battle, a struggle for existence, and thus believing
render itself "the unfit" to analyze its own symptoms which predicate peri-
odical collapse of the structure it has reared upon the soil of an earthquake
thought. And yet, in contrast, the open mind which may have won its
freedom through valor, going forth into the world of men and thoughts
and things, discerns basic simples everywhere and in all things. To such
mind the confusion of the world is no mystery.

It is no part of my business here, nor of my intent, to go into the technical refinements, the subtleties of reaction, and the plastic sense of balance and free movement that enter into the structural theory and actuality
of the Imperial Hotel. Mr. Wright may do this if he so sees fit. The vast,
sumptuous building, in all its aspects: structural, utilitarian, and aesthetic,
was the embodiment, and is now the revelation, of a single thought tena-
ciously held by a seer and a prophet, a craftsman, a master-builder.

This most significant architectural monument that the modern world can show, stands today uninjured because it was thought-built, so to stand. It was not and is not an imposition upon the Japanese, but a free will contribution to the finest elements of their culture. The fame of the building and its author is now world-wide; and we will let it go at that.

Meanwhile, I declare as my real business and my true intent herein, to be that of one of enquiring mind who seeks in this disaster the realities behind its terrifying mask.

THE WORLD'S FAIR — AND AFTER

Sullivan died on April 14, 1924. For two years prior to his death, he had been writing a series of reminiscences and recapitulations, which were published serially in the *Journal* of the American Institute of Architects. In writing these, Sullivan went back, notably, to the events which led to the 1893 World's Fair in Chicago, and those which followed after it. He did so not only to lament or recriminate, but to re-affirm, with the touchingly diminished coherence of a dying man, his unshaken belief in democracy and its ideal expression in architecture. The passages which follow, from the concluding section of *The Autobiography of An Idea*, begin at the point where an Act of Congress, passed in 1890, had authorized an exposition to celebrate the four hundredth anniversary of the discovery of America.

Chicago was ripe and ready for such an undertaking. It had the required enthusiasm and the will. It won out in a contest between the cities. The prize was now in hand. It was to be the city's crowning glory. A superb site on the lake adjoined the southern section of the city. This site was so to be transformed and embellished by the magic of American prowess, particularly in its architectural aspects, as to set forth the genius of the land in that great creative art. It was to be a dream city, where one might revel in beauty. It was to be called The White City by the Lake.

Now arose above the horizon the small white cloud. It came from eastward. It came borne upon the winds of predestination. Who could fancy that a harmless white cloud might cast a white shadow? Who could forecast the shape of that shadow? It was here that one man's unbalanced mind spread a gauze-like pall of fatality. That one man's unconscious stupor in bigness, and in the droll phantasy of hero-worship, did his best and his worst, according to his lights, which were dim except the one projector by the harsh light of which he saw all things illuminated and grown bombastically big in chauvinistic outlines. Here was to be the test of American culture, and here it failed. Dreamers may dream; but of what avail the dream if it be but a dream of misinterpretation? If the dream, in such as case, rise not in vision far above the general level of intelligence, and prophesy through the medium of clear thinking, true interpretation—why dream at all? Why not rest content as children of Barnum, easy in the faith that one of them is born every minute. Such in effect was the method adopted in practice while the phrase-makers tossed their slogans to and fro.

At the beginning it was tentatively assumed that the firm of Burnham & Root might undertake the work in its entirety. The idea was sound in principle—one hand, one great work—a superb revelation of America's potency—an oration, a portrayal, to arouse that which was hidden, to call it forth into the light. But the work of ten years cannot be done in two. It would require two years to grasp and analyze the problem and effect a synthesis. Less than three years were available for the initiation and completion of the work entire, ready for installation of exhibits. The idea was in consequence dismissed. As a matter of fact there was not an architect in the land equal to the undertaking. No veteran mind seasoned to the strategy and tactics involved in a wholly successful issue. Otherwise there might have arisen a gorgeous Garden City, reflex of one mind, truly interpreting the aspirations and the heart's desire of the many, every detail carefully considered, every function given its due form, with the sense of humanity at its best, a suffusing atmosphere; and within the Garden City might be built another city to remain and endure as a memorial, within the parkland by the blue waters, oriented toward the rising sun, a token of a covenant of things to be, a symbol of the city's basic significance as offspring of the prairie, the lake and the portage.

But hustle was the word. Make it big, make it stunning, knock 'em down! The cry was well meant as things go.

So in the fall of 1890 John Root was officially appointed consulting architect, and Daniel Burnham, Chief of Construction.

Later, with the kindly assistance of Edward T. Jefferey, Chairman of the Committee on Buildings and Grounds, Burnham selected five architects from the East and five from the West, ten in all. Burnham and Jefferey loved each other dearly. The thought of one was the thought of both, as it were—sometimes. Burnham had believed that he might best serve his country by placing all of the work exclusively with Eastern architects; solely, he averred, on account of their surpassing culture. With exquisite delicacy and tact, Jefferey, at a meeting of the Committee, persuaded

Daniel, come to Judgment, to add the Western men to the list of his nominations.

A gathering of these architects took place in February, 1891. After an examination of the site, which by this time was dreary enough in its state of raw upheaval, the company retired for active conference. John Root was not there. In faith he could not come. He had made his rendezvous the month before. Graceland was now his home. Soon above him would be reared a Celtic cross. Louis missed him sadly. Who now would take up the foils he had dropped on his way, from hands that were once so strong? There was none! The shadow of the white cloud had already fallen.

The meeting came to order. Richard Hunt, acknowledged dean of his profession, in the chair, Louis Sullivan acting as secretary. Burnham arose to make his address of welcome. He was not facile on his feet, but it soon became noticeable that he was progressively and grossly apologizing to the Eastern men for the presence of their benighted brethren of the West.

Dick Hunt interrupted: Hell, we haven't come out here on a missionary expedition. Let's get to work. Everyone agreed. Burnham came out of his somnambulistic vagary and joined in. He was keen enough to understand that Uncle Dick had done him a needed favor. For Burnham learned slowly but surely, within the limits of his understanding.

A layout was submitted to the Board as a basis for discussion. It was rearranged on two axes at right angles. The buildings were disposed accordingly. By an amicable arrangement each architect was given such building as he preferred, after consultation. The meeting then adjourned.

The story of the building of the Fair is foreign to the purpose of this narrative, which is to deal with its more serious aspects, implications and results. Suffice it that Burnham performed in a masterful way, displaying executive capacity. He became open-minded, just, magnanimous. He did his great share.

The work completed, the gates thrown open 1 May, 1893, the crowds flowed in from every quarter, continued to flow throughout a fair-weather summer and a serenely beautiful October. Then came the end. The gates were closed.

These crowds were astonished. They beheld what was for them an amazing revelation of the architectural art, of which previously they in comparison had known nothing. To them it was a veritable Apocalypse, a message inspired from on high. Upon it their imagination shaped new ideals. They went away, spreading again over the land, returning to their homes, each one of them carrying in the soul the shadow of the white cloud, each of them permeated by the most subtle and slow-acting of poisons; an imperceptible miasm within the white shadow of a higher culture. A vast multitude, exposed, unprepared, they had not had time nor occasion to become immune to forms of sophistication not their own, to a higher and more dexterously insidious plausibility. Thus they departed joyously, carriers of contagion, unaware that what they had beheld and believed to be truth was to prove, in historic fact, an appalling calamity. For what they saw was not at all what they believed they saw, but an imposition of the spurious upon their eyesight, a naked exhibitionism of charlatanry in the higher feudal and domineering culture, conjoined with expert salesmanship of the materials of decay. Adventitiously, to make the stage setting complete, it happened by way of apparent but unreal contrast that the structure representing the United States Government was of an incredible vulgarity, while the building at the peak of the north axis, stationed there as a symbol of The Great State of Illinois matched it as a lewd exhibit of drooling imbecility and political debauchery. The distribution at the northern end of the grounds of many state and foreign headquarters relieved the sense of stark immensity. South of them, and placed on the border of a small lake, stood the Palace of the Arts, the most vitriolic of them all— the most impudently thievish. The landscape work, in its genial distribution of lagoons, wooded islands, lawns, shrubbery and plantings, did much to soften an otherwise mechanical display; while far in the southeast corner, floating in a small lagoon or harbor, were replicas of the three caravels of Columbus, and on an adjacent artificial mound a representation of the Convent of La Rabida. Otherwhere there was no evidence of Columbus and his daring deed, his sufferings, and his melancholy end. No keynote, no dramatic setting forth of that deed which, recently, has aroused some discussion as to whether the discovery of America had proven to be a blessing or a curse to the world of mankind.

Following the white cloud, even as a companion in iniquity, came the gray cloud. It overwhelmed the land with a pall of desolation. It dropped its blinding bolt. Its hurricane swept away the pyramided paper structures of speculation. Its downpour washed away fancied gains; its raindrops, loaded with a lethal toxin, fell alike upon the unjust and the just, as in retribution, demanding an atonement in human sacrifice. The thunder ceased to roll, the rain became a mist and cleared, the storm subsided, all was still. Overhead hung the gray cloud of panic from horizon to

horizon. Slowly it thinned, in time became translucent, vanished, revealing the white cloud which, in platoons, unseen, had overrun the blue.
Now again shone the sun. Prosperity awakened from its torpor, rubbed
its eyes and prepared for further follies.

It is said that history repeats itself. This is not so. What is mistaken for
repetition is the recurrent feudal rhythm of exaltation and despair. Its progressive wavelike movement in action is implicit in the feudal thought, and
inevitable, and so long as the feudal thought holds dominion in the minds
of men, just so long and no longer will calamity follow upon the appearance of prosperity. The end is insanity, the crumbling and the passing of
the race, for life is ever saying to Man: If you wish to be destroyed I
will destroy you. The white cloud is the feudal idea. The gray cloud, the
nemesis contained within that idea. The feudal idea is dual, it holds to
the concept of good and evil. The democratic idea is single, integral. It
holds to the good alone. Its faith lies in the beneficence of its power, in
its direct appeal to life. Its vision revals an inspiring vista of accomplishment. Its common sense recognizes man as by nature sound to the core,
and kindly. It as clearly sees, in the feudal scheme, a continuous warfare—
as well in so-called times of peace as in sanguinary battle. It views all this
as lunacy, for its own word is kindness. It bases its faith upon the heart
in preference to the intellect, though knowing well the power of the latter
when controlled. It knows that the intellect, alone, runs amuck, and per-
forms unspeakable cruelties; that the heart alone is divine. For it is the
heart that welcomes Life and would cherish it, would shield it against the
cannibalism of the intellect.

From the height of its Columbian Ecstacy, Chicago drooped and subsided with the rest, in a common sickness, the nausea of overstimulation.
This in turn passed, toward the end of the decade, and the old game began
again with intensified fury, to come to a sudden halt in 1907. There are
those who say this panic was artificial and deliberate, that the battle of
the saber-toothed tigers and the mastodons was on.

Meanwhile the virus of the World's Fair, after a period of incubation
in the architectural profession and in the population at large, especially
the influential, began to show unmistakable signs of the nature of the
contagion. There came a violent outbreak of the Classic and the Renaissance in the East, which slowly spread westward, contaminating all that
it touched, both at its source and outward. The selling campaign of the
bogus antique was remarkably well managed through skillful publicity
and propaganda, by those who were first to see its commercial possibili-

ties. The market was ripe, made so through the hebetude of the populace, big business men, and eminent educators alike. By the time the market had been saturated, all sense of reality was gone. In its place had come deep-seated illusions, hallucinations, absence of pupillary reaction to light, absence of knee-reaction—symptoms all of progressive cerebral meningitis: The blanketing of the brain. Thus Architecture died in the land of the free and the home of the brave—in a land declaring its fervid democracy, its inventiveness, its resourcefulness, its unique daring, enterprise and progress. Thus did the virus of a culture, snobbish and alien to the land, perform its work of disintegration; and thus ever works the pallid academic mind, denying the real, exalting the fictitious and the false, incapable of adjusting itself to the flow of living things, to the reality and the pathos of man's follies, to the valiant hope that ever causes him to aspire, and again to aspire; that never lifts a hand in aid because it cannot; that turns its back upon man because that is its tradition; a culture lost in ghostly *mésalliance* with abstractions, when what the world needs is courage, common sense and human sympathy, and a moral standard that is plain, valid and livable.

The damage wrought by the World's Fair will last for half a century from its date, if not longer. It has penetrated deep into the constitution of the American mind, effecting there lesions significant of dementia.

Meanwhile the architectural generation immediately succeeding the Classic and Renaissance merchants, are seeking to secure a special immunity from the inroads of common sense, through a process of vaccination with the lymph of every known European style, period and accident, and to this all-around process, when it breaks out, is to be added the benediction of good taste. Thus we have now the abounding freedom of Eclecticism, the winning smile of taste, but no architecture. For Architecture, be it known, is dead. Let us therefore lightly dance upon its grave, strewing roses as we glide. Indeed let us gather, in procession, in the night. in the rain, and make soulful, fluent, epicene orations to the living dead we neuters eulogize.

Surely the profession has made marvelous improvements in trade methods, over the old-fashioned way. here is now a dazzling display of merchandise, all imported, excepting to be sure our own cherished colonial, which maintains our Anglo-Saxon tradition in its purity. We have Tudor for colleges and residences; Roman for banks, and railway stations and libraries—or Greek if you like—some customers prefer the Ionic to the Doric. We have French, English and Italian Gothic, Classic and

Renaissance for churches. In fact we are prepared to satisfy, in any manner of taste. Residences we offer in Italian or Louis Quinze. We make a small charge for alterations and adaptations. Our service we guarantee as exceptional and exclusive. Our importations are direct. We have our own agents abroad. We maintain also a commercial department, in which a selective taste is not so necessary. Its province is to solve engineering problems of all kinds, matters of cost, income, maintenance, taxes, renewals, depreciation, obsolescence; and as well maintenance of contact, sales pressure, sales resistance, flotations, and further matters of the sort. We maintain also an industrial department in which leading critics unite in saying we have made most significant departures in design. These structures, however, are apart from our fashionable trade. Our business is founded and maintained on an ideal service, and a part of that service we believe to consist in an elevation of the public taste, a setting forth of the true standards of design, in pure form, a system of education by example, the gradual formation of a background of culture for the masses. In this endeavor we have the generous support of the architectural schools, of the colleges and universities, of men of wealth, and of those whose perspicacity has carred them to the pinnacle of eminence in finance, industry, commerce, education, and statesmanship. Therefore we feel that we are in thorough accord with the spirit of our times as expressed in its activities, in its broad democratic tolerance, and its ever-youthful enthusiasms. It is this sense of solidity, solidarity and security that makes us bold, inspires us with the high courage to continue in our self-imposed task. We look for our reward solely in the conviction of duty done; our profound belief that we are preparing the way for the coming generation through the power of our example, our counsel and our teachings, to the end that they may express, better than we ourselves have done, the deep, the sincere, the wholesome aspirations of our people and of our land, as yet not fully articulated by the higher culture, in spite of our best efforts toward that end. This task we are quite aware we must eventually leave to the young who are crowding upon us, and we wish them joy in their great adventure when we relinquish our all.

In the better aspects of eclecticism and taste, that is to say, in those aspects which reveal a certain depth of artistic feeling and a physical sense of materials, rather than mere scene-painting or archæology, however clever, there is to be discovered a hope and a forecast. For it is within the range of possibilities, one may even go so far as to say probabilities, that out of the very richness and multiplicity of the architectural phenom-

ena called styles there may arise within the architectural mind a perception growing slowly, perhaps suddenly, into clearness, that architecture
in its material nature and in its animating essence is a *plastic art.* This
truth, so long resisted because of the limited intellectual boundaries and
deficient sympathy of academic training, must eventually prevail because
founded upon a culture of common sense and human recognition. Its
power is as gentle and as irresistible as that of the Springtime—to which
it may be likened, or to sunrise following the night and its stars, and
herein lies beneath the surface and even on the surface the inspiration of
our High Optimism, with its unceasing faith in man as free spirit! as creator, possessed of a physical sense indistinguishable from the spiritual,
and of innate plastic powers whose fecundity and beneficence surpass our
present scope of imagination. Dogma and rule of the dead are passing.
The Great *Modern* Inversion, for which the world of mankind has been
preparing purblindly through the ages, is now under way in its world-
wide awakening. The thought of the multitudes is changing, withdrawing
its consent, its acquiescence; the dream of the multitudes is metamorphos-
ing, philosophy is becoming human and immersing itself in the flow of
life; science is pushing the spectres back into the invisible whence they
came. The world is in travail, smeared with blood, amid the glint of
bayonets; the feudal idea has reached the pitch of its insanity, yet by the
way of compensation the veils are lifting rapidly, all the veils of hypocrisy and sinister intent, all the veils of plausible, insidious speech, of
propaganda, of perfidy, of betrayal. It requires courage to remain steadfast in faith in the presence of such pollution. Yet it is precisely such
courage that marks man in his power as free spirit. For beneath this corruption the enlightened one perceives the everlasting aspirations of mankind, the ever-yearning heart in its search for kindness, peace and a safe
anchorage within its world, and to such, the compassionate one gives out
words of encouragement and prophecy, even as the gray clouds hover
from horizon to horizon; a prophecy that this cloud shall melt away, and
reveal aloft a shining white cloud, in the blue, announcing the new man
and the new culture of faith.

It seems fitting, therefore, that this work should close with the same
child-dream in which it began. The dream of a beauteous, beneficent
power, which came when, winter past, the orchards burst into bloom, and
the song of spring was heard in the land.

That dream has never ceased. That faith has never wearied. With the
passage of the years, the dream, the faith, ever expanding in power, be-

came all-inclusive; and with the progress of the dream and the faith, there emerged in confirmation a vague outline, growing year after year more luminous and clear. When the golden hour tolled, all mists departed, and there shone forth as in a vision, the reality of MAN, as Free Spirit, as Creator, as Container of illimitable powers, for the joy and the peace of mankind.

It was this unseen nearby presence, messenger of Life in its flowing, that sang its song of spring to the child, and the child heard what no one heard; the child saw what no one saw.

It is questionable how much of social value one who has had access to the treasures of the past, access to the best and the worst in the thought of his day, may leave behind him in his fruitage, as a quantum—an IDEA.

This narrator agrees, in such connection, that the initial instinct of the child, as set forth, is the basis of all fruitful ideas, and that the growth in power of such ideas is in itself a work of instinct; that, if it has been convincingly shown that instinct is primary and intellect secondary in all the great works of man, this portrayal is justified.

It is further the belief of this narrator, in this connection, that if he has succeeded in setting clearly forth the basic fruitful power of the IDEA permeating and dominating this narrative of a life-experience, physical and spiritual, he has done well in thus making a record in words to be pondered in the heart.

PART TWO

THE PIVOTAL THEMES

FUNCTION AND FORM

His genius as an architect enabled Sullivan to explore the concept 'form follows function' in action and inaugurate one whole aspect of modern art; disuse of that genius led him to explore the significance of the same insight in human life and in the natural world. The most explicit statement and development of this insight is found in his *Kindergarten Chats,* first published in *Interstate Architect & Builder,* between February, 1901 and February, 1902. These "chats" take place between the author and an imaginary graduate of an architectural school; the one reproduced here came, as the opening exchange makes clear, immediately after another on the nature of language.

You were going to tell me more about language, and you—

No, I was not. I began to tell you something about function and form, when you interrupted; and that is what I am to do now.

That is so; we didn't finish, did we?

We can never finish. We may talk for long, and get only a start; but it will be a right start, I believe. We may, perhaps, see where the end lies, but it will be and remain like a star in the sky, unreachable and of unknown distance; or it will be like life itself, elusive to the last—even in death; or it will be like a phantom beacon on a phantom stormy sea; or as a voice, calling, afar in the woods; or, like the shadow of a cloud upon a cloud, it will glide, diaphanous and imponderable, floating in the still air of the spirit.

What's that you are talking about?

The interrelation of function and form. It has no beginning, no ending. It is immeasurably small, immeasurably vast; inscrutably mobile, infinitely serene; intimately complex yet simple.

But you surely told me to listen, not to the words, but to the thought. How can I follow, if you are always thinking away ahead of the words? You seem to take delight in it.

That is true. I will specify: Now, it stands to reason that a thing looks like what it is, and, vice versa, it is what it looks like. I will stop here, to make exception of certain little straight, brown canker-worms that I have picked from rose-bushes. They looked like little brown, dead twigs at first. But speaking generally, outward appearances resemble inner purposes. For instances: the form, oak-tree, resembles and expresses the purpose or function, oak; the form, pine-tree, resembles and indicates the function, pine; the form, horse, resembles and is the logical output of the function, horse; the form, spider, resembles and is the tangible evidence of the function, spider. So the form, wave, looks like the function, wave; the form, cloud, speaks to us of the function, cloud; the form, rain, indicates the function, rain; the form, bird, tells us of the function, bird; the form, eagle, is the function, eagle, made visible; the form, beak of that eagle, the function, beak of that eagle. And so does the form, rose-bush, authenticate its function, rose-bush; the form, rose-branch, tells of the function, rose-branch; the form, rose-bud, speaks for the function, rosebud; the form, full-blown rose, recites the poem, full-blown rose. And so does the form, man, stand for the function, man; the form, John Doe, means the function, John Doe; the form, smile, makes us aware of the function, smile; so, when I say: a man named John Doe smiles—we have a little series of functions and forms which are inseparably related, and yet they seem very casual to us. If I say, John Doe speaks and stretches out his hand, as he smiles, I add a little to the sum of the functions and the forms, but I do not affect their validity or their continuity. If I say, he speaks ungrammatically and with a lisp, I merely modify a little the form your own impressions are taking as you listen; if I say, that, as he smiled, and stretched out his hand, and began speaking, with a lisp and ungrammatically, his lip trembled and a tear formed in his eye—are not function and form moving in their rhythm, are you not moving in your rhythm while you listen, am I not moving in my rhythm as I speak? If I add that, as he spoke, he sank into a chair, his hat fell from his relaxing fingers, his face blanched, his eyelids drooped, his head turned a little, have I done more than add to your impression and my sympathy? I have not in reality added or detached; I have not made or unmade; I speak, you listen—John Doe lived. He did not know anything or care anything about form or function; but he lived them both; he disbursed them both as he went along through life. He lived and he died. You and I live and we shall die. But John Doe lived the life of John Doe, not of John Smith: that was his function and such were his forms. And so the form, Roman architecture, means, if it means anything at all, the function

Roman; the form American architecture, will mean, if it ever succeeds in meaning anything, American life; the form, John-Doe architecture, should there be such an architecture, must mean nothing, if it means not John Doe. I do not lie when I tell you John Doe lisped, you do not lie when you listen, he did not lie when he lisped; then why all this lying architecture? Why does John-Doe architecture pretend it is John-Smith architecture? Are we a nation of liars? I think not. That we architects are a sect, a cult of prevaricators, is another matter. And so, in man-made things, the form, literature, means nothing more or less than the function, literature; the form, music, the function, music; the form, knife, the function, knife; the form, axe, the function, axe; the form, engine, the function, engine. And again, in nature, the form, water, the function, water; the form, rivulet, the function, rivulet; the form, river, the function, river; the form, lake, the function, lake; the form, reeds, the function, reeds; the forms, fly above the water and bass below the water—their related functions; and so the fisherman in the boat; and so on, and on, and on—unceasingly, endlessly, constantly, eternally—through the range of the physical world—visual, microscopic, and telescopic, the world of the senses, the world of the intellect, the world of the heart, the world of the soul: the physical world of man we believe we know, and the borderland of that world we know not—that world of the silent, immeasurable, creative spirit, of whose infinite function all these things are but the varied manifestations in form, in form more or less tangible, more or less imponderable—a borderland delicate as the dawn of life, grim as fate, human as the smile of a friend—a universe wherein all is function, all is form: a frightful phantasm, driving the mind to despair, or, as we will, a glorious revelation of that power which holds us in an invisible, a benign, a relentless—a wondrous hand...Like sees and begets its like. That which exists in spirit ever seeks and finds its physical counterpart in form, its visible image; an uncouth thought, an uncouth form; a monstrous thought, a monstrous form; a thought in decadence, a form in decadence; a living thought, a living form. Light means light—a shadow means eclipse. How many shadows do men cast! How many live in shadows! How many walk in darkness! How many struggle in their night! How many wander, all forlorn, in the verge of Death's deep valley! How many are mired in the black pit! How many drag others thereunto! Great is the light that shines. Profound the shadow that Man casts upon his own spirit! Opaque and moribund that man who gives forth, not a light, but a shadow in his daily walk. A dense, material, moving phantom, he, who stands before the sun and puts his art in obscuration! Stand out of my light! Stand out of our light! I say! Platoons of dead men! This is the day when strikes the hour upon high noon, within a cloudless sky! Avast the sun! Avaunt, the clay that doth eclipse it! Shall the hour sound, and no man answer cheerily its call? Shall the sun shine and no flower bloom in gladness? Shall the joyous heavens find no answer to their smile, but sullen turbid stares? It cannot be, it shall not be: for of the wilderness I'll make a song of spring that shall dispel its gloomy wintry skies and icy snows, and make awake to sweet rejuvenance the lark, the soaring, singing lark that doth abide within the hearts—of all the young!

Is there then form in everything?

Form in everything and anything, everywhere and at every instant. According to their nature, their function, some forms are definite, some indefinite; some are nebulous, others concrete and sharp; some symmetrical, others purely rhythmical. Some are abstract, others material. Some appeal to the eye, some to the ear, some to the touch, some to the sense of smell, some to any one or all or any combination of these. But all, without fail, stand for relationships between the immaterial and the material, between the subjective and the objective—between the Infinite Spirit and the finite mind. Through our sense we know substantially all that we may know. The imagination, intuition, reason, are but exalted forms of the physical senses, as we call them. For Man there is nothing but the physical; what he calls his spirituality is but the most exalted reach of his animalism. Little by little, Man, through his senses, divines the Infinite. His highest thoughts, his most delicate yearnings arise, through an imperceptible birth and growth, from the material sense of touch. From hunger arose the cravings of his soul. From urgent passions have the sweetest vows of his heart arisen. From savage instincts came the force and powers of his mind. All is growth, all is decadence. Functions are born of functions, and in turn, give birth or death to others. Forms emerge from forms, and others arise or descend from these. All are related, interwoven, intermeshed, interconnected, interblended. They exosmose and endosmose. They sway and swirl and mix and drift interminably. They shape, they reform, they dissipate. They respond, correspond, attract, repel, coalesce, disappear, reappear, merge, and emerge: slowly or swiftly, gently or with cataclysmic force—from chaos into chaos, from death into life, from life into death, from rest into motion, from motion into rest, from darkness into light, from light into darkness, from sorrow into joy, from joy into sorrow, from purity into foulness, from foulness into purity, from growth into decadence, from decadence into growth. All is form, all is function—ceaselessly unfolding and infolding—and the heart of Man unfolds and infolds with them: Man, the one spectator before whom this drama spreads its appalling, its inspiring harmony of drift and splendor, as the centuries toll and toll the flight of broad-pinioned Time, soaring, from eternity to eternity: while the mite sucks the juices of the petal, and the ant industriously wanders here and there and here and there again, the song-bird twitters on the bough, the violet gives her perfume sweetly forth in innocence. All is function, all is form, but the fragrance of them is rhythm, the language of them is rhythm: for rhythm is the very wedding-march and ceremonial that quickens into song the unison of form and function, or the dirge of their farewell, as they move apart, and pass into the silent watches of that wondrous night we call the past. So goes the story on its endless way.

THE CREATIVE IMPULSE

To the principle that "form follows function" Sullivan eventually added another, less coherent and incisive, but also fruitful: man's sense of his aloneness in the universe is the source of his need and capacity to shape the world in his own image. These ideas Sullivan developed in the course of a voracious program of reading that fastened with particular avidity on the advanced works of the day in history, sociology, and psychology, and on popularizations of the major discoveries in physical science. But he was never a retailer of other people's ideas: he used them all in an attempt to contemplate the source and character of his own genius, and its relations with nature and society. "The Creative Impulse," the last but two of the dialogues that make up his *Kindergarten Chats,* contains ideas Sullivan found essential in his subsequent attempts to relate art and democracy in a general philosophy of life.

You have a singular habit of assuming, when you suddenly make a compact statement, novel in character, that I am capable of digesting it at once. For instance, I am still puzzling over your statement that every problem contains and suggests its own solution; and that to seek the solution elsewhere is a waste of time. Now I can't see that a problem contains its solution; still less can I see that it suggests it.

I admit the impeachment. It is likely to happen, when one has given years of thought to a particular subject, that his working idea concerning it is apt to concentrate into a statement so terse that, while axiomatic to himself, it is not self-evident to others.

That is just where I stand: it is not self-evident to me. My training tended the other way. And yet the suggestion excites my vivid curiosity. It sounds neat if nothing more.

I have come to regard as valuable those truths only which are universal. And it is a bit surprising to note how many truths are universal or may be expanded into a universal application. I don't suppose that anyone who succeeds in solving a problem really goes out of it for the solution; and this assumption doubtless also accounts for innumerable failures. And the failures certainly are self-evident: the world is filled with débris of this sort. Particularly is this characteristic of the intellectuals. The unsophisticated man is often better qualified to go straight to the core of a matter: by a process of feeling to sense its reality. Now to give a very simple case: if you are given a peanut-pod and the problem is to find the peanut, you simply open the pod and there is your peanut. The conditions are extremely simple, but the truth is there: the germ of a universal truth, which, with sufficiently extended experience will formulate itself in an axiom, or what scientists call a law: for to scientists, truths are laws: in which little word you may incidentally note the survival of an autocratic notion of the universe.

If we gradually enlarge our problem, we find its husk of conditions becoming complicated, and its contained germ of solution less and less obvious. But when we have solved our problem by confining our attention to it, we find the law holds good. And when we have had further experience, we become aware that the very nature of the limiting conditions suggests to us what must be the nature and the limitations of the solution. If you are searching for a peanut you come to know by experience that you will not find it within the burr of a chestnut. Thus a given problem takes on the character of individuality, of identity. And you become aware that your solution must partake of that identity. If you come across a problem which does not possess an identity, you know by such token that the problem is not a problem but a figment. As the problem becomes more complex it becomes the more necessary to know all the conditions, to have all the data, and especially to make sure as to the limitations. Now suppose we extend the problem to its broad human limit and pose it as the problem of Democracy. The conditions seem enormously complicated and complex, and sternly limited by what is called human nature; the solution not only doubtful but nowhere in sight. Yet, let us but patiently stick to our law, and we finally, perhaps after many years, penetrate this vast husk of humanity and fictions, and find the germ of the solution to be individual man himself, and the fundamental nature of man within him. Having discovered one man, his spirit and his powers, we have discovered all men. Having discovered man, the problem reverses, takes on a new, a constructive aspect; an aspect and purpose born of the desire to create. So I will leave you to make your own specific applications of the law as the need arises, and proceed to talk about what is uppermost in my mind, and yet which will grow rather naturally out of your inquiry. And, by the way, what sort of problem do you fancy you presented, in your precious self, when first you came to me?

What I want to talk about concerns this query: What underlies man's desire to create? It surely must have in it much of the nature of his problems.

To begin with, man must originally have had the notion that he could make rather than that he could create. His idea was to do something, to fashion something, for his immediate use; to satisfy his immediate physical wants. And this germinal notion still survives, in its simplicity, through all the complexities of ensuing civilizations, up to the present day of our calendar. Hence we may assume as a basis that the idea of doing something came into being before the idea of creating something. That man the worker, in biological sequence, preceded man the inquirer, the thinker, the poet—the creator. We are probably justified, moreover, in believing that the power to work and the power of emotion, while contemporaneous in man, were not equally satisfied, that in man's emotional nature lay a germ, an unshapen idea, which gradually grew in assertiveness within him and sought outward realization. This germ was the inarticulate beginning of the desire to express himself wholly; the earliest indication of his need of an art of expression; the latent beginning of the CREATIVE IMPULSE.

Now, the particularly delicate point involved is: Why did man wish to create? Was it not that he felt lonely? That he desired emotional, psychic companionship? Was not this subdued and shadowy anxiety, a problem shaping for him, gradually but vaguely pressing for solution? Now, how did early man solve this unique problem which would prostrate a modern mind if it were suddenly new? Still guided emotionally by instinct, he sought the solution by instinct, and found it precisely where it was— within himself. He did not formulate laws on the subject; he simply acted out his instinct—his instinct of reproduction. He infused his bare work with the quality of his emotions and thus found in them the companionship he yearned for—because they were of himself. His growing intellect might have gone on satisfying his physical needs and amplifying their expression. Instinct alone, in inspiring the work of his hand and his intellect, could satisfy the craving of his heart, the hunger of his soul. Thus man unconsciously began to create in his own image. His work slowly grew in power of impulse, in power of expression. As civilizations arose, man's work in those outwardly differing civilizations evinced his temperamental variation. In some, the intellectual force predominates, in others, the emotions. Seldom have they approached a balance. Never did they achieve it. For such achievement was beyond the range of the feudal mind. It lies in the domain of sanity.

In our own day, sadly enough, as I have told you, Instinct has departed, in form if not in substance. To its beautifully varied powers we, unconscious of their origin, give many beautiful names; to the primal impulse which we emptily call instinct we apply terms of obloquy and reproach. And we do this, not because we are over-civilized, but because we are half-civilized. We have given to intellect a loose rein, utterly regardless or ignorant of the fact that in the end it would surely run amuck and attempt to drive us like sheep over the precipice or into the morass of social suicide.

Now, therefore, arises again, this time for us, the selfsame problem that confronted early man. There exists in us the same power to make something, the same vague, instinctive yearning for emotional and psychic companionship, the same inarticulate desire to image ourselves forth. But intellect has long held repressive sway, while Instinct has been biding its time. We have been practical so long that what we have imaged forth is relatively monstrous, and by sane standards unreal, untrue to man's oneness: true only to his dualism. Modern man is a traitor to himself in suppressing one-half of himself. In a measure he realizes this, and makes attempts at betterment, as he calls it, feeble, miscellaneous, and misdirected, employing but a minute part of his power in endeavoring to effect that consummation he so devotedly worships and which he calls Compromise. In other words, he is attempting the impossible task of eating his cake and keeping it. It is true that he is constantly putting forth multitudinous intellectual images of himself and the unique character of these works indicates the corresponding status of his intellectual reach. The fact that he is not putting forth equal works based on instinct shows as clearly his intention that the intellect shall continue to dominate the heart: that he is practical. Therefore modern man's attempts at solving the basic problem of life have been unsuccessful, because he has looked everywhere for a solution, or a suggestion of solution, except within the problem itself.

It is always fatal to a solution to approach a problem with a preconception or fixed attitude of mind; with a mind made up as to what the nature of the solution will be, must be, ought to be, shall be. And yet modern man has made this specific, particularly grave blunder. He has begun by surrounding the husk containing the germ of solution—a husk already thick enough—with a fibrous super-husk of intellectual misconceptions concerning man, his powers and his relation to his fellow man. In other words, he has attempted to solve a problem wholly altruistic in nature by the application of methods wholly selfish and therefore external in nature. In fact, we might pause here to say that man, throughout his history, has preponderatingly sought explanations in the external instead of seeking them as he should, in the internal. This mental attitude accounts accurately for the phenomenon that man projected out of himself that vast sombre and inexorable image of himself which he has called Fate.

The man of the past has shown to us his power to create multiform images of himself in his feudal status. These images arose in actuality of physical form, or as marvelous airy fabrics of his emotional dreams, his spiritual hunger for companionship, directly from the need, the impulse, to create. Yet he did not know (though doubtless he may have felt) that these many things he created, these many systems he created, the many gods he created, were but sublime projections of himself into the outer world; which creations, as visioned forth by him, awakened a reaction within his inner world; and that, in his simultaneous outer and inner world he found the companionship he sought; he felt at home among the family of images of himself—his veritable progeny. And thus his civilizations, with all their contained institutions, were the collective image of the multitudes, the instinctive unconscious output of their powers, the visible glorifying symbol which the voice of nature—Instinct—told them was theirs, but which Intellect assured them in their waking, toiling hours could not possibly be of them but was a gift to them from on high. And as the lowly as well as the highborn were under the sway of intellect, the multitudes believed and consented. Hence there is not and never was such thing (except in passive moments) as a government existing independently of the consent of the governed. The feudal governments, past and present, have rested upon the foundation [of the] feudal thought of the people. Our civilizations have thus been superstructures erected upon such intellectually and emotionally ethereal, yet physical, solid, foundation.

However—and let this be particularly noted—when the massive thought of the multitudes changes, the civilizations, the institutions supported and sustained by that thought, correspondingly change with it, for no civilization, no institution, can long exist after the creative impulse, the emotional desire, the intellectual consent of the multitudes, is withdrawn. For such civilization has by such token ceased to be their image. It no longer responds to their dreams. Or, it may be, their dream fades, and the image fades or is destroyed. Usually in past times these changes have progressed slowly. In modern times there is a visible tendency toward acceleration. And, be it further noted that in all the glory of the past, man had not solved the problem of man.

Now comes to us a new yearning, a new sense of loneliness, a new anxiety for companionship. The old images, the old gods, the old procedures no longer satisfy. Slowly there is awakening and stirring in modern man, a new desire, a new, a vaster creative impulse, a new movement of instinct. This is what makes the aspect of our world today so thrilling, so dramatic, so potent in new solutions, in new creations. The thought of modern man is swiftly shaping itself, with self-impelling power, upon the new-appearing center of gravity within himself; about a new conjunction of Intellect and emotion, a new assertion of Instinct, a new and concentrated creative impulse; a new desire to see his new self imaged in new institutions, giving him a new satisfaction, a new sense of fulfilled companionship. Engrossed now in the analytical stage, he soon will enter the constructive stage. For the creative impulse, intimately subjective in origin, fulfills its function in objective realities.

All this may seem a digression from our main theme, but I have made it purposely, that you may locate wide boundaries and concentrate upon simple initiatives. That you may see the day that man will soon, with open eyes, find himself confronted by portentous images of himself which he will reluctantly recognize as such. That with selfsame open eyes he will recognize his prudery and prurience of intellect *in extenso* and, for his own healing, will become ashamed.

Furthermore, while what I have said may cause our art to seem insignificantly small in comparison, we may easily note, in concentrating our thought upon it, that it is indissolubly a part of the larger undertaking, and in our application thereto of an analytical creative impulse phasing into a synthetic, constructive, creative impulse, we are doing our special work in connection with the greatest adventure the spirit of man ever has entered.

So let your art be of, for, and by this new creative impulse of our day, that it may in due time put forth true images of man's free spirit.

PART THREE

DEMOCRACY AND THE
SPIRIT OF MAN

SELECTIONS FROM NATURAL THINKING

By 1905, Sullivan had sunk to that nearly permanent level of un-
employment and indigence which was to lead, a year later, to the
auction of his private property, and from which he never emerged.
Meanwhile he had filled his idleness with an intense inner seeking.
What is man's relationship to the universe? What is his relationship to his fellows? Sullivan made two major attempts to answer
these questions. The first of these, a book-length manuscript in the
Burnham Library of the Art Institute of Chicago, was read, according to a note on the title page, before the Chicago Architectural
Club on February 13, 1905. There is no record of how this formidably long and didactic speech was received at the time. No part
of it has been published hitherto. Read today, it offers us, among
many rewarding passages, three which provide crucial statements of
points of view Sullivan was to elaborate at greater length, on a
more philosophical scale and in a more messianic tone, in *Democracy: A Man-Search.*

"Consent to Listen"

Listen:

I have never sought to tell what Life is, because I do not know what
it is. I have patiently rummaged the books, kept fairly in touch with
the delicate probings of latter-day science, but have found no man who
can tell others what Life is. The Nazarene, seeking, could not tell. He
could but hint of it in parable and symbol—images like the dawn of an
unseen sun.

I have regarded the daybreak; the plant, growing from its seed; have
looked deep into human eyes; have watched, as from a tower, the revolving spectacle of the seasons, and the drama of generations of men. Yet
I do not know and cannot know what Life is, nor can any man.

Nevertheless it is precisely of Life that I would speak; of that diaphanous, pellucid essence which has baffled all men, in all times, and which, Sphinx-like, will forever baffle them. Indeed, strange as it may seem, it is of this very inscrutable Life that I must perforce speak to you. For it is to be the animating spirit of that which I am to portray, as well as of that mental attitude in which I ask you: listen.

Therefore consent to listen—as the apple of Newton consented to fall. If there be an attracting element in that which I am to think and say, if there be in it any potency of natural suasion, there must likewise come to your hearts and minds a certain responsive ripening, else are my words and your hearing vain.

For no mere force of gravity ever unloosed an unripe or an unconditional apple, however subtle or constant the earth's drawing power may be; for it is not in the program of normal Life that the apple shall approach the earth until its time is ripe—until it has consented.

Therefore I say that in this sense listening is the ripened faculty of hearing. Hearing can ripen into listening only through the consent of the mind. If the mind is unwilling or impotent, hearing by the ears avails not, for the brain is deaf; and hence one great channel for the flow of impressions from without is choked at the end, and useless for the entrance and exit of thought.

But if the mind not only consents, but is eager with desire, then is the mind normal in its relation to Life, and the channel of hearing is open to an endless flow of impressions from every source of sound. Now there is no sound without its significance; and what the meaning may be, it is of the refinement of listening to discern and retain. Therefore train yourselves to listen; for in this attitude of the mind lies the beginning of natural thinking.

And so with the eyes. They may see without seeing, in the sense that the mind does not consent to receive that which the eye sees. Thus is another channel from the outer world to the inner man blockaded by an unwilling brain, and the natural returning flow of thought through the eyes is estopped.

As there is no word which bears the same popular relation to seeing, that listening bears to hearing, the word *listen* itself may, by a little turn of its significance be applied here; and to *listen with the eyes* becomes an understandable term because it implies a willingness and receptivity of the brain.

But a strong word may be applied to seeing—it is *focus*—which means in its live sense, the outpushing or the indrawing, the spreading or the concentration of vision as a mechanism of natural thinking. And, in this same sense, we focalize our hearing—that which we see and hear becomes local or comprehensive to our consciousness; provided always that the brain reacts in sympathy with the external impressions that are brought to it.

It is of prime importance to us then, that the eye has this power of localizing on the object; for from the locating of a series of objects arises the sense of perspective or a consciousness of differences in position.

It is fortunate for us that literal words may, by common consent, be used in a figurative sense. Otherwise how could we so readily turn the idea of physical perspective into its fuller correlative, mental perspective.

In this same sense may we speak of focussing the sense of touch, and of the perspective, of that same—and thus how readily does the physical word "touch" evoke its psychological companion, "feeling"—and thus how readily may we associate with the senses of touch and sight as well as with the sense of hearing, the idea of listening.

It may sound strange to you at first, if I say, listen with the eyes, listen with the fingers, or the entire muscular or even the entire physiological system. But, in so doing I am in reality but expanding the local meaning of the symbol or word "listening" into a comprehensive association with that mental, emotional, and psychic state or landscape of human perspective we call "feeling." And feeling, in turn, has its power of focus.

In thus transposing and modulating words, I am indicating to you my conviction that under normal, or as I prefer to say, natural conditions, of mind and body, the physical, the mental, and the spiritual are in essence one. That is to say, while the eye and the brain appear to be different things, while the senses and the mind appear to be and are generally spoken of as different things, they in reality are but phases or aspects of one thing: and that one thing is Life. What Life is I have already said that I do not know. But, apparently, it seems a force or essence infinitely simple in power and equally infinite in complexity of manifestation.

If then, as I hold, natural thinking is a vital process, it must be of Life, and possess the simplicity of Life in its power, the complexity of Life in its manifestations.

By power do not understand mere force, mechanical strength, might, warfare, or strenuousness. This misconception is too general. The great powers of nature, are silent. The lightning is but a little power—and noisy. The dew-fall is a great power—and quiet. Life itself, the greatest of powers, is infinitely silent, serene, deep, and constant; so still as to be inaudible to our sense of hearing, but, nevertheless, in a measure tangible to the higher, finer sense of listening—that listening which is of our whole being—which therefore is of Life itself. Indeed when we thus listen, it is as Life listening to itself, so vital, so powerful in quality is Natural Thought.

Few stop to consider the really elaborate complexity of the simple things we encounter near at hand and every day. For instance, the simple act of walking. It seems commonplace enough; and not only is it so, but also, and at the same time, it is a marvel of complex coordination. So remarkably complex, in fact, that it would require volumes of print backed by the highest conceivable technical skill in expression to render its analysis relatively clear, accurate and exhaustive, and to make its synthesis fully appreciable to the mind, even assuming the mind could grasp it. Every day we walk, and think nothing of it; we simply do it; and believe that we do it. It does not occur to us that it is Life that is walking.

But on the other hand, thinking, which is in reality as simple and natural in its Life-quality as is walking, is held up to us as a purely artificial acquirement. Something in the nature of an accomplishment reserved for those who have leisure. And we, in our folly, accept this feudal notion. Your shrewd business man does not believe this because, after the manner of so-called 'horse sense,' he knows better. Your horny-handed working man is beginning not to believe it because there are arising pale glimmerings in his brain of a conviction that by thinking, only, can he survive in freedom. But your scholar, your man of culture, and even your teachers are prone so to believe—because of the Feudal Tradition. It is a wondrous pity that they do not know better. It seems not to occur to them that thinking, like walking, is a natural process: That it is the essence, Life, that thinks, just as it is the essence, Life, that walks.

Therefore I repeat; the prevailing estimate of thinking is Feudal because it tacitly or openly denies this power except to a limited class; whreas the true or natural view of thinking is Democratic, because it holds a natural power of thought to be the portion of all without distinction. Our troubles and our distortions of thought are traceable largely to the fact that the people do not as yet fully grasp the magic power of this simple truth.

Perhaps you do not quite understand what I mean by Feudal and by Democratic.

It is quite essential that you should both know and understand, if ever you are to hope to think rationally, and independently.

FEUDALISM, (without a pun) signifies for the few. It means, in essence, denial; repression, segregation; class distinction; aristocracy; robbery of your fellow men in every way, shape and manner. It means, specifically, irresponsibility, unaccountability. It leads directly to usurpation, and, finally, to a declaration of divine right. It is the insanity of civilization because it breeds the disease, the dishonesty, the crime, the cant, the hypocrisy of civilization. It prefers to receive rather than to give. It is founded on selfishness. Its power lies in the corrupted Dollar; this power means Death. The aspiration and goal of Feudalism is Absolutism.

DEMOCRACY, signifies of by and for the people. It means equal rights, responsibility toward the neighbor and kindliness toward him. It means that we receive our individual divinity from nature, as a gift at birth. It implies the brotherhood of man, and universal love because of universal accountability. The rock of its foundation is Character. Its motive force is natural thought. Its animating principle is Life. Its aspiration, its goal, the uplifting of man. Justice is its life blood.

Therefore: Every unjust judge, every crooked merchant, every hypocritical preacher, every evasive workman, every hide-bound teacher, every lofty-nosed scholar, in short every man who betrays a trust is, in the essence of his thought and drift of his action, Feudal. In short, the Dishonest Man is Feudal.

Your true scientist is a Democrat; so is your manly man; your real philosopher; your real scholar; your true teacher; your real mechanic, or any real man laboring with hands and brain; so is your man who helps his fellow men; and, greatest and best of all, every Honest Man is a Democrat.

How poignant is this word Honesty.

It is as the sharp rising of the sun upon abodes of darkness.

Honesty is human light—and the assertion of human right.

Dishonesty is darkness, and the denial of Justice.

You should consent to know, and to understand clearly, if you are to follow my thought, that Feudalism and Democracy, are at war to the death in this our own land and day.

Nominally we are a Democracy. Really we are a confusion of Feudalism and Democracy. Or perhaps it were more apt to say, we are a Democracy afflicted with the hereditary taint of Feudalism. The hope of Democracy lies in speedy education in natural thinking. Else will Feudalism surely crush it.

Conditions in our American civilization have shaped with ever growing momentum; and are now moving with appalling swiftness toward a crisis. Hostile and vast forces are forming and defining—you will live in an era of great happenings. The eyes of the world are upon our land wherein there has begun to unfold on a gigantic stage the greatest of all historical dramas: The conflict, under strictly modern conditions, between those that would bind and those that would loosen.

So when you hear, and afterward recall what I shall later on say of a Democratic Art, you must surely feel something of my meaning—and grasp something of its forecast.

All outer Life seems shifting and changing. And our inner Life shifts and changes: We are not today what we were yesterday. We will not be tomorrow what we are today.

This change or flow is precisely what stimulates thought. Were we and all objects around us stationary, there could be no thought. Thought therefore is synonymous and synchronous with change; and it is change that makes us conscious of Life and the Flow of Life—for change and flow are phenomena of Life.

This change is not erratic. It is regular and ordered, and follows a law that we call rhythm. A law, a flow so constant in its double aspect that we call one manifestation of it Growth, and its corollary Death.

These various considerations lead us to look on Life as:

1. Individual to ourselves.

2. As characteristic of objects external to us.

3. As a great aspiring force both external to us and permeating us, operating on a grand scale, and balanced, on an equally grand scale by a subsidence called death.

4. As an essence so vast, so compelling, so completely integral, that death disappears; individual Life vanishes; and there remains in our consciousness a sense, vague, grandiose, exalting, strangely attracting, deeply convincing: The sense of an Infinite that is Complete.

It is to this Infinite that the natural man listens.

It is to this Infinite that all Nature hearkens; and interprets—for Nature ever listens, ever consents.

As Nature, listening, consents, she passes through her wondrous changes. As man listening, consents, he hears the flow of an inexhaustible energy; he perceives a vast RESERVOIR OF LIFE on which he may draw as he will; and, ever listening may ever truly hear; and, ever drawing, come nearer.

It is the constant flow throughout all Nature, of the effusion of this Infinite energy that gives to each object its Identity.

How It does this no man knows—for the flowing is the processional of ever-baffling Life.

As Life itself, hangs, as a veil, between us and the Infinite, the more we wilfully and noisily pursue, the further the veil and that behind the veil recede. But the more deeply and silently we listen and consent, standing righteously before the fair face of Nature, and the open countenance of Man, the nearer comes the veil; and That behind it.

Throughout this vast flow, and the reaction of the mind upon it, this much seems certain: That the Infinite makes its divisibility apparent to us in countless forms of Life—and that we may note in the special form or physical expression of the individual life, and in each and every of its manifestations, one of the numberless ramifications of the Infinite, and feel the conviction that the Infinite is partly intelligible to us, even though It be ultimately inscrutable.

It is this partial intelligibility that fills the soul with hope and it is this hope that is the animating function of that living form or expression of the Infinite that I am calling NATURAL THOUGHT.

At the risk of seeming prolix I must insist, very earnestly, upon the great practical value in our daily lives of this conviction that the Infinite is partly intelligible, and wholly useful to us.

All the more must I impress it upon you, because precisely the contrary is taught, and because it is generally and tacitly assumed by the unthinking and the cynical that the Infinite is apart from us. Under such conditions of belief the Infinite has become in our minds an academic, an abstract symbol, instead of a living presence—and our unison with it official, delegated, perfunctory, and occasional.

The simple conception of the Infinite, that I am herein setting forth, has been so distorted for us by the theologians, the ecclesiastics of all denominations, creeds, and sects, so cobwebbed, and obscured and blended with the conception of a Deity, that the Infinite has become, literally, in practice a thing remote from us. The conception of a personal Feudal God, so deeply impressed on us for so many centuries, has deprived us of a serenity of soul which might be ours—has taken our thought away from our fellow men, away from Nature, and away from happiness. Through long inactivity we have at last forgotten how to seek.

It seems ironical therefore that I should so earnestly wish to make the Infinite attractive to you. And so it could be, were the conception of the Infinite that I herein picture, other than simple, natural and fitted for a Democratic day.

And yet the suggestion of irony is not to be wondered at. For the traditional notions, however sincere, were based upon the conception of the Infinite as a monarch, and our relations to him distant—with the sense of fear and our own sinful unworthiness predominant. In other words, the traditional notion was and is deeply pessimistic.

With the rise of Democracy as a world force, a change in conception was inevitable; and the changed conception has been flowing and shaping, with the spread of humanity, toward a more consciously optimistic, practical, and natural basis—toward a sense of our own personal responsibility and accountability, in which fear is supplanted by Justice; toward a conception more direct and immediate—more concerned with our physical and humble surroundings, more concerned with wholesome spiritual balance. It remains to give to this conception the perfecting flow of sublimity and true companionship.

It is then of a new thought, born of that liberty of brain sprung of Democracy, that the Infinite is near to us, immediately concerns us and is manifest in things close at hand, things which under the old regime of thinking were called commonplace.

As pioneers, the sciences Physics, Biology, and Psychology have opened and are preparing the way. Logic and Political Economy have remained Feudal, and obstructive, as I shall later show.

The crying need of the world is now for a New Philosophy—one that shall tally with modern manifestations—one that will embrace humanity, as the most important of phenomena.

On the outline of such a philosophy I am endeavoring to sketch when I speak of natural thinking. For such thinking must, as a prerequisite, rest upon an elevated, a humane, an enlightened and natural appreciation of the Infinite—on adequate realization of our close identity with It, with Nature, and with our Fellow Men.

Thus in our study of the Infinite we begin to see, throughout Its manifestations, how varied, how serene are they; and in our minds the conception of whim, is supplanted by the conception of order and stability; the notion of caprice transforms itself into the finer consciousness of rhythmic change and flow.

But above all comes the growing consciousness and satisfaction that our Life, through our intelligence, can and will draw upon the Great Life. That our minds may draw from the energy of the Great Mind. And thus is opened to our minds the clarity of the truth that that which makes us nonconductors of the flow of Infinite energy, is our diffidence, our superstitions, or our apathy toward our natural and attainable relationship with the Infinite.

Further comes the conviction that to do this we must be as conductors;

that the filaments we call our nervous system, must indeed be live wires; that, just as to hear we must listen, so to draw our current from the Infinite we must regard it not as an abstract symbol of power, but, in sincere and noble humility, as a living presence—for us, the immediate presence of Ultimate Life. Thus should the mind of man listen through the calm eyes of sympathy, and take account and profit of the fact that he, is in a sense, infinite, because he lives and reasons.

Thus, in turn, the Infinite appeals to us in a series of manifestations coming from afar off and reaching close into our lives:

1st: As an ultimate conception of Inscrutable Life, of limitless grandeur.

2nd: As an essence animating the universe from the Infinitely vast to the infinitely minute.

3rd: As a spirit animating what we broadly call Nature:

4th: As an energy fructifying what we broadly call living forms, and their endless reproduction.

5th: As an impulse animating each individual manifestation of life and shaping its identity.

6th: As an energy inspiring things not generally called living, but which science is daily showing are in fact alive.

7th: As an essence flowing through the almost incomprehensibly small, in a manner substantially identical with its flow through the incomprehensibly great.

8th: As the energizing principle of suspected but undiscovered surrounding forces which are unknown as yet to us.

9th: As the ultimate essence of that which we believe must remain unknowable.

10th: As a principle filling all vital aspiring organisms, and withdrawing as such from all decaying organisms.

11th: As the living, luminous, value of our individual bodies and souls, and of all our natural thoughts.

12th: As ever present in the commonest nearest things: as ever present in the smile, the fleeting thought.

13th: As the one permanent fact of Being. The spirit of Creation and of existence; the essence and balance of All.

This grouping I put forth as a practical working basis—as an immediate and pervasive fact.

I purposely herein have separated it from the religious conceptions that have descended to us, because these have as their axis of revolution the thought of a hereafter.

I wish to deal with the present. I deem it vastly more important. What becomes of a man's soul in a theoretical hereafter, is of insignificant value to the people at large in comparison with the social or anti-social use he puts it to here.

If we grasp the conception that the Infinite is a direct, ever present ever active force, we have reached a solid permanent foundation for a constructive sequence and a mechanism of natural thinking. For natural thought, partaking inevitably of the quality of the Infinite, must work beneficently. Natural thinking is as yet largely latent in the people—but its potential power is ever acting and shaping.

Therefore in view of all these considerations I begin my discourse with an appeal to the faculty of listening: Because listening is the link between ourselves and the Infinite.

A definition of this link is substantially as follows:

All our impressions of the outer world reach us through the channels of the senses.

The outer world is constantly pressing upon us in a manner somewhat like the pressure of the atmosphere. Forces are constantly streaming upon us from without—the radiations of countless energies. They seek constantly to penetrate the vital and perfect channels of the senses, mechanisms of entrancing perfection, miracles of use, precisely adapted to this end; and, mark you, the pressure is ceaseless.

It is not the eye that sees; it is the pressure of external forces, reaching the brain, through the mechanisms of the eye, that stimulates the form of thought we call vision. In this sense we do not see objects, objects see us—which is the primary truth.

It is a physiological inversion to say that we see objects. We might as well say that we warm ourselves at a stove—we do not—it is the radiant heat that warms us—we receive the warmth, we do not create it. It is not will on our part—it is receptivity.

Thus these outer forces seek ever to reach the brain, and do reach it; but the brain must consent to receive them; when it so consents we have as a resultant reaction mechanical or objective vision.

But they, the forces, strive also to reach through the brain to that of which the heart is the most delicate index; but to achieve this the brain must consent to their passage; when it so consents we have an added and finer vision that we call sympathy, and which in turn reacts upon objective vision.

Still do the forces press on, seeking to reach our inmost being called the soul. And for this the brain and the heart must consent—then have we that finest and ultimate quality of vision that we call psychological or spiritual insight, whose reactions are general, specific and comprehensive. The internal reaction of these activities upon the brain arouses the faculties of conscious thought and reason.

Thus does the Infinite penetrate to the soul of Man and there in part reveal Itself—if Man consent; if the individual consent.

If man refuse, if the individual refuse—it does not enter—and thus man, in his perversity, in his ignorance or in his bondage, is left Godless.

This means in essence and in fact that he is left without the power to receive and the reactive power to create—and is an animal automaton.

For the Infinite is a force quite beyond measure, even as it holds the stars in their balance, even as it holds the microscopic creature in its balance.

And thus in every sense a gateway to the inner man if he bar not the vestibules of being.

And thus the myriad forces of the Infinite in countless manifestations ever and constantly seek man; but they are gentle forces; easily debarred.

It is the true function of education not to debar them, but vividly the contrary: to yield them access, that the brain, the heart, the soul may fructify, even as the flower is fructified; even as it is of nature that all things should be fertile—for fertility is of the Infinite.

Education and Natural Thinking

The truth that all forms of human natural thought, however ramified, spring from the same source, is borne out by the reflection that all
vital wholesome thought is a reaction from wholesome natural external
stimuli. The free flow to the brain of such stimuli means richness and
honesty of thought, the shutting off of such natural stimuli, or what is
worse, the substitution of artificial stimuli means perversion, poverty,
and dishonesty of thought. In this sense we reach a recognition of a
vital quality in a real science of political economy, only when we learn
to know the people and their natural wants.

It is therefore of my main contention against prevailing educational
methods, that their general, traditional tendency is to shut off Nature's
stimuli and substitute book stimuli, or else the spectres of mediaeval
theological doctrine. Inasmuch as the people discern and shape their
real, their true thoughts slowly and wastefully, it is the manifest duty
of educators to discern, anticipate, lead, economize and conserve the true
forces of the people.

From this arraignment I specifically except the Kindergarten, manual
training school, gymnasium, and athletic field which are the best in
educational method that we have. And I urge the extension of the essence of Kindergarten, manual training, gymnastic, and athletic methods
into the so-called higher education, that matters physical, intellectual and
spiritual be brought intimately, and objectively into our lives, and that
our lives be brought physically and spiritually into the open air.

For there is no complexity of thought that does not spring from a
simple basis, and that may not be traced to that basis. The relationship
between complexity and simplicity is not so generally understood as it
should be, but this is the law: Whatever is organically complex may be
traced to a simple origin, and whatever is organically simple contains
the potency of complex expansion and organization. By this test you
may test any thought or any feeling, or any expression of thought and
feeling. In precise elucidation of this law I have stated to you that the
vastly complex technical expressions of the arts, sciences, industries, in
short, all forms of productive human thinking, spring from the same
common source, namely the ultimate simplicity of the Infinite, operating
directly and effusively upon the human body and brain, through the

ever present, ever active forces of Nature. And that the highly complex organizations of Nature and of natural Human Thought ramifying into every form of expression, are but an organically complex elaboration of the simplicity, the oneness of the Infinite.

Therefore while always acknowledging the inscrutability of the Infinite, we are always warranted, precisely because of the limitless complexity of Its manifestations, in assuming it to be an essence that signifies to our reason an ultimate pro-creative simplicity.

We are logically led to this view because each and every analysis of complex organisms of thought, as well as of vegetable and animal phenomena, and of organizations of so-called material things, leads the mind, ever searching, ever onward, toward increasing simplicity of origin. This origin and this simplicity recede further into the vastness of Life while at the same time approaching ever closer in the near at hand and commonplace, as we pursue. Even while remaining unreachable, they are always expanding yet concentrating; always becoming more unreal, yet more real; always remote yet always immanent—until the finite mind realizes that it is and must ever remain finite. And yet there ever abides the profound conviction that, through operation of an inscrutably subtle force of spiritual attracting, the finite mind will ever continue to seek. That such seeking signifies the ineradicable hunger of the mind, the heart, the soul. These considerations show also, in view of social necessity, that man must keep his feet on the solid ground of humanity while contemplating the wonders and seeking the purpose of the Infinite.

We are warranted therefore in the sane conception that, if we cannot know the Infinite, we may approach It; and that the Infinite has established a means of communication, whereby, if the senses, the mind, the heart, the soul of Man consent and listen, he communicates with Man not in terms of speech, but in terms of vital energy—in terms of Life.

Therefore can we never know what Life is, because it is a communication from the Infinite; and, in this sense, to know would be to vanish.

And likewise are we warranted in an equally sane conception that the Infinite has provided for Man a means of communication, not so much with Itself as an ultimate, but with that phase of Itself which it imparts to Nature, and hence with that phase of Itself which it imparts through the immediate agency of Nature to each Individual Man, whose senses, mind, heart, and soul consent, listen, and receive its vital message, and desires to transmit it to his fellows through the intelligence and honesty of his daily activities.

Thus, logically, is the first and constant, active, daily duty of man-kind, the duty of man to man; the duty of the individual to his fellows; the duty of his fellows to the individual. For the Infinite has provided the unfailing current of energy, the channels for its passage, the brain, heart, and soul to receive and react, and methods of communication of simplicity and complexity marvelously vital and akin to mankind and to Itself.

Therefore is it the vital, the practical function of all human thought, to draw from the Infinite, and transmit to Humanity.

This is the psychic foundation of Democracy—the living simple germ of Natural Thinking: And thus have I shown that the Infinite is ever seeking Man.

Therefore is all normal thought, however varied its forms of expression and communication, and by whatever names its various subdivisions may be called—fine arts, commerce, science, industry—essentially the same, because of common origin of their real, their true functions in the benifi-cence of the Infinite.

And therefore, is all abnormal thought such as has perversely shut out, or, in innocence and helplessness has had shut out from it the In-finite; because the brain would not or could not consent to listen—and has thus debarred the Infinite appeal.

Thus is normal or natural thought shown to be altruistic and benevo-lently constructive in its origin, nature, and purpose.

Thus is abnormal thought inevitably selfish and destructive.

Thus are Feudalism, Aristocracy, Absolutism, and Priesthood explained.

Thus is Democracy explained.

No brain, heart or soul can or will give birth to abnormal thought, if the individual possessor of them, has from infancy received a normal vital education in natural living and natural thinking.

In our study of social science, altogether too much importance has been attached to heredity and too little to environment. In my view there is no normal heredity but that which Nature intended, namely, health, vigor and beauty.

As one views humanity broadly and in detail as it exists today, we note that by virtue of the law of differentiation, that is to say, the passage from the simple to the complex, there has arisen a slight pre-ponderance, varying with the individual, of one form of susceptibility to external impressions, an added variation in the form of reaction or response thereto, with another added variable in the power of quality of expression, or the giving out of these reactions.

These variations of susceptibility we call collectively temperament; and we proceed to sub-divide temperament in accordance with the variability in reaction of the four great internal agencies—the body, brain, heart, and soul.

Thus we speak of the poetic temperament, the commercial temperament, the artistic temperament, the legal mind, the mechanical mind, etc.

This sounds simple enough; but let me give you a rather vivid arithmetical illustration of what it signifies.

We have five senses and four agencies of reaction.

If men were all alike, that is to say cast all, precisely in one inflexible mould, we would have from each man $5 \times 4 = 20$ simple arithmetical reactions from the Infinite.

But man is multitudinous and manifold, therefore, we have $1 \times 2 \times 3 \times 4 \times 5 \times 6 \times 7 \times 8 \times 9 = 362890$ normal and collective reactions between Man and the Infinite.

But this, even, is merely elementary, and a simple beginning.

Let us next make the very reasonable estimate that each channel of sense and each of the four agencies of reaction has the power of 1000 separate adjustments: the permutations and combinations at once soar in a cloud of numerals toward mathematical infinity, and hint at vital Infinity.

Now let us apply the law of integration or the persistence of fundamental unity in the ever expanding complexity of variations. At once this nebulous haze of numbers and what they represent, condenses toward first principles and Infinite Unity.

If therefore we arrive at such illuminating results with a few, ordinary, everyday numerals, what must the permultations and combinations of the visible universe, with its untold millions of variables, all vital, signify to the soul of Man—itself infinite-like in variability!

And, if in all the splendor of this spread of simplicity in complexity we call the Universe, ranging from the infinitely vast to the infinitesimally small and striving gently and incessantly to manifest itself in the Life and in all the affairs of the people, we perceive at the last analysis an Infinite Serenity; it is not our manifest right, our compelling duty to enquire why the soul of Man, the souls of all men, should not reflect this serenity? They so do in part; and this ever beautifying reflection of the Infinite Serenity is irrevocably what we call REASON—Man's highest attribute—implying his highest duty.

When you think such thoughts as you are in duty bound to think them, do you not shudder at the spectacle of mental trickery, of mental weakness and poverty, of crime, of pauperism, of aristocracy, of a misguided and wayward Priesthood, Catholic and Protestant, and do you not yearn for the coming of that Education which shall be Honest because Natural, which shall fill a people with serenity and fruitfulness, and which shall flower in a perfect Democracy—exhibiting a completely worked out science of political, or, rather, social economy? Such thoughts are well worth thinking: Indeed it is necessary to think them.

But to return to our immediate theme—that of the natural inspiration and productivity of the individual—this individual with five mechanisms of sense and four mechanisms of reaction. What are his individual possibilities, regardless of his special variation from the mass?

We will assume him, as is reasonable, physically normal at birth; that is to say, blessed with health as nature intended, and that he has grown until he takes notice of things, that is to say until things take notice of him. The child has the energy of the race behind it and the ever-present external impulses about it. All is prepared: All is ready.

Do you know of any reason why this child should not grow up into a natural and high productive man? Do you know of any reason why, under existing conditions, he will probably grow up into a man barren in mind, heart and soul? I do—UNNATURAL EDUCATION.

In grown up men, however rich, however 'successful,' as we say, I see so much of this poverty of heart and mind.

On the other hand, if this child be endowed with extraordinary powers and initiative, exceptionally favored with independent strength, instinctive response to Nature's appeal, instinctive repulsion from his artificial human surroundings he may ultimately break through and beyond his environment and the repression of tradition and the schools. Among grown men I see a few such—but, alas, how few!

This latter condition is what heartless, heedless English philosophy calls the 'survival of the fittest'—a doctrine, I might say a device, essentially Aristocratic when applied to humans. I call it Waste, the *inevitable waste entailed by prior false thinking*. I call it a senseless social crime that, out of our natural fecundities, we produce so few great men.

Now let us suppose that this normal child is educated to manhood, by a natural system, a system that seeks bodily health, liberates the faculties, bring them normal food, and sanely guides their abounding activities. Will not the result be a man useful and productive to the full extent of his faculties? Will not humanity be, to that extent, thereby enriched?

Most assuredly it will be so. In a humane and democratic philosophy there is not room for such thing as an unfit human being—except in a very limited and strictly pathologic sense—and indeed this would disappear.

I assure you most earnestly it is my conviction that the ordinary normal body and brain are at birth gifted with possibilities, probabilities, indeed certainties of functional power, that should be cherished and developed—not suppressed, surely not poo-hooed. That this body, this brain should be given pure, natural food, to maturity; that the heart should be nourished with the purity of human surroundings and aspiration, that the soul should be nurtured upon the purity of its relationship to the Infinite, that character should be formed, judgment balanced, in short, Democracy taught; and this, ever in the home, ever in the open air, ever in a series of public democratic schools; no privacy, no sectarianism, no grip of endowment, no chance for a priest of any denomination to implant in the young mind, a distorted and outraging conception of the Infinite, and the destructive, cancerous doctrine that a man is responsible first to his conscience—the reflection of a mediaeval god—and second, and *only as* secondary, responsible to his fellow man and his fellow men. We can see clearly enough in the past and in today what the doctrine of non-responsibility means. It means the subversion of Democracy; it means psychic impoverishment at the tender and plastic beginning of individual lives.

Therefore the first objective of Education is to develop health and character, to form active habits of body and mind which shall crystallize around simple wholesome notions of honesty, justice, responsibility— thus shaping the good, all around, fearless, independent, and useful citizen. The citizen who does not fear either to speak the truth or to hear it spoken.

The second objective is to differentiate capacity, and develop it to the highest degree, by giving it nutrition, exercise, roundness and finish— meanwhile never losing sight of citizenship, never forgetting the ultimate end—the individual man's part, his specific duty to do his share throughout all his life, in shaping a vigorous, sane, beautiful, and gentle Democracy.

If the infant, the child, the adolescent, the man, is taught that might does not make right, that honesty is sufficient in itself, that to do good to others, constitutes the nearest approach to happiness, that manly gentleness is very manly, that to cherish the conviction and contribute to the end that through natural thinking, disease and crime will disappear and Democracy emerge sweet, wholesome, triumphant and lasting, to what superb realizations may we not look forward?

This sounds like a dream; but I assure you that if it be a dream, it is a dream that contains within itself the means and the certainty of realization. My dreams do not rest idly on soft cushions. They seek action. They do not fear the bugaboo, the Dollar. They do not fear the sway of organized Feudalism. They know their own power.

As to the element of time required for these realizations, the happenings on a grand scale, of the coming few years will help determine. For I have told you with emphatic warnings, that the curtain is now and here rising on one of the greatest national dramas in history—a greater curtain, indeed, is rising to reveal a world-drama.

Turn for a moment the searchlight of this drama upon the murk, the filth, the squalor, and disorganization of this our own city of Chicago. What does the light reveal? Simply and solely unnatural thinking, benumbed brains, present and prior.

Can any good come out of this mire? Yes! Chicago is but temporarily a social blot, and of itself would perish. But it is immersed within the streaming energy of a far-flung vital atmosphere, vast fertile prairies, and great lakes. It is a huge ganglion in the plexus of national Life. But because it has not yet consented to listen, it is not as yet conscious of its real destiny—hence its revolting barbarism.

Can any great and vital thought arise here? Certainly! For the same reason.

Will Democracy some day flourish here? Surely so! For the same reason.

Will Democracy radiate from here for the same reasons? It will.

Chicago has tried her ignorant, brutal, and selfish best to escape from Nature. But she cannot, except temporarily. Nature's pressure is too powerful, too silent, too continuous. Nature will have her way, she will slowly, surely prevail over men. The city cannot escape its destiny.

SELECTIONS FROM DEMOCRACY: A MAN-SEARCH

Three years after he had composed the urgent manifesto which is "Natural Thinking," Sullivan had completed the first draft and revision of what he considered his magnum opus. But by now his mood had darkened: the fundamental optimism of his vision clashed at every point with the misery and frustration of his personal life. Besides, the attempt to make a comprehensive, relatively systematic statement of his philosophy exposed Sullivan to grave difficulties. Much of *Democracy: A Man-Search* lacks coherence, and its long stretches of scolding alienate the reader. A pity: for the poet and prophet in Sullivan were rarely more eloquent, and more fecund even in their extravagancies, than they show themselves in certain passages. Here we find statements of his ultimate vision, so far as he was capable of expressing it in words rather than in stone: was he mistaken in thinking that some such vision is necessary to give meaning to the life of modern man? The passages which follow are reproduced, with permission, from *Democracy: A Man-Search,* edited by Elaine Hedges and published in 1961 by Wayne State University Press.

"What is the Use"

The cry of the old world. The tragic cry of the heart.

How often is it heard, how oftener is it unheard? It was the cry of yesterdays, it is the cry of today, of this hour. It has been uttered in every tone, every accent, every modulation, in badinage, in cynicism, in ferocity, in despair. It is a question answering and unanswered. From the depths it rises as bubbles.

Yet this cry will not down. It ever seeks an answer, expecting none, satisfied with none, denying all answers, while ever, through the ages, through the rise and fall of civilization, it raises its persistent mournful query.

It compels attention. At the very outset it appears, raising a fateful, deprecating hand, as a guardian of the hinge of the door we would open.

To ignore this first demand is to ignore all—to end in folly. Is but to write a word upon the door and then depart in foolish hope, leaving it closed.

Shall we then, too, write our little word upon the door, and, satisfied, depart as cheerful madmen, or shall we, when we are at the wall wherein this door is set, the wall that rises up for every one who thinks alertly, look first at this pensive figure in the stillness and the twilight to see if indeed it be not a ghost, a phantom, and at least lay hold upon the handle of the door, and pull, to see, if it in truth be not unlocked, and then to swing it open, and see what?—*Reality?* and the sunshine?

How often has this specter said to me, said it persuasively, said in frozen tones:

'What is the use? Why are you here, alone, in this still hour? This is no door. The wall alone is real. It was raised by Fate and not by Man. For what is Man? I am the questioner. Hark!—there is no answer save the soft hush of my knuckle-bone upon the adamant. What is the use? Return whence you came. It is vain to look at me so steadfastly. For I am real; you are unreal.

'Courage? Others have had that. You are not the first to come. Others have come long before. Others have come, believing, also, that there was a door.

'Millions upon shadowy millions have come. They did not even know a wall was here, they broke their hearts against it—and are gone. Did not Job of old, come to this wall, sit here beside me in sackcloth, wailing? Did he not cry to his God: 'O, for an umpire between Thee and me!' He saw me not.

'Did not your Jesus come here, radiant, sweet, proclaiming joy, and a door that would open? Had he not courage? But his cross came here too. It was planted here beside what you call a door. To that cross he was nailed, the iron passed into his soul, with dying gasp he cried aloud: 'My God, why hast thou forsaken me!'—with dimming eyes, he saw the wall that Fate had reared. He saw me not. It was I who stood at the foot of his cross. Alone I. Nor did I move, there was no need, the cross was planted here beside me. And many a cross before that one, has been set up here, many since, many are to come. And many a noble heart's desire has been slain here, and many shall be—the hearts of those I could not and cannot dissuade, of those who believed me phantom and believed their own dreams real.

'Do not tell me of Siegfried, his re-forging of the splintered sword, of Siegfried and the Dragon, of Siegfried and the circle of fire, holding sweet life within. Those are but fables, illusions of hope, dramas of the North. Do not tell me that spring-sun melts winter's ice. For that does not avail. Winter comes again remorselessly, to freeze the heart of Spring, to still the soul, to lock up all in ice, to cover all in snow, to blanket all with stillness. For Spring is man's destruction; it drives him mad even as it flees before oncoming death. The twinkle you call Life is futile in flight from dark to dark. Have not countless millions lived, have not these same swarms died like flies, utterly forgotten? What is the use? Ask not me, ask Death, great peaceful Death, what is the use? For death answers with its one word—death!

'You talk of freedom? Vain!—You are free to die! Close but your eyes —all things die. You would do good? Vain! Illusion that you are, what is this good, but a sure road to destruction! You do not believe! Try it— and die.

'Do you not know you are blockaded, and a vagrant on the high seas? Do you not know that man has ever said, evil is real—that in his heart this is the thing he surely knows?

'Did not your great King Solomon say: Vanity of Vanities—all is vanity and vexation of spirit. Are you then grown wiser!

'Does not your priest say that your hope is after death? For he must lie that he may live—just as all men have ever done, do now, and must ever do. There is no hope, here or there—for hope is man's illusion.

'You say that a God reigns over all? The God kills you as he kills all. He daily tears the heart and throws it on the earth. He daily breaks the back. Sorrow is your companion, not God. Sorrow is merciful. For did not your God kill the one man who asked to be his son, who asked of him to be as a merciful father here, and take away the bitter cup? Your God! Vain! This God is your Betrayer!

'You would earn the gratitude of men? Fool! You wish vipers at your heel, dogs at your throat? You would slap men in the face to earn their gratitude? You would call them by their real names, not Mr. This, not the Honorable That, but Thief, Liar, Scoundrel, Hypocrite, Coward, Murderer, Betrayer—to earn their gratitude! What is the Use? Keep quiet; or you in turn will ask an unseen God to take away the bitter cup— the sign of gratitude. And you shall, as you should, be denied. And then you will come here again, this time with your cross, here, where I am forever and forever, and your breaking heart shall surely say, My God, My God, why hast Thou forsaken also me!—as I have heard it said, long, long, long. I will be here when you are gone. Here as ever; here by the door of illusion; the door of hope; the door of Justice, which the light of wit have writ upon, and safely gone their way. But the door at which the great heart breaks. Here will I wait for the Next; and I shall see the same passion, the same agony, the same ending, as I have seen from the beginning, as I shall see unto the last.

'Go. Return to the hearts of your people. Be vile and you shall live— for such keep away from the door.

'I am your friend. I would warn. For I am old.

'You would make a book into a door? You would turn it on the hinge of Life, believing that as it slowly opens there will spread a prospect of which men have dreamed and which is now become real—a promised land for which man was thought by his God, and by his God's handmaid, Nature, furnished as a home, and that his neighbor therein is his friend?

'You would show that this wall was built by men, and might be removed by men at a breath if but so they willed? Vain! Go write your words in the desert sands while a tempest sweeps. Go write them with your fingertip in the quiet pool. It were one. For Life is but a mocking mirror—and a storm—and dust. And man is but a useless finger, moved by a useless soul, writing therein.

'Go. Return to the follies in which you were born—your birthright— your inheritance which all respect. For your coming is but madness here.

'Return! Awake! Sit down—and write that all is for the best. That the Lord giveth—to some; and taketh away—from others. That thus it has been, that thus it shall be, that thus it should be. That a Providence regards the sparrow's fall. That He will consider man—hereafter, in due time. But do not write that man must seek man now. For that you will be rended as they turn. Thus would you write your knell, thus would you come to me for the last time.

'I am your friend. You have seen me. But you know not who or what I am. Nor shall any. So, go—before you persuade yourself that neither the wall is here nor I. For that is self-destruction. I am here, invisible alone to the blind—And here I shall remain.

'You would call as a voice in the wild? Go pluck at the stars—they are near. Speak softly—the mountains will come. Say 'peace' to the flood, say 'wait,' to the sun, pray and your God will answer—so will the Wilderness answer. For have you not heard: 'I asked them for bread, they gave me a stone'? Go: Ask the stars for meat and drink, but ask not man for Justice. The sun will give you his light without stint. So your own will give you hate.'

'What is the use? What is the use?

'Ask now your futile soul, your futile God:—What is the use? They will deceive you now as ever—for such is your heart's desire.

'But ask not me—For I am Truth.

'You will not go! You will stay here by me, and see Fate face to face! You will lay your hand upon the door! And throw it open wide! That all may see! You will not come again! You are here now! You will not bring a cross! You will blow down the wall with a breath! Spring shall— once and for all, prevail! You know the meaning of the seasons! You questioned them before you questioned me! Beware!—Siegfried! There is a crow, a forest and a spear! And there are men—and passions cold as ice! And there are sheep which bleat and run away!

'You say you have hailed the sun? You say there is a greater sun that would rise and shine into the hearts of men! You say: Light, Light! More Light!

'Siegfried! Beware!

'What is the use! What is the use!

'The Great Sun rises but to set.

'Night! Night! Eternal night is Man's repose.

"'Tis there, alone, the wicked cease from troubling, and the weary and the righteous are hushed.

'Siegfried, Siegfried! Shall I have warned you, alas, in vain? If so: Farewell until we meet.

'The Great Sun-Star now seeks to break apart the night!

'So: Go! This time in peace.'

"Too Busy"

. . . In a study of Democracy as a philosophy of life, it is of prime importance to arrive at the real thought of a people. The trail to this thought, is defined by the acts of a people. Beyond the thoughts of a people lie the origins of these thoughts. These origins are of a twofold nature; the one phase arising as a reaction from specific environment, the other coming as a flow and pressure of tradition. For the study of environment we have the facts of daily life; and for the study of social tradition we pass from a survey of the present through the gateway of history, which opens to view the prior environments and the flow of men's thoughts, the flow of racial and national thoughts through them, with the many reacting modifications. Thus History, in its humanistic use gives a view of the rhythmic flow of man's thoughts into acts, and the reaction of his thoughts from his acts, in an imposing, an inspiring drift, from the dawn of recorded events to the present hour.

Daily the continuity and significance of this historic flow is becoming clearer; and daily the consciousness is increasing in clarity and power that this flow has been ever onward—never backward—and that the race is moving toward a new domain. With the aid of this historical consciousness we may look with clearer eye upon the happenings of our own day, and realize, to the full, what it means when a great people comes to a crucial parting of the ways. This interest is rendered the more acute, the more solicitous, because of the awakening consciousness of the people of the world. This modern phenomenon is a something new under the sun. The import of the slow but sure awakening of the world-people lies in the instinctive urge of its arousing latent power, and the uses to which that power will be put.

The deepest of our own internal stresses has arisen from the act and the fact, that we, of all peoples, have said, the most flippantly and fatalistically, 'What is the use?' This query we have posited against the spiritual first-principle whereupon depends our wholesome life as a people.

There are many reasons why, with us, liberty has become license, and freedom a menace to that very individualism by which we lay such store. But the appalling aspect of our fatalism and instability is revealed in the thought, the act, the fact, that with us, betrayal has become a fine art—

the one art that we have assiduously cultivated. The consquences of such betrayal in thought, in act and in fact, must be included in the reckoning.

If our studies are to eventuate in substantial good, we must face our facts as facts. For we shall find, as we progress, that the broader, the simpler the fact, the more intense is the personal application of the principle within it. Our fixed purpose is clearly and broadly to present vital aspects, in our man-search. And in our search for man we must pass from the facts of his acts, to and through his thoughts, until we reach his core. Inasmuch as he can go nowhere that his acts do not reveal him, we shall surely find him. The study of a people can have but one fruitful end, and that: to find the individual—and reckon with him. If we had not a sound and sane balance in which to weigh our social values, such attempts to search out man through his larger expression in a people would be futile. But the nature and accuracy of our Balance will be set forth, as speedily as the ground plan of our work will permit; for this delicate and supreme balance that we shall put to use is naught else than the integrity of the Life-impulse.

Thus the unwelcome part of our task, the very hard part of it, is to look steadily at that which is worst in ourselves.

We are not a happy people. We say we are; but the saying is negatived by our manifest unrest, our obvious lack of equipoise, our progressive disintegration. To be sure there is a certain broad division in this regard between the city dwellers and the country dwellers; but the distinction is superficial—wherever you may go you are sure to find anxiety close under the surface. Now why should a flourishing people be anxious, and why should a free people be anxious, unless it be, perchance, that the prosperity and the freedom are unreal? Why does the stress of living bcome daily tenser in a land overflowing, in a land whose resources have not as yet been drawn upon in an intensive way? A land in which famine is unknown:—Or, should we stop here, and say, a land in which a widespread spiritual famine prevails, though seemingly unknown and unsuspected?

Righteous indignation we have with us, to be sure; but toward what end does that avail? Plain perception of the few, but simple, realities of life will count for more. To make these realities stand forth clear is the whole of our task.

Schools, colleges, universities we have; but what do these avail, in

that they do not sow the seeds of simple, vital truths—truths as essential
to a democratic life as are air, food and water to the physical life?

Of what avail are they if they do not inculcate the little truth that
betrayal is fatal to the aspiration of Democracy? If they do not teach
the plain truth that integrity is the mainstay of Democracy. To be sure
they declare they teach these things; but in thought, in act, in fact they
do not. For there is all the difference in the world between the conventional repetition of a traditional ghostly precept, and the clear, powerful
presentation of the reasonableness behind a living truth; however small,
however negligible that truth may appear within the immense maze of
our civilization.

For this failure in efficiency of teaching there is naturally, a reason.
This reason, this reluctance, this evasion, it will be a part of our work to
search out.

Whence has come the minute and diversified ramification of graft?
Did it originate in the big? By no means. It has come from the sanction
of innumerable individuals; it has grown out of innumerable small desires,
and merely flourished and flowered conspicuously in the big. For it is not
a primary fact that thoughts work downward from what we call the top.
The reality is that the few at the top derive their power for good or evil
and are supported and sustained in that power directly and solely by the
desire and sanction of the many; that is, by the thoughts of the multitude.

At any given time there exists a prevailing thought of all the people
considered as a unit; and upon the creative power, uplift and sanction of
this thought rests the special power of those whom this thought chooses to
exalt, because of definite accord with it. This accord of thought is the key
to the flowering of any aspect of any civilization. But as this dominant
thought of the people waxes, wanes and changes, so does the power of the
sanctioned—individuals or institutions—wax, wane, and change accordingly and with marvellous precision. As long as the few remain sane they
clearly understand this sanction and its nature. When the sense of delegated power drives them mad, as invariably it does when the passion of
possession seizes them as a mania, they forget the sanction, and go down—
after a brutal but useless struggle to retain the power, which, in their illusion, they have believed to be their own. This mad dream of power invariably takes the form of a desire to enslave all the people—and evolves
a most plausible, cunning and intricate system of treachery. When the
people awake to the object lesson, the feudal fabric, vast though it be, falls
to the ground. Thus individuals come and go, but the people move on. The

vanity of the sanctioned few inexorably leads them to believe that they determine the orbit in which the many move. No superstition could be more fantastic. The orbit, the inertia, the momentum, the creative power lies in the imagination and will of the people. It has always been so; it is so now. Hence, special virtues are exalted when the multitudes so feel and will; and when the exaltation of vice is particularly in evidence, it is a sure sign that these are dominant within the thought of the people. Hence if graft prevails it is a plain sign that the average man is in thought a grafter, that he sanctions graft. The fact that he will variously disclaim this allegation signifies nothing further than an indication of the variety of mask he elects to wear upon his secret thought. For the physical, tangible fact of graft is here; you meet it everywhere, under every imaginable guise, disguise, and disclaimer; therefore the creative cause is here also: for it is irrational to suppose that any broad social manifestation may exist unnurtured by the sanction of these secret thoughts which determine the expression of the will of a people. It cannot feed upon itself. It rises and falls as sensitively as the stream of a fountain. For the stream of a fountain cannot exist of itself. It is but an expression of water, pressure, and an organized mechanism.

It is our business to search out man regardless of his phrases and his attitudinizing. And it is to be a part of our business, in such search, to utilize the knowledge that the great forces of nature are silent, and that what really counts in human affairs is the concurrence of minute individual agencies released by a simple silent power—the power of Choice.

Thus the will of a people but expresses the gathered choice of its individuals. And the will or choice of the specific individual, has, ever, a minute origin. It is his choice, his initiative, his will, his imagination, at the small, sharp, ever-recurrent parting of his ways. It is his conscious, deliberate estimate of the values of gain and loss, in the large and the small way. It is his immediate answer to the query: What is the use? It is his individual response to the query: Which way?; the individual expression of his conception of liberty; the exact expression of his secret estimate of himself, of his neighbor, and of the world.

That is to say: Every man, in every thought, hence in every act, casts a real ballot—the kind that counts and is surely Life-counted—either for Feudalism or for Democracy.

And thus it comes, that such individual choosing—a continuous intimate process—taken in bulk and continuously, constitutes the real plebiscite, the real referendum—the real initiative, the real creative act—which sanctions or changes the social status. It is just here that we, a multitudinous people, are very busy now.

In our search we shall see how deep we are engrossed in a mania of destruction. How far with us the feudal madness has progressed, and we shall search, also, if there be a leaven of work within the surging power of our thought as a people; a ferment which may bring about a massive change.

Viewpoint

It has been the fashion among philosophers to assume that mind is something apart from the Cosmos and that there is another something, apart in the Cosmos, called the objective reality. Hence there is assumed to be a pure reason, and a thing in itself concerning which the pure reason reasons. This is called transcendentalism. It is supposed to stand for the uttermost reach of intellect. In actuality, in comparison with that men daily *do*, it is crude. The wayside weeds shame it. The real moonlight makes of it a will-o-the-wisp. The vigor of health turns it to nonsense.

Now such view is definitely laid to one side in this work, as particularly lacking in the truly human sense of humor, kindliness, and sympathy.

In place of it is set forth the conception that all is life—that the Cosmos is life—that the desire and the flesh of man is life—that what we call Nature is life—that what we call motion is life— that all things within us (as we say) and without us (as we say) are modes of life: and that there is, in essence neither a within nor a without, neither subjective nor objective; that our thoughts concerning phenomena—in sympathy, and therefore in reality—are modes of life interplaying with modes of life, and that the interplay of phenomena is likewise thus related to us. That the animus of Life is Spirit. That the simplest thing is intelligible only when with our life we cordially accept it as life, and with our spirit accept it as spirit.

It is assumed the day is passing, wherein men seriously believe in a rigid dualism—in the fetish of matter as a something acted upon by another something called energy or force; in the fetish of mind as an active something apart from another passive fetish called Nature; in the fetish of soul as apart from a fetish called body.

For such conceptions are but survivals of the day and the night, of the feudal notions of good and evil, of the phantasmal notions of sin and redemption—Survivals of the notion of an external God—as though there could be anything external—external to what? Survivals of the notion that man is apart from nature, exterior to nature—where could man go to get away from nature? Survivals of the notion that nature is apart from man, external to man—where would nature go to get away from man?

Thus, is here set up the conception that in all things the individual man may see himself, because Life is integral, therefore nothing is really foreign to man—not even his neighbor—and man has been really foreign to nothing—not even to his God.

But man has assumed otherwise—and has paid the price. That singular perversion of his intellect, called vanity, and that equally singular intellectual repression of his heart, called hypocrisy, have obscured his sanity of vision. So, to fortify himself in his vanity and hypocrisy, to 'prove' that his vision is clear, he has invented philosophies, doctrines, religions, dogmas galore—vain and hypocritical as himself.

Stubbornly has man refused to see himself in the neighbor: 'What! Brother to vermin like that?,' he has said. Yet if he will look upon the meanest and most wretched of his kind, look close, he will see in the meanness and wretchedness of that other the meanness of his own vanity and the wretchedness of his own hypocrisy. He will see, in 'vermin like that,' the vermin that crawl within his intellect.

For man cannot escape the neighbor—where will he go to escape the neighbor? And the neighbor cannot escape him—where will the neighbor go to escape him?

And if a man resolutely sets out to search for man, will he not find him? Surely he will. For where can the man escape—there is nowhere to go. But the man does not believe this—he thinks he has anywhere and everywhere to go—that is part of his folly, that is the key to his illusion. For does not the man say: I am, I possess, I do this and do that! Do I not harness nature? Am I not above the brutes? And thus does he nurse his round of illusions, thus does he cherish his monomania, thus does he foster his illusory segregation from the rest—and thus is his pride complete. But thus also, does he prepare himself for us as a specimen, and make himself ready for us that we may condense the totality of his environment upon him from all directions—because in his fatuity he believes he is not like other men.

And if we take one of the mean and wretched, one of the "vermin," show to him one of the exalted, and say to him: Neighbor, would you like to see yourself?—Behold what you have created! He would surely say: No, it cannot be possible. Yet it is not merely possible, it is actual. For the man, the vermin believes not so much that he is not like the exalted, as that the exalted are not like him. And this is the key to his illusions. He does not know himself when he sees himself in the mighty; for he is a dreamer; his vanity lies in the luxury of self-abasement, his hypocrisy in his secret disdain of his kind. He is as complicated in his pride and stubborness as the artificial few whose furniture is philosophy, economics, theology, etc. His fetish like their own is Self. He is as much a snob as they. And yet he is man, whose thinking and feeling are none the more or less inane, luxurious, and futile than theirs. For his vision is neither more nor less obscure than theirs in essence and in practical application in the way of life. For him, as for them, the neighbor is a stranger—and man an unknown quantity. Because he, too, believes that there are two things— himself and something which is not himself. He too has his pure reason and his objective reality. He too is a transcendentalist. So his folly is neither greater nor less than theirs. His sense of humor and kindliness is as wanting as theirs; and the gift of fear is the common possession—it is that which unites all men in the mutual antagonism we call civilization, whose handmaiden we say is Reason.

But we have a sieve through which to sift, and we shall sift through man.

Meanwhile, allowing the pure reason and the thing-in-itself to repose on the shelf, we will proceed. For eyes and ears, a little sensibility, a little looking back, around and forward, a scent of the trail, a little awareness, are all the baggage we need. For have we not man in his environment always with us? What more do we need? What more should we need? Have we not the man-of-the-Past, as well as the man of today? And have we not as a sure guide the sound of his eternal cry: What is the use? In our thought do we not carry the man to come?

The Great City

This is the Great City. It is the crux of things.

Men are crowded here, hence they must be put to test.

We see them better, than scattered sparsely over the land. We see them in their bulk. We shall see better what they create! We shall see the direct consequences of their thinking. We shall see the axle-thought at work! turning the other thoughts about itself and making them work! And we shall see men clinging to the rim of the fly-wheel, men on the spokes, men hidden in the axle—as the wheel ponderously turns, day in day out, night in night out. And we shall see the iron truth of it. And this truth shall suddenly become alive and jump into a horrid, kaleidoscope smear, before our eyes. So will I make the iron feudal truth within, you within me, within us all—jump out alive!—stare at us, whine at our hearts, and look formidably into our souls—face to face in the open. The darkened soul of the Great City shall confront our own—like unto like.

For had I not found this truth in myself, I could not have found it in you. And had I not glimpsed it in the Great City, I could not have found it in myself. For what I saw in the Great City was the soul of its people confronting my own, like unto like! And I could not escape! There was nowhere to go but that soul would follow mine and inhabit it.

Hence I know that in the Great City men now see dimly in the daylight. See things human with untaught glassy eyes. They see not their fellow men because of the great pestilential City they have created. They see not the City they have created because of the crowding and surging pestilence of their fellowmen.

But, just so sure as the men living in the Great City and continuously creating and sustaining it as it is, *once see it as it is!* and their fellow men *as they are,* within it; all the men, women and children within; as they are—two millions of them in all (What Power!!)—they will, that hour, begin to destroy it, and to remake it.

As it stands today, they see men of all kinds, everywhere, and do not know what they are. They see the city, everywhere, and do not know what it is—For they are, one and all, insensible, in the world-old trance of Feudalism! Hence they wander, phantom-like, and create, phantom-like, unheeding a crowded world of realities within which they move as wantons, even as they jostle realities, look squarely at them—and see nothing.

Behold! This is the Great City! How many hearts break daily here? Who knows? Who cares? What other useful end can there be for hearts, in the Great City?

What sorrow is here in the Great City? Who knows? Who cares? Do you care? Do I care?—provided it be not our sorrow? And if it be our sorrow do we not think the Great City heartless indeed? Does it not weigh upon us like iron; does it not seem monstrous, and stone cold? And who cares about our sorrow? Why should anyone care? Are we so different in thought and act that our sorrow particularly signifies? Why complain, if we would receive and have not given? Why curse?—when we have helped create the gloom? Let us then accept our logic. Let us not whine—if we cannot see and think and feel and act to better purpose than to create sorrow.

How many poor are here? Who knows! Who cares! Do the poor themselves care? Do the rich care? Do we care? Obviously, graphically not. For the poor are here; the poor, the demented, the crippled, the criminal and the outcast, are all here in the Great City. They are our thought, our deed—as well as their own. And are the poor therefore white-winged and as angels? Or are they the sinners, and the rich they favor, white-winged and pure? No! Poor and rich, the broken, the demented, outcast, criminal are, all, just like you and me! There is something interchangeable in us that fits exactly with them all. That something is a *thought!* It is the *Feudal Thought;* the axle-thought of all civilizations of the past and of today. That thought which has been hugged secretly and blazoned openly by the Man of the past—and which we hug and blazon this day. Only we mask it. We call it, good-times, or hard-times, as the case may be; we call it by every name but its own. We even call it Charity; we even call it Religion! We even call it Philosophy! When you get down to our last thought—it is the same in all. *Therefore!* things are exactly as they are! The conventionality whereby one man is called a priest, another a pauper, this one is called an economist, another an imbecile, one a scholar, another a thief, one a senator, another a blacksmith, does not make an iota of difference when we come to deal with the simple, the obvious, and the fundamental in man—stripped of all subterfuge, casuistry, sophistry, fine language, fine art and fine nonsense, and scientific self-deception.

Thus do we see ourselves pictured forth in the great city. Anything and everything we see there, is ourselves.

All the people think in terms of murk and filth, wealth and poverty, crime and misfortune, and the rest of the long list? And there is the thought, pictured for you, point blank, in the open, where all may see. The smoke, the filth, the rich, the poor, are merely parts of a great picture —the picture of the Great City. The picture itself but the open showing of our own thought at *work!* continually painting fleeting and permanent pictures for us all to see and heed.

Had you thought the many pictures and the great picture not here because you had not noticed? Do you think, now, that they will vanish if you disclaim them? Do you think that ever again you can draw a veil of words to hide them? Not so! That is the pedestal on which you have long stood in an illusion of wordy, fanciful isolation. On that pedestal, in that isolation you shall never again stand. For I shall cause it to dissolve—and your feet shall come to the earth.

From now on you are to remain with me on the level! (It is high enough.) You shall keep your feet on the ground, and you shall see with a clearing eye. For I will unroll picture after picture before you. Pictures all real, all so different and yet all of a kind; For they will be views of the great moving panorama Man himself has painted, as, from the beginning, he has spread, in many colors, the many scenes, some sombre, some gay, vivid, tremulous, revolting, inspiring—spread them all upon the fair Earth; has drawn and painted them all out of the dream stuff of the single thought wherewith he has driven himself, like chaff before a whirlwind of his own, on the path of Time and Destiny: The soul-disturbing thought of self—the abandoned ego!

The Man of the Past thus has helped paint the pictures we now see. Therefore he shall go with us, a shadowy, but real companion, as we walk the streets of the Great City, seeking realities, seeking the how and why— seeking ourselves therein!—and seeking beyond!

Now you, in your list of practical difficulties, complain of corrupt politicians, in the Great City—shoals of them. Now who has corrupted them! Did not you? Did not I? Did not they themselves? Have not we all? Have they not accepted corruption because we asked them to, because we set them alluring examples, because we sanctioned them, because we drove them, willing, unwilling, or hesitating, or wishing, though they might be? Were they not, in fact, as chaff before the silent whirlwind of our stormy heart's desire, our secret predatory thought, within our multitudinous sanctuaries of one? That sanctuary of the poor man as well as the rich man, that sanctuary of the ditch, the coal mine, the railroad yard and the mill, as well as of the pulpit, the altar, the university, the editorial chamber and the private office? Are they not therefore a picture of our thought? The thought of all the people? Look at them near and square, look at them as brothers; not on terms of superiority or inferiority as you would like, but on terms of likeness, as you must! Look near and searchingly; get up close! Are they not your very image? Can you not see clearly the thought you hold in common with them? Does not that thought join your hands with theirs in fellowship?—those whom you affect to despise? Are they not your secret thought *at work* in the open? whoever you may be, rich or poor, or in between—or in any walk of life!

Do you suppose that because you have held up your hands in pious horror and have bellowed or squeaked in protest, that you are immune to responsibility? Do you assert that righteous indignation is other than a farcical pharse? Search your memory from the cradle up! Test your life-thought with acid reality. You know! I know!

Do you suppose that because you have remained sadly silent, that you are immune? Do you suppose that because you have pitied the depravity *of others* that you are immune? Do you suppose that because you have led an upright life, as you call it, that you are immune? Do you believe yourself immune because you place your trust in Jesus and the feudal God, and the Sunday school, and heaven, and all the rest, and are of the elect? Do you really believe that you can thus escape the shrill call to personal responsibility and accountability here! The cock-crow of dawning Democracy! That cry which shall awaken men to realities!. That cry which shall awaken men to you! and to themselves!

If you have so thought, then you have another thought coming. A thought that I shall lead to the threshold of your door and cause to enter your soul. And there it may grow and amplify until it brings you to a genuine and willing utterance.

If I hold you in the hollow of my hand, it is so because you yourself have revealed the closed circle of your thinking and the narrow boundaries of your sympathy—and in the so doing have revealed to me my own, and thus have shown me the way.

But do not fear. For if I shall show you many pictures, and explain them all clearly, it is to be solely that you may see at last how it must have come about that all the little pictures and the great picture are your true portrait—the likeness of each and all of us.

Rest assured I shall not assert you are essentially either worse or better than any other man. For the tie between us all is indissoluble; and the responsibility is universal as well as specific, joint as well as several—and so is the hope!

And if I remove from you the garment of your hypocrisy, I will also remove your humbleness, and banish your fear of Life. Because I will reveal Life to you in all its sweetness, grandeur and regenerative power. I will outline to you who and what you really are. So that, henceforth, you will walk the streets of the Great City or the pathless open fields alike, companioned by a new thought that shall have grown within you—a thought that will be not entirely of self, and will have parted company with murder.

Be not irresolute. It is yours yet to pass through many a gruesome scene, to view ever deeper and nearer the tragedy of human life. The bitterness of its folly. But, in due time there will appear an imposing parting of the ways. And then the choice will be left to you. Your sanctuary of one will then have become enlarged to the size of the great round Earth. Then! —choose you must! Men will know your choice; for you will be in the open with them all. And before that time I shall have made plain to you, plain as daylight to you, who and what they are.

Meanwhile there is no escape. You are surrounded in advance. The circling investiture of circumstance is historically closed. Nor shall I need to send you the conventional invitation to capitulate. It will not be necessary. For I will cause your citadel to dissolve—leaving you alone in the open. And then I will cause the investing army of your own phantom thoughts to dissolve—leaving you alone with your own spirit—as a freeman should be.

As together we walk the streets of the Great City, roaming here and there, passing a mansion on a boulevard, and then, elsewhere passing sweat-shops lining streets not called boulevards because not respectable enough, not well enough paved, not tree-planted and grass-platted, vacant of fair equipages going and coming, and children prettily dressed; but crowded with other things, unseemly; do you believe there is no connection between the two pictures, the two realities? Do you think there is really not a modern ghost, making a modern trinity of our one, ancient, persistent thought? Uniting parent and offspring in one? Is not the sweat-shop the parent? Is not the mansion the child? Does not the man in the mansion know it? Is he not content? Is not the mother on whom he sponges seemingly resigned? Is it not fate! Have we not been told that an all-wise providence has thus arranged for the good of all? That it is through the benevolence of the rich that the poor are given work? That were it not for the

Charity of the rich the poor might sometimes starve? Have not the poor long drawn inspiration from this comforting thought? Did not the poor create this thought out of their sweet, sad dream?—as they have created all things? Is it not also our thought? Are we not, all, agreed? Is it not therefore our portrait, one and all?—this little picture in the great city!

And thus, ever unfolding, as we cross and recross many paths, appear picture upon picture, revealing in vibrant form and varied coloring the multitudinous aspects of a single thought the people hold and stand for— some in overwhelming contrasts, others blending into a gray insipid monotone. Pictures painted not by artists, so-called, but by ourselves—by all the people. Pictures, without frames, conjoining, interblending to form a huge, graphic image of the totality of our thoughts, and the singleness thereof as interpreted in our complicated, tangled and thwarted lives.

It may have been your habit of mind to consider drama as occasional; episodic; an artful presentation merely, as set forth on a stage within an isolated house called a theatre; and more or less well done, more or less inane, as the case might be. That is but a little truth. The broader, unescapable truth, is that you are ever in the midst of a drama; a drama in the open. You are both spectator and actor therein. It is the drama of the Great City. This drama is unfolded within the action of the greater drama of Land and People. The drama of Land and People is in turn enfolded within the greater drama of the nations and peoples of the Earth. This latter drama is but the tidal continuation of the still greater drama of history; and the urge of it all sets forth the stupendous and pitiful drama of Man, moving passionately through the ages, and as passionately moving today; ever-seeking, ever-thwarted Man! It is this great drama of the soul of man that we are slowly to unfold. It is the background, the vista, the ever pressing drift, now nearing culmination for weal or woe, on which we must set our gaze, and concentrate our hearts and minds. It is the one drama! and in it man (the spirit and summation of mankind) the sole actor, has moved and moves in solitude through the great wilderness and teeming world of nature, through darknes and light, ever, in a darkling dream, seeking to know man, seeking to know God—and tragically unaware! unaware!

And thus, in the drama of the Great City, are enfolded lesser and lesser dramas—dramas growing ever acuter, more poignant, more intimate as they grow ever, but in seeming, only, smaller and less significant; dramas innumerable in the open, dramas of the day and the night. The lesser drama keys to the greater drama, the greater a key to the lesser, and the least. Dramas, without end, within a roof and a wall. Terrible and subtle tragedies behind closed doors; behind the door the breath of Life has blown to, to hold in tight the sordid and calloused soul—the wrecker of thousands of his fellow-men; to hold in tight the terrible, the solitary drama of one, bitterly alone behind the door that Life has blown to in disgust with man. A flash! and it is done! A drama of the wretched home: Enter the man, drunk unto mania, surly, irritable, A surging word of reproach; an oath and a blow; a woman prostrate, huddled screaming children; a maudlin interval; and then a man, outstretched, snoring on the floor in the night stillness, in the sanctuary of one home, behind the closed door, behind the veil where we are told we cannot enter because there is no trail and all are safe in solitude.

But there is a trail. It leads from the forlorn home direct to the working-man's saloon and there it parts in two straight lines, running, one to the brewer, the other to the rectifier—both poisoners, both cowards—(they both struck the woman). From the wife beater, beaten wife, children, brewer, and rectifier run lines straight as the crow flies to you and me (we also brutalized the man, struck the woman, terrified and degraded the children), and from us, they run straight to every man, woman and child in the land—and come back to us; and between all the people in the land they cross-connect, and connect us in endless combinations.

Have you deemed the inter-relations of human life and civilization impossible of precise definition? Have you agreed to be thwarted? and that the aggregate of human life is a mere blur, a smear, all grays except a few bright spots for the favored—and that there is no simple definite meaning underlying it all?

Do you think there is no center of gravity? No definite direction of urge, merely because the man on the street seems commonplace to you, and you to him? He the practical man; you, the practical man—inane dreamers both—visionaries, spending your lives dreaming difficulties and hence creating them—never dreaming a solution.

Awake! The hour is drawing near when all this must be changed—or we undone!

Wake! Be a man! Do you really deem it incredible that all these varied, endlessly flowing and intermingling pictures and dramas, have sprung, and can and now do spring from a single thought all men have held in common, and have not ceased to hold? Do you really believe that violent opposites cannot contain the same truth? Do you really consider

differences more significant than similarities? Have you been betrayed by
words, not knowing the meaning of words?

Are you then the closet-philosopher, who has spun a theory of thought,
but has not gone abroad among men in the world of stress—where he
might clearly see that acts, and *acts alone* identify thoughts. Where he
might see the mind, the heart, the soul of man clearly, indubitably set
forth in the actual pictures and the actual dramas of man's individual and
collective life? Open to the view of all—even to the dull, dreaming, inconsequential, frivolous philosopher of abstractions!

Why should we bother with the rubbish of abstractions when we have
the palpitating living thing? Why should we take a tortuous and obscure
way, which never arrives, when there is a clear way straight from deed
to man?

Awake! Let your heart expand until you become aware that you are
not alone! until you become aware that between you and every human
there is a thread of thought connecting all together. Binding all—brain to
brain, heart to heart, soul to soul, body to body, life to life. A thread more
ethereal than gossamer, stronger than steel. A thread we cannot break, a
living thread from whose band there is no escape-and yet a thread which
may transmit a new universal impulse that shall prove our salvation.

Had you thought it possible really to isolate yourself from your fellows?
To evade and deny the tie? To evade and deny your responsibility, your
manhood? You cannot! Along these delicate threads, these live wires, I
will pass like a current, and, entering intimately into your secret depths,
will shift your ballast; and you will feel the awakening shock of an enlarging consciousness as I bring you to an even keel.

I will search your mind as never mind has been searched. I will search
your heart as never heart has been searched. I will search your soul as
never soul has been searched. To me you are no secret. To know you I have
merely to look at any other man, high or low, rich or poor, in the ditch
or on the throne of the vicar of God on earth. And if I look at a thousand
men, I shall see but yourself in a thousand occupations or situations, the
same You—called by a thousand other names. So shall I place you, at last,
squarely before yourself and before all—in the open, and in secret, whoever you are, wherever you are, and whenever you are. And I shall set
humanity square before you in the open, and in the secret longing. Square
in the daylight—face to face!

As we walk together in the heart of the Great City, is there aught greeting our eyes to suggest or even hint the nearby presence of a noble Lake,

the teeming prairies, green and radiant, half-encircling the Great and gloomy City? Do you think the picture of the City one thing, the picture of the fair broad water and land another thing? The drama of the City one thing, the drama of the open another?—the drama of the open air, the open sky, the open waters and the open land! Do you perhaps deem them paradoxical? No. Undeceive yourself! Open your eyes! The two pictures are but parts of a larger; the two dramas but responsive and coordinate scenes of a greater, simultaneous drama: Picture and drama the same; and, together, merged into one living image, which marks us, as with a fateful and monitory finger; and then moves to the one thought within us from which the mirage of a seeming paradox has come forth to obscure the city and the open.

Spare your explanations, your excuses, practical, sentimental, historical, scientific, benevolent and what not withal. I have listened to the chatter for many a year. Patiently I have read on page after page of many a book, endlessly, concerning an exquisite and delicately rapturous difference between tweedledum and tweedledee; knowing well, in decency, that the real proposition (so deftly set aside) had nothing to do with either tweedledum or tweedledee, but vitally concerned you and me! Over and over I have seen the hair split into a thousandth part, and, meanwhile, I have seen simple men DO!!—simple things—and do them well!

Thus have I come to know to my sorrow and waste of time the inanity of the wise, pious, wordy, over-educated poseurs—and their joint and several inefficiency. By way of compensation I have learned their lesson.

But they are busier than they opine. I shall show you in picture and drama their color, form and movements. I shall show you just how, why and where they fit into the scheme of the little dramas and the great drama. We shall run along the live wires reaching to them, and binding them to us all in the fierce, disconsolate, and impassioned stress of real life. That life, calling, calling—calling!

So, too, in the drama, shall appear the man on the street. He *says* he would not do certain things. But in the great drama I shall point him out to you in the act of killing by thought, by word, by deed, by influence, by indirection. We shall run along his wire like Nemesis! Because he is a liar, a thief, a scoundrel and an assassin—and because he has declared his religion to be his most precious possession—Because he has been benevolent and charitable with the loot of his murders. I shall show him to you sitting silent, or wandering like a madman. And in the great moving picture I shall point out to you, as therein clearly set forth in sharpest definition, just what the word practical means, as used by him; just what his word business signifies; and just what economy, as he understands it, signifies for him, for you, for me, and for every man, woman and child on earth. No doubt he lies; sometimes even to himself. But the lies, the hypocrisy, the turpitude, the concealments, avail not. For, unwittingly, the man on the street, he who is no dreamer, no visionary, who believes himself no artist, no poet, is painting on the great picture, his great and little share, and revealing there, with a precision unattainable by him in conscious speech, the startling truth concerning himself and us all—where we may see.

What a curious notion men have, concerning themselves, their thoughts, their sayings, their doings; with what a curious hebetude they minimize and maximize their parts in the roaring farce, the vaudeville, the melodrama, the tragedy of the Great City and the far-flung Land. How like semi-mechanical figures they go this way and that, not dreaming their dream is come true; not surmising that daily, as a sheer reality, it mocks them, jeers them, warns them, ridicules them—and seduces them into dreaming anew! And yet no one laughs!

Think of a civilization, a city, a land in which men are honest at their peril, and speak truth at their risk! And yet no one laughs! No one smiles.

Think! of a civilization in which the predatory, the relentless, the parasite, the saintly, the feudally benevolent pull the wool over our eyes—knowing us for the sheep we are!—And no one laughs! Preacher and teacher pulling the wool over our eyes—and their own. All of us eagerly pulling the feudal wool over our own eyes—And not a smile!—all serious and fanatic, in a vast silence, and emptiness of sympathy. Truly our feudal denial of reality has at last undermined not only our sense of human tenderness, but even our sense of humor. Thus no one weeps at the dream come true.

Had you supposed that the poet, only, could see such dramas? Only an artist paint such pictures? Do you still worship genius as a fetish, and still consider it a thing apart from the common? Undeceive yourself! Unglue your eyes! We are all poets—every one of us. All artists. All geniuses. Only—we deny it; we decry it; we say it *cannot* be so! And *why* do we deny it! Primarily, because we are cowards. Broadly, because we deny any and everything that is real; narrowly, because we decry anything new—we revile anything true—we ridicule anything that is broadly sympathetic—and, most conclusively, because we persistently mistake our reverse-sight for insight. Under the age-old stupefaction of our feudal education and training we deny life—and affirm death. We lack a knowledge, an insight into the simplicity and naturalness of that illumination that is called genius, merely because we have no use for it. We do not know that it is a universal quality resident in all things, and neither more nor less mysterious than the open air, the sky, the land, the water and— the neighbor. Genius is the simplest thing in the world. It is the only simple thing in the world of men. *Therefore* it is common, to all men. Now if you can even partly dissolve and reshape your notions concerning genius, you will have taken the first step toward an understanding of man; and toward a perception of those latent powers within him which it is the function of Democracy to call forth. Genius is the simple unsophisticated power to see, hear, and feel Life! Therefore genius in Man is nothing other than the historic aspiration of Democracy. That deepest, simplest instinctive aspiration of the human heart, which has glided through every form of Feudalism; an impulse so small, so simple, so persistent, so integral with the spirit of man, that it cannot be exterminated. It is that one, little thing, in all the people, which you cannot fool all the time. Of all our imbecilities, the suppression of genius is the most pathetic, deplorable and utterly inane.

Burdened with our darkened and grotesque notions concerning genius (which is equivalent to saying our obscure notions concerning the beneficent All-Life), is it to be wondered at that we deem great things (as we call them) difficult, and great men (as we call them) necessarily rare?

Have you ever stopped to reflect that the education you have received in school, college, university, and are still receiving in the greater school of practical life has been and is Feudal?! with all the manifold inversions of human thought that that word, that reality, contains and breeds? No, of course you have not. How do I know? *Results!!*—results set clearly forth in the pictures and dramas you have made and are making!—you who are no artist, no poet—Yet have the power to paint most startling pictures, and create most revolting and heart-rending dramas! I don't bother to look at you, or to talk to *you*; I look at the insane, the destitute, the criminal, the vicious, the corrupt, the restless, the tuberculous, the anaemic, the outcast, the criminal rich, the financial rottenness, the political rottenness, the poisoning packer, the treacherous lawyer, the unscrupulous business man, the timid and hypocritical priest and preacher, that you have created and are sanctioning this day!—out of your feudal thought. Is it to be wondered that you are a hypocrite?—(and it doesn't

make the slightest difference whether you are a conscious or an unconscious hypocrite—the *result*, in practice, is the same). Is it to be wondered
that at times you look upon men as through the ravening eyes of a wolf;
and at other times through the timid and flattering eyes of a cur? Is it
to be wondered that hate, envy, malice, vengeance, jealousy, greed, anxiety,
pessimism and, at times, despair, have a home in your soul? Is it a wonder you do not know who or what you are? No wonder you do not know
who or what the neighbor is. No wonder you think genius is necessarily
rare. No wonder you suspect nothing of the all-inclusive beneficence of
nature—of that gentle power which is ever seeking to make real men, and
is ever thwarted by your kind—of that life-giving power which ever faithfully and hourly is striving to make a real man of you—and is being hourly thwarted by you. No wonder you have neither sought nor found man!
And still less wonder you have neither sought nor found, nor had curiosity
concerning that Spirit of Democracy which for so long and with such
patience and wistfulness, has waited, until you be ready, that it may enter
and illumine your thought, and establish therein the consciousness of your
integrity. No wonder, instead, that you slammed the door shut in its face
and sordid terror (lest this Spirit of Life enter—lest the genius of Life—
the power of Life enter—to make you human)!—slammed the door that
you might be alone with your darkened egoism within a roof and a wall
of self. No wonder you have so heavy a countenance as you walk the streets
of the Great City—alone, bitterly alone, helplessly alone amidst the shoals
of faces, among the half-humans, the feudal humans—who are moving
swiftly or slowly towards nothing whatsoever but graves. Because brutally
they have struck kindly and smiling Nature in the face—in return for her
smile. No wonder you cannot see these faces, ghostly and pictorial as they
are, dramatic as they are, eloquent as they are of the feudal thought you
and they have held and hold in common—and which your forebears and
theirs held in common—The feudal thought which wears out the heart, un-
balances the mind, devastates the soul and wrecks the hopes of mankind.
That feudal thought which has brought hitherto civilizations to decay; and
is now, swiftly disintegrating and inflaming our own. That! is our Crisis!
That is what our Crisis means! That is what makes a terrible reversal,
revulsion and cataclysmic revolution, not only possible, probable, but
imminent. That is what renders imperative the prompt liberation and
diffusion of the aspiring spirit and the kindliness of Democracy. That
spirit, so long thwarted and denied utterance, that it has accumulated
intensive explosive power within the subconsciousness of men. That is

what the printing press, land lines, and ocean cables mean, in the last analysis. That is what the teaching of the Nazarene means in the last analysis. Our hour is on the wing. Democracy is at last about to be born. Whether in anguish, alarm and terror, or in peace, reasonableness and joy—remains to be seen. But one thing is palpable: our equilibrium is unstable. It is trembling delicately in its balance. And soon, we are going-one way or the other. It is high time that you get busy thinking about realities. It is high time you begin to understand what this prosperity of ours means *under the surface;* in the pictures and dramas, in the open (and in yourself)! *This* is the thought you will want to take with you into your sanctuary of one, behind the veil. This is the thought that will cause the feudal mighty to dissolve as though they never had been. You had better get busy forgetting your "practical difficulties!" and learn how simple, how masterful, thought and act can become, when you will them to become so. How quickly problems can be solved when we make up our minds that they shall be solved.

It is then equally no wonder you deem benevolence and charity sweet and lovely things; no wonder you do not see that these two fetid-sweet feudal words are but the names of two ghastly, grinning skeletons in the ring of our grim and ponderous dance of death; and that you and your kind, (all of us—feudal) are but phantoms joining with them, hand in hand, clattering, running and clamoring around and about dazed and momentarily terrorized manhood; and that all the fine words, all the fine deceptions, are but a weird and sombre song of the Modern crucifixion. No wonder you cannot see that what you call Business is the name of another such phantom; and the laws of trade—as you call them—others; Industry—as you call it—another; and society as you call it—another; the rich man—another; and the poor man—another. Can you not hear them all?—like the murmur of a keen wintry wind driving through a bare forest—singing the song of the Great City? Can you not hear it? It is roaring on, day in, day out; night in, night out; in the churches, in the asylums, in the jails; in the mansions, in the shanties; in the pest house, in the hospitals, in the police stations; in the mills, the factories, the ditch, the marts of trade; in the hotels, the theatres, the boarding houses; in the sweat shops, the rear of saloons, in the private office, in the newspaper sanctuary, in political committee rooms: Everywhere—anywhere! Cease-lessly! Here in a whisper—there it passes in a wink, a nod, a tip, a sign—there amid clangor and clamor, and bustle and hustle, buying and selling, hooting and yelling—There it is! For you to see! For you to hear—in the

Great City! In the Great City where you and I are walking side by side, looking into the faces of the passers-by; observing the traffic in the streets, and over the streets, and along the streets, dropping in here and there and everywhere, by day and by night, only to hear the same song with its endless, teeming variations in pitch and key and intonation and volume— in smooth flow, in rabid discord—in fine words and ribald words and crude words—in pious prayers and in strings of oaths—It is always the same, always with the same refrain—The Dance of Death and the Song of Death! For we are indeed a busy people—none busier—We have no time—we are greatly occupied—and business is businss—so we say.

And do you think the Great City really is alone, in a gloomy isolation? Alone in its murk and jargon? Not so. There are filaments. They go forth from its engorged and inflamed nerve centers:—Ganglions quivering with incessant messages that flick out to the land and come in from the Land— Ties to other great cities, to smaller cities, to every village in the far-flung Land—Ties to the whole great World of Land and the Isles of the seas. The Great City! It is a man-created Monster—shuddering with the load of traffic in and the burden of traffic out; traffic following the gleaming, parallel threads, far, far throughout the Land, and coming, far, from everywhere, constantly approaching, nearing, and arriving. And the monster groans and sighs. Ever pregnant, as it were, with its one darkling need, it brings forth, every day, the infinitude of things of which it dreams —such as they are, and they live for an hour or a day, or they are absorbed and elaborated into its tissues and further irritate and inflame and engorge and impoverish and congest, and dull its semi-consciousness; as it grows and waxes huger, and becomes heavier and heavier upon the Land and the People: Broadening, elongating and holding within itself multitudes—a fantastic and passionate mass. The Great City is shaped Titanic, rough, and hulked in a human semblance. Its passion is a mystical, distracting devastating urge and confusion: Bewildering, vast, oceanic to those who do not see—but heavily feel—and lament, or cure or flaunt. Clear and gross enough to those who see that the monster is without a definable brain—and without seeing eyes—bringing forth blindly, struggling turgidly, quivering and working without a clear thought—A Caliban in the Midsummer-night dream of a new century, in a Land magnificently fair and filled with shimmering and hovering gayety and beauty and wistfulness and delight—and a winging spirit of the Land, that laughs it to scorn, because the Monster does not yet know how to wish to be glad.

No! the Great City is not alone. It is in purblind touch with the world;

and the borning thought of the world disturbs it. Within its massive bulk a consciousness is struggling toward the slowly envoluming light of a dawning day. That is all. And the seasons sweep over it in untiring succession. And the great shadow, night, sweeps over it silently. And the great orb of day moves over it, dazzling and silent—as the Monster broods in a fateful mood—dreaming by day and by night, its inchoate and turgid dream—in the midst of the steadfast prairie—by the steadfast Lake. Unaware, unaware! For the Great Feudal City, the man-created monster, has not yet dreamed of man.

And there are other great Feudal Cities in the Land. One lies in the East near the sea. It is the Great Feudal City of the little feudal pennies. It is stark and ferocious; clean and callous. Blasé, glutted and irritable, it is ever ravenously hungry, with a dyspeptic and maddening hunger for pennies. It, also, is a monster. It has one eye that sees everywhere, that can spy a penny a thousand miles and more away, hidden though that penny be in the tall grass, in the pocket of a poor man. It may be the last penny—just one—but the all-ferreting eye detects it—and forthwith the penny begins to move toward the Great Feudal City by the sea. That is all—is it not enough? When you wake up you will think it is enough.

And there is another Great Feudal City in the east. It lies not far south of the one-eyed monster and is tied to it by cables of feudal power— surcharged with viciously crossing high-tension currents. This third city is clean and rather fair to look upon. It also is a monster—with a bland, smiling face,—which is right and proper—for, here all treachery culminates. For, in like manner, as the little pennies flow to the City by the Sea, so all the little treacheries throughout the land, rippling gaily on in rivulets, conjoin and conjoin and debouch here and there in irresistible volume. Hence, here, in this City with the smiling face, this Capital City of the Land, the American people achieve their heart's desire—for here they are betrayed in bulk. And yet there is a truth in treachery. Hence this City is a mirror, our great national soul-mirror, accurately giving back a faithful and fateful reflection of all the people in all the land. Look into it—you will see the apple of your eye. If you do not like the image— Change! So much for Great Feudal Cities. Let us pass on.

Feudalism

The most ancient of sanctioned laws is the law of the right of might. It it tacitly approved by the man of today. In his practical dealings he knows none other, except by whim, caprice or benevolence. In theory he speaks of the might of right, which, with him, is a palliative abstraction. Thus is his intellect divided between cowardice and courage, between abstract and concrete, between crooked and straight thinking, as man's intellect has always been divided: a vertiable house against itself.

The inception of the law of the right of might lies within the beginnings of a law of self-preservation at first tacitly assumed, afterward consciously and constructively formulated, and which men have unanimously agreed to call Nature's first law, because the concept of the right of might has been their own first law and last appeal, not only in large affairs, but in the little and the littlest.

In other words, man has always held that, to preserve himself he must dominate the neighbor or be his slave; for right meant both dominion and servitude.

What may therefore be called pure or unadulterated Feudalism (that is, Feudalism unadulterated by Democracy), meant, in essence, master and slave, and was expressed in fact, in the broad compensatory aspects, dominion and servitude. That is, servitude and dominion moved about the same intellectual center of gravity, which center was none other than that conception of self-preservation in the individual and the mass which evoked the spirit of might and exalted it as right.

Hence, all the civilizations of the past, expressing as they did faith in the righteousness of the theory of self-preservation, are feudal, and, inasmuch as our own civilization is based in practice and in doctrine upon exactly the same concept, it too is feudal.

Hence equally, if in the modern movement of individual and mass thought there comes about a weakening of the notion that servitude is necessary to self-preservation, there must come with it, logically and inevitably, the notion that dominion also, is unnecessary to self-preservation. Such change of thought, therefore, if it comes, will in the nature of things, constitute the intellectual beginning of the downfall of Feudalism as a social doctrine and practical rule of conduct.

Also, in the past the spirit of cunning came forth companion to the spirit of might. Thenceforward the man of cunning and the man of might were right. Both sprang from a normal desire for power. And both became perversions of man's natural powers because of a primary misconception that constitutes the tragedy of historic man. To this dark tragedy therefore, we give the name Feudalism.

Out of the multitude's dream of the glory of might sprang the coarse warrior. Out of the lowliest dream of the sanctity of cunning glided the humble priest. Out of coarse warrior grew resplendent potentate. Out of humble priest grew resplendent high-priest. Therewith began an alliance between these two. For they stood for the fiercely and subtly attracting and repelling aspects of man's unstable and marvellous intellect warring within itself and yet seeking, within and without itself, stability and peace. Jealousy, envy, fear, suspicion, hatred, mutual tolerance, were the portion of prince and priest. For each needed each. Each was complementary and supplementary to the other. Each was so necessary to the self-preservation of the other that each strove to master and subjugate each—that warrior or witch might achieve sole dominion over the minds, and domination of the bodies and property of men; control and direction of the thought, the will and the energy of the multitudes. That there should be those to have and hold dominion over them for the common good was the intellectual desire and attitude of the multitudes. It seemed to them right. For to them might and cunning, force and craft, wisdom and power, glory and omnipotence were attributes with which they had as it seemed worthily to them, endued and endowed the Gods as the highest renunciation of their social powers in the hope of compensatory salvation from mysterious evil. It was indeed their dream—their dream of wisdom and omnipotence. For to them sacrifice and salvation, death and transfiguration, were as much one in thought as were servitude and dominion—as vivid as master and man— they seemed right—they implied self-preservation—it was the only way as it seemed to them. It seemed real to them—this phantom of vicarious self-preservation in the persons of the elect and exalted—as real as it seems to us.

Thus the dream of absolution, as an ambition and a goal, came boldly and bodily imaged forth of the multitudes to lure on prince and priest. And thus, in the dream of the lowly, came the ferment of man's intellectual madness. For the dream of force and cunning, of glory and power, of dominion and servitude, of master and man, made his world unreal.

Thus the basis of Feudalism is an intellectual conception. For, be it understood, historic man high and low laid stress upon the rectitude of his intellect. He was sure it could not fail him. He made scant allowance for the fact, that, for every position his vainglorious intellect assumed, a convincing response would arise from his senses—for between the senses and the intellect of man exists a most curious interrelationship of mutual dominion and servitude—just as the same subtle relationship has ever existed between rich and poor, lowly and exalted, prince and priest.

Thus it was that, in the past, the priest, in his tense secretive ambition, sought theocratic absolutism through wily shifting of the sense of certitude of the warrior, and hence the subjugation of the warrior and the longed-for control of his physical power over the multitudes—that the vicar of heaven might be prince of the earth—for the earth and the multitudes have ever been real to the priest. He alone has glimpsed the reality of power over man. He alone has understood the terrible power of gentleness. He, alone, has perceived all folly but his own.

The warrior also sought a theocratic absolutism, through subjugation of the priest, by shifting his sense of security in graft, and thus seizing upon the control and utilization of the subtlety of the priest's power over the fears and hopes of people: that the prince of earth might become potentate of heaven. In the view of each, subjugation was the sole evidence of power, and such power alone was deemed by all men to be at once God-like and earth-like. The multitudes believed that man might become a God. Prince and priest knew that the multitudes could be completely subjugated only through manipulation of this idea. Each so acted. Thus came each at the throat of each, and thus was sometimes priest under-wolf, sometimes warrior, in the keen, icy struggle for dominion as acknowledged leader of the pack that preyed upon the world of men, as the world of men was ready to prey upon them.

Thus were the forming civilizations grandiose, ferocious, intensely imaginative, introspective, esoteric, mystical, verbose and drastically practical. These were the shapings of organized Feudalism, with all its mysticism of rich and poor, strong and weak, darkness and light, good and evil, exalted and lowly. For it was divinely ordained—so all men said. Thus in our own day we believe our sanctioned ferocious civilization to be divinely ordained. Thus civilization and feudalism have been in fact synonymous terms throughout all recorded history.

It is typical of our traditional view of ancient, mediaeval and modern Feudalism (or, as we call it, the history of civilization) that we have been taught, from the cradle, in season and out of season, in all occasions, in all times and places, to see it completely in reverse of its reality. We have been taught that this phantasm was and is man, instead of being taught that it was and is man's mirage; and that by the guidance of that mirage, we might somewhere find the reality—man—and that the man-search is the true business of men. For the institution of Feudalism worked in appearance from the top down. The show and parade and semblance of power were all at the top. In this radiance of reflected power, the source of power, in the thought of the multitudes, was invisible. It has not been officially set forth to us that the spiritual idea of Feudalism had its being in man's self-created vision of the external and miraculous. The vision, the image, of the God was of an immensity of external power and wisdom. God was on high. Hence, with pictorial fitness and literalness, power and wisdom seemed to descend from the God—the highest of all—to the highest of earth, the potentate and priest, and from them seemed as visibly to descend to the multitudes. Sometimes indeed, as seemed dramatically fitting to an imaginative people, the God himself descended to earth. Hence were the exalted called exalted by themselves and by their lowly. For exalted and lowly, rich and poor, each possessed each in a marvellous bond of sympathy and union. They worshipped in common a feudal God. And the God-conception is ever in exact accord with the social conception. This same idea plainly survives and is potent with us. It still remains the intellectual pivot of our civilization. Hence with us still exists that same clandestine bond of sympathetic union between rich and poor, powerful and weak, betrayer and betrayed. Each adores each with the old feudal infatuation. Quarrels are but preludes to luxurious reconciliations. We still believe power and wisdom descend from a God, we still believe in the miraculous and in magic. We have not yet learned to identify power and wisdom with ourselves; hence we fail to understand that which is very plain and specific, namely, that force and cunning are but social perversions of our own normal power and wisdom. Hence our thought has remained basically feudal; and our Democracy thus far is little else than a vague, wistful dream not yet grown clear enough to come true—because we are not ready, in our drowsy and luxurious heaviness, to make the required intellectual inversion of our traditional concept of the right of might and cunning.

So the man of the past created his civilizations in the image of his thought, and in the same identical image created he his God. His civilizations, in their flowering thus became the picture, the drama of that idea or thought which he conceived to be most profoundly spiritual, most real, most solid, most nearly everlasting.

Hence, while Feudalism arose in fact out of man's most simple selfishness, it became in its times of glory a marvellous sublimation of that same selfishness. It became, indeed, transfigured into a vast and opulent poem of ferocity, cruelty, and cunning—the apotheosis of plunder, graft, extravagance, splendor and abject misery—and a riot of duplicity—exactly like our own.

Surely Feudalism was and is a simple and absorbing passion of man. In it he has glaringly displayed one phase of himself—his abnormal ego.

But a new passion is about to arise within the soul of man—the passion of Democracy—which shall inspire his intellect to set forth in unexampled clarity and spiritual beauty that still simpler phase of himself which, during all these ages, he has, in fear, himself kept submerged—in his normal ego. For the passion of Democracy is the passion of the modern world-shaping consciousness of man: the consciousness that power and wisdom reside in and arise from the multitudes; the consciousness that man, normally, is simply unselfish; and that, in the reasoned exercise of that unselfishness, lies the sublimity of his spiritual power, his simplest and cleanest manhood.

So viewed, Feudalism has been man's stupendous, world-old phantasm; his witching mirage; the eidolon of his fear of the All-Life; his altogether pathetic failure to find the simple and sound foundation of his own nature.

Under the sway of the spell of the Feudal illusion, under the powerful thrall of its gorgeous and miraculous and miserable dream, the world of men still sleeps within the great world of Reality.

Verily no passion of a God could equal the passion of man. It is incalculable. Nor has man yet invented a God that could suffer as man has suffered, or aspire as man has aspired. Feudal man indeed curiously underrated his intellectual powers, and, therefore, caught but fleeting and flitting glimpses of his own integrity.

Such is Feudalism: The great shadow of man's intellectual self-eclipse. The great veil, which he has drawn before the countenance of Life. The opalescent and glamorous mist with which he has obscured the dream-clear purity of vision of his own spirit.

Thus how closely are we of today drawn to the man of the past. In what bond of affection are we. How visibly is he of us; and how noteworthy are we dreaming our new dream of Democracy within his ancient dream of Feudalism. To our dawning and clearing world-embracing and timeless sympathy how vivid, how real is he, as we vision him forth in his long ago!

Democracy

Notwithstanding the law of predatory and subservient self-preservation is the most ancient, and likewise the most modernly sanctioned of man-enunciated laws, it is a pressing truth that Integrity ever has been and remains the valid law of the cosmos—that cosmos with which, in spite of his favorite beliefs and unfaiths, man is so integral that in no sense can he get away from it.

That is, while man's intellectually formulated social law has sanctioned might and cowardice because he believed them right, the vast and friendly domain of nature within which he has moved and moves has ever set forth the oneness of all things to be right.

The inception of this law, principle, or urge, or spirit, of integrity—this most ancient and modern thing in the cosmos—dates back not only through man's intellectual law of selfish self-preservation, but, indefinitely far beyond that to the primordial law, aspect, or urge of self-creation. That is, as we fundamentally and conjointly among all the peoples of the world understand such things, it is the law of oneness of the infinite Spirit, or that, to which we, and all peoples of the past, have, under varying synonyms, given the conventional name, God. For the term God, or its equivalent, has ever stood, among all the peoples of the past, and really still so stands with us as a symbol of what we mean in everyday language by the term, right, or integrity. That is, reliability, safety, security, balance, equipoise, peace, certitude; or in language of wider horizon, wholeness, creative and preservative power, wisdom, and goodness.

It is of the profoundest and simplest instinct of man that he has ever clandestinely as it were, felt himself at one with the integrity of all things; that he has surreptitiously and furtively felt and known himself to be co-continuous with the vast primordial, spiritual integrity, and it is precisely of this deeper faith of instinct, that man's feudalism has been a prolonged intellectual perturbation. And in this perturbation, this aberration, is bound up the drama of his sorrows, and his bitter discontent with life.

Man's turning toward integrity was but an episode of his indolence, of his ease, of his meditative solitude, of his temporary safety. But the moment he set eyes on the stranger (the other man) presto, all was changed, and the calm of universal integrity was dispelled by the storm of seeming individual diversity. For, lo, this other man, the neighbor of earth, was forsooth a stranger, hence an obscure enemy. And yet man has also ever been more than ready to welcome this stranger, if but he dared; for in him, also, he has perceived an obscure friend. Thus are seen the original urges of Feudalism and Democracy. Feudalism has ever been the urge of that phantasmal fear or lust which regarded the other man as enemy or prey; Democracy ever that urge which regarded the other man, the stranger, as friend, likeness and equal. Hence, in the historic drama of the civilizations the sane kindly and original urge of Democracy ever has been the victim of the subsequent fiercely treacherous and destructive delusion and mania of Feudalism. That is, Feudalism in essence, has ever stood and now still stands for man's mad intellectual treachery to mankind, Democracy for his fidelity. The one tends toward spiritual disintegration and the betrayal of the heart, hence toward social downfall, and the other toward social strength, stability and wholesomeness.

So it is with Feudalism and Democracy, and so have these twain ever seemed to war within the being of man, and thus has man ever kept his intellect and his heart estranged. And thus has man oscillated in his career, now coldly intellectual, now feverishly emotional, now fast, now loose, now honest, now dishonest, now rich, now poor, now victor, now vanquished, now eminent, now obscure, now virtuous, now vile, now hero, now dastard. Thus during all his career man has known no balance but the beguiling equilibrium between his cold lust and his hot lust. It is true that in the cold bursts of his asceticism and the hot bursts of his abandon, man has equally achieved marvels—marvels of intellect, marvels of emotional crisis and of physical accomplishment. But it is just as true that he never knew where he stood. His feet have been off the ground, and his head and heart have separated and wandered anywhere and everywhere. For he ever thought himself a law unto himself—which was actually right, but passingly wrong. In man's sane social balance, it is strictly fitting that he be a law unto himself, for in such poise he recognizes and acclaims the fundamental law of integrity; but in his feudal unbalance (really his feudal insanity), when he declares himself a law unto himself, it is but to declare himself anarchic to the primordial law of integrity. For it means simply this: that he wishes to apply a law to himself of his own fantastic devising—he forgets that there are others. But the real man, the sane man knows that no law can apply validly to himself that does not in equal and fullest measure apply to all others, and this corrective thought must tend at once to bring into equilibrium his overturning and collapsing intellect which has led him into the ghost-like supposition that a social law might be found, applicable to him alone, and not equally, unequivocally and fully to all men.

Thus are the appeals of our modern predatory great ones, to a higher law, both right and wrong, both fantastic and normal. Wrong intellectually, right in this that the predatory urge, is after all, but a profoundly obscure desire to be of use to others. It is but an intellecual perversion of the normal activity of the brain—the decay of the real ego.

There is a fundamental urge in man which causes him to hunger for work, which causes in him a deep desire to give his whole life-energy to the service of his fellow men. And this urge is clearly discernible to the sympathetic eye, throughout all the history of Feudalism. In other words, man's heart has always been right. All his confusion has been wrought by his vanity and absurdity of intellect. The splendid urge of his imagination and his will has been misconstrued by him, and it is his own intellect that has prepared the pitfalls into which he has sunk, even as he believed himself on the scent of something socially real. It is not that Feudalism represents what is bad in man's heart—for there is nothing bad there. It really represents the instability, the incertitude, the perplexity, the bombast, the stubbornness and, alas, the cowardice of his intellect.

If you wish to know how true and trite this is all set forth in the reeking feudalism of our modern democracy, you have but to touch with your fingertip anywhere—no matter where. Try first the places in which you are convinced it cannot possibly exist: There you will find it in its over-ripeness. Touch with your finger the high places, the sacred places, the choice places, the pure places, the reputable and eminent places—you will find it there—but you will find it everywhere else—in the obscure and lowly places as well—and you will find it, equally, throughout all the past.

The feudal desire to do "good" to others is the righteous as well as the wicked man's delusion; for he has omitted, first, to take account of himself. He believes he is really a law unto himself. Truly he is; but not unto himself alone.

It is not because men are essentially vicious, that they are feudal, it is merely because they do not clearly understand the essential and concrete nature of their relationship to their fellows, to the earth, and to the spirit of integrity.

The discernment of this spiritual relationship is therefore of the essence of Democracy—for Democracy is the New Way. And the unfolding of a law of self which shall likewise be the integral law of all, is the manifest mission of the man of today. Else why regard with such wistful interest the man of the past!

It will be seen therefore that what we are here choosing to call Democracy or The New Way, is but the ancient primordial urge within us of integrity or oneness. And it is this very urge of nature (Nature's true first-law of preservation) that is awakening within the heart of modern man the desire to seek a fundamental law of social integrity or oneness, wherein each man shall be truly a law unto himself. For that basic law shall imply the liberation of his free creative and integral spirit. It shall be an organic law, or human utterance, not for one man or a few men, but for all men.

This is of the essential nature of Democracy. For Democracy and the oneness of all things are one. Thus, even within the depths of historic feudalism, one perceives the primal urge of man's spirit toward Democracy.

So, if feudal man has been a wanderer and a seeker, far from himself, far from man, far from the earth and far from his God—Democracy is but his home-coming.

The tragedy of the man of the past lies in this, that his unstable intellect led him to believe that his normal power consisted in dominion over his fellow men; that is, in the right and therefore the rightness of might and cunning.

It obscured to his common sense the manifest fact that cunning is but the perversion of a normal desire to accomplish useful and beneficent social results, just as force is but a perversion of man's natural power to create social integrity, beneficence and peace.

Thus, since Feudalism has for foundation and superstructure a false attitude of the intellect, and as its entire fabric of thought, in all its aspects of institutions, manners, methods and processes is becoming daily more clearly artificial, futile, extravagant, mischievous and cruel, it cannot longer stand as an intellectual proposition, but must crumble and fall before the searching powers of modern critical and creative integrity of thought. Its phantasmal conception of the dual nature of man must vanish before the increasing light of our clear and radiant conception of man's reality, the inexhaustible fertility of his powers, and the vividness of his integrity.

In the course of Feudalism the head was wrong, the heart essentially right.

In Democracy both head and heart are right.

Thus throughout all history the vast phantom of Feudalism filled the Earth and the Heavens.

But today: The free spirit of man draws near!

The Multitudes

It is said that human nature always has been the same. That is true. But it has not been pointed out with suavity and persistence that human nature has ever expressed itself through two significant phases or aspects, which, by whatever name they hitherto may have been called or miscalled, we are here for most pressing purposes of reinforcement naming the feudal and the democratic.

To be sure, much has been said concerning good and evil. Variously it has been assumed that good and evil are abstract external powers acting upon man while independent of him, yet he not independent of them. And yet good and evil manifestly are man himself appearing alternately in two phases or modes of himself, both arising from the same radical or root of self and readily explaining him, even to himself—would he but pause and listen.

There is no dualism in good and evil. Man merely has thought there was; it has been his spectacular divertissement. There is no dualism in the cosmos. Man flippantly or solemnly has thought there was; it has been his opulent dissipation. The universal spirit in integral. Hence is man integral. The belief in dualism has been man's specific self-poison secreted from his luxurious fear of seen and unseen Life; his turning in upon himself as a lover of himself, now in panic of incertitude, now of certitude. He would not let himself alone. He did not know how to do so in a quiet way. In this belief, therefore, lies the kernel of his philosophy of despair—his extremest, most tranquil and most solitary luxury—the epitome of his self-complacence, his self-pity, his self-love, his self-aversion and his self-absorbed, intellectual disdain of his own manhood. He would not accept it: always he made a mental reservation—a terrible protest when self-driven to extremities.

Feudalism has ever been the potent expression of man's illusion of dualism. In it are involved the coupled and dual notions of Master and Man, of Rich and Poor, of Good People and Bad People, of good God and bad Devil, of Vice and Virtue. So vivid have such mental images seemed to man, so real, so specious, so certain, so right, so changeless, so graphic, so sharply projected upon the screen of his outer world, so God-made, God-ordained, stable, eternal, God-sanctified and God-engloried; that man has not ventured to doubt his senses; has not presumed to suspect their abject and affectionate servitude to his domineering and profoundly unbalanced intellect. Hence he has said: whatever is is right—it must be right because it is.

Thus out of the self-imposed dualism of man's egregious and little-understood intellect sprang Gods of caprice, by turns cruel and kind because feudal man, that is, dually imaginative man was so. Also sprang out of the mournful fatality of his prefervid dualism Gods utterly removed from him. Out of it sprang likewise the bird-like notion that man's soul was separate from himself, even as an eagle and its nest; a something that had come silently and formidably from the air to inhabit his body conveniently as a house. It seemed to him obvious it must be so; for man in his insistent dualism has been profoundly phantom and most curiously a dreamer and a fanciful image-maker. Therefore always was there a double; always were there two things, not one thing. Hence was his own single thought divided against him. Hence could he not find himself to know himself—because he was divided against himself and in conflict against himself, in mutiny against himself, in rebellion against himself, and in conspiracy with himself against himself. Still less could he find and know the neighbor—who is but himself. Hence was he divided in his thought against the neighbor, and strove, mutinied, rebelled, and conspired against the neighbor. Hence was his thought troubled and phantasmal concerning the relationship of himself and the neighbor, and therefore concerning all other things and all other Gods, and especially concerning his own spirit, his own integrity. Always, therefore the bewildering and agonizing notion that there was something external and estranged from man. Always the notion that there was something internal and still estranged from him, flattering him, placating him, imprecating him, discrediting him, watching him, intriguing, conspiring, ready as a wild beast to overthrow and destroy him, and yet strangely fearing him and as strangely docile, willing to be slave. Always the notion of two great powers without: Good and Evil. Always the notion of two strange, furtive, abysmal powers within: Good and Evil. Never the notion of one power without and within: the All-Spirit, man himself! Under the domination of so arrogant, so melodramatic a fear, hope, distrust, frenzy of incertitude, and frenzy of certitude which man so avidly harbored, how could man find man? How could man emerge from his feudalism? From his petulant, fickle, abnormal ego?

It is to this very notion of dualism, this supremely drastic notion of the phantasmal, external, theatrical nature of good and evil, that there was given the sharpest cleavage, the most precise, superb, mystical and elegant separateness by the brilliantly constructive minds which absorbed the notion of loneliness and strangeness and companionship from the people, the multitudes, the lowly, and reared of it vast verbal and ceremonial edifices in philosophies, religions, governments and wars. And yet man ever truly strove to find man. But he believed the neighbor double, while man is surely single; hence he failed to find. And to this failure of the multitudes and of their chosen exalted, the warriors, philosophers, the poets, artists and priests—to this colossally simple failure—we give the name Feudalism. For in it is summed up the breaking of the hearts of the multitudes carrying with them their exalted, in a veritable surf of tidal urge and ebb against that wall of their own uprearing which they called Fate, or God, or the Gods, but which they never called man. Thus through the ages has the notion of good and evil obsessed and distracted the minds of the peoples of the world—the exalted, the multitudes, the lowly—earth-creepers, heaven-stormers, hell-evokers all, in a liturgy and litany, in a paean and dirge of self-denial—of denial of Life and of man's reality—as they pursued the dual ghosts. For most surely they believed good and evil to be spirits, even as their forebears had believed the darkness and the light, the night and the day to be powerful spirits inscrutable in their great lairs, and coming forth potent for weal or woe. Such is man in the dark side and the light side of his marvellous, fruitful, and prodigiously active and fertile imagination. It is in amazement therefore that we regard man when we begin to get a glimpse of his natural powers; and it is with awakening amazement that we regard the multitudes of earth when we begin to realize that it has all come from them; that what they sanction is sanctioned, and that, per contra, not a solitary institution can exist, not a government can exist, not a church can exist, not an army can exist, not a formal God can exist that we do not sanction. Hence it is the multitude that have ever been the primal social power, because the multitudes stand for the individual in mass, and because the multitude itself finds its own center of gravity within its own mass-thought. The mass-thought of the multitudes has hitherto been animated by the conception of dualism—by the notion of light and darkness as powers, by the outgrowing notion of good and evil as powers, by the notion of a terrible disturbance within the soul, by the notion of complete incertitude and caprice, by the consequent notion of fear and the consequent notion of escape from the bondage of self into the free and open field of servitude of dominion. For to the primitive-minded, superstitious and phantasmal man servitude was a form of freedom; that freedom from self-struggle which came to him through yielding obedience. So yielded he obedience to his Gods. Also, dominion seemed to him a form of freedom; another way of escape from lonely self-struggle and self-slavery: an escape into the open world of conquest, and of creating out of other men a host, an army of offense and defense, that he might carry his struggles into a greater, higher world than his little world of inefficient self—that he might secure the freedom of glory and power visibly, that he might dominate visibly the terrible powers within and without and be secure; that he might aspire even to emulate the powers of his gods; that he might indeed perhaps himself become a god on earth and thus achieve complete freedom. For man ever has searched for the Gods, has striven to emulate them, to rival them, to dominate them, has conspired and rebelled against them. For man in his heart ached for freedom; for man in his intellect keenly sought freedom—the freedom of dominion or servitude. Also in his heart he wished peace, the peace, the tranquility of a complete dominion or a complete servitude. Also in his spirit he wished peace and freedom—the freedom of Death or of Life; the peace of a death everlasting or of a life eternal. Thus were the fears, aspirations and conduct of the man of the past essentially the same as the fears, aspirations and conduct of the man of today. But turn his dualism of mind into singleness of mind and you turn Feudalism into Democracy.

The incertitude, the lack of confidence of the multitudes of the past made them timorous, modest, bashful, self-deprecatory, self-abasing, self-effacing—and prodigiously generous, amazingly fluent of heart; quick to anger, quick to anything and everything and likewise slow to anything and everything; hence active-minded, suspicious, crafty, fickle; hence slow-minded, docile, swinish, contented. Hence resenting change until excited; hence insisting madly upon change when excited. Desiring mostly a change in moods rather than methods. Reviling the rulers if the rulers were tyrant, blessing the rulers if the rulers were lavish. Reviling the Gods if the Gods failed, blessing the Gods if the Gods fulfilled. Such is feudal man, today and then; such the multitudes then and now; such the exalted, the chosen. Such was master then, such is master now—and such is slave. Names change, the names of men and gods, of institutions and processes, methods and customs and manners and clothing; but what was feudal then is feudal now, and what is feudal now was feudal then. It is all the same; for men are all alike and have ever been. The American slave is the Egyptian slave, the Russian slave is the Egyptian slave, the German slave is the Egyptian slave, the Chinese slave is the Egyptian slave. It is all one; and the masters of today are the masters of ancient Egypt; it is all one thought, one motive, one impulse, one urge, one phantasm held in common through the ages by the multitudes of earth and so held in common with them by us, of today.

Thus have the multitudes been ever arrogant and bashful, keen and oblivious: ever stupidly and sturdily trusting, ever sturdily and profoundly fickle. Thus have they ever stood amazed before their own creations, believing them the while the work of powers on high. Thus have they stood dazed and timid and diffident before that which they created with their own hands and feet and backs, out of the sweat of their bodies and their dreams. Thus have armies impressed them—as though vast glittering armies were not molded of themselves, by themselves, the multitudes. Thus have temples and palaces and dungeons impressed them, as though temples and palaces and dungeons were not made and dreamed out of the abodes of the thoughts of the lowly, and thus have governments impressed them; and religions; and luxury and pomp; and the appalling pride of caste; thus great engineering works; thus great poems, and the sciences. They all seemed miraculous, divine; they were all simply and intensely human, ineffably of the multitudes, universally of man's spirit. They all arose out of the dreams of the multitudes, from out the fertility and fragrance of earth, and floated on high into the light air of their wonderment, even as vapor of earth's moisture arises and forms in feathery and towering clouds in the firmament. Who would suppose that such cloud-like civilizations could arise to the heights from the sweaty dreams of the forgotten and discredited millions of the earth; surely not a feudal dreamer; surely not a Pharisee.

So, has man, the earth-creeper, been abashed and easily confused, because he knew not himself nor his powers. Hence he has not known the nature and the power of his dreams, nor how surely they come true to his multitudes, whatsoe'er the dreams might be. Man's lowly and resplendent feudal dream has come true as a likeness to him through the ages. He is now softly dreaming the dream of Democracy. It will shape within his image-world, earth-man that he is, and come vividly true to him in the ancient, primal and ever-youthful power of the earth's wistful multitudes. For, lo, it is the dream of the infinite spirit of Integrity shaping true through the aeons. For man is the dreamer. When widest awake he most vividly dreams—and most dramatically acts his own dream. And when fullest awake he is nevertheless and always most profundly asleep and dreaming within the dream of the All-Spirit, as a part thereof. But man seldom awakens—even for a moment—such dreamer is he! Truly what a spectacle is the drama of man, the lowly creator! and, behold, before him outspread, the multitudes of his Works and his Gods on heavenly high and on the fair Earth. Truly, the Man-Search is worth while.

Thus is the God-idea ever a mystic symbol of the Man-idea.

The pure God is ever the pure man.

The dream-God is the dream man.

The Lord God is ever the pirate, the plunderer, in action.

The over-wise God is ever the priest at his work.

The political God is ever the intriguer in his mess.

The property of God always has slaves and lowly ones.

For man creates no God greater than himself: He can utilize no God better or worse than himself. That he can create and utilize such a God is a figment, an illusion. Let there be no mistake concerning man and his Gods. For the Gods are as plain, as simple, as phantom, as man.

That man has created great and beautiful Gods, sets forth man's great and beautiful powers.

When man frankly worshipped the storm as a storm, he was wiser than when he worshipped the storm as a spirit.

When he feared the night as night, he was truer to himself than when he feared the night as a spirit.

And when he worshipped the sun, as the sun, he was simpler, more thoughtful, more sympathetic, than when he worshipped the sun as a God. But he thought not so; for he, extravagant and over-anxious, neither grasped nor could understand the simplicity and beautiful clarity of his own powers.

Thus as man became more and more sophisticated, his God became sophisticated, secretive and withdrawn.

When man was direct with his God, his God was exactly as direct with man—neither more nor less—for the God was exactly the man.

When man is phantasmal in his intellect, all things react phantasmally upon him. When man shall become lucid, all things will become lucid. When man shall become natural mentally, all things will become natural to him.

So powerful is man's thought that, as he thinks, so the universe reacts upon him. He calls the Universe to himself: Evokes it: It replies. Thus man creates a Universe by the power of his thought. For no universe can exist for him other than such universe as he is willing to select and approve. And likewise, no God can exist for him other than such God as he willingly prefigures in expectancy and welcome. If he creates a God of Hell it is because such God is welcome to his thought, and he embraces such a God in clamorous unison, for his purposes of wrath. If he creates a Prince of Darkness, it is because he wishes such a Prince. Man's thought is powerful beyond the present willingness of that thought to conceive itself. He does not know himself—so eccentric, and hot, and cold, and furious and weak has he been. He has as yet but a glimpse of himself. In his sublime innocency he has told how the God has made revelation of Himself. Let us reveal man to man. Let us write the poem of Man: the hitherto unwritten: the poem of the primacy of the Man-Child. This is the modern revelation—the Logos of our Time. For such is the Man-Search—the Poem of Man—in his naked mentality, in his supreme desire to fructify and create with his passionate, virile, impatient intellect. Such is man—the dispenser of power. And such, when calm, is the greatness of man: passionate, intolerant, arrogant and imperious man—in his desire to overcome the Earth, to breed great children from his brain. For man is the brain of passion, and his hitherto most passionate and daring outburst is the creation of the gods. But man must be calmed in his energy, and the torrent and flood of his thoughts diverted to the lowlands. Thus will man become sane through relief. Man, the wanderer, the seeker, the poet, the aspirer—creating gods as a wayfarer in passing.

Therefore: As man became mystic the God became mystic. As man became hysteric, the God became hysteric. As man became cataleptic, the God became cataleptic. As man became a trader, the God became a trader. As man made bargains with God, so the God made bargains with man. As man became a politician, the God became a politician. Hence, as man betrays his fellows, so the God betrayed the multitudes and the elect. As man became mighty, his God became mighty. When man was warrior, the God was warrior. When man was agriculturist, the God was agriculturist. As man began to create, so he invented a Creator-God. As man dreamed in tranquility, so he put forth a God which dreamed in tranquility. As man surmised how the Universe was "made" so he "made" a God, who "made" the Universe that way. Thus has man ever been erratic in his dealings with his God, because erratic in his dealings with himself and the neighbor. His God has been the symbol of his hypocrisy. For man has not sought a God of integrity. Hence has man's God, as a symbol, failed to create peace on earth and good will to men. For man has not wholly desired either peace or good will. What he really desired was either dominion or servitude: Either to win or to lose. Feudal man could have no use for such God of integrity other than to beguile the multitudes therewith and thereby; and the multitudes had no permanent use for such God: For the multitudes wished to win or lose.

Man has ever hoped that he might at once be crooked and straight; and if not both, then successfully crooked. He has not in all his history hoped to be straight alone. Hence has his God been a symbol of specious duplicity.

So soon as man desires in his heart to be honest, just so soon will he create an honest God—an image of his own integrity.

So long as man is a liar, he will have for his God an omniscient and omnipresent liar, an infinitely wise beguiler.

So long as man is himself a man-destroyer, he will have a man-destroyer for his God: A glorious and kindly destroyer, a parasite-God, one that glories in the opulent abasement of the poor and unfortunate; one that gives to those that have, familiarly, and takes as familiarly, from those that have not.

Whatever the social view is, such is the God-view. In times of master and man, the God is a mighty ruler, the man a sinful slave. In all the God-images, the social status is ever taken for granted, always was. In times of poetic imagination, the God is a poet and highly imaginative. In times of wickedness and downfall, it is the God that sorrows and is bereft of his people. Thus is the heart of the people the heart of the God; the soul of the people the soul of the God—the thought of the people the thought of the God.

This is the marvel of the bond between man and his God: it is the historic self-love, self-chastisement, self-regulation, self-destruction and self-glorification of man. Truly man has ever celebrated himself: in God-images of his moods and whims and passions. Endless are the aspects of his Gods. And when, at times, he has had one Great God, ruler of all the Gods, then was that God symbol and vast image of man's sublimest hopes and fears and momentary understandings.

As God-maker, Man has given us a glimpse of his inexhaustible natural powers.

Now let him try his skill and power at man-making.

Still, the God-idea has always been man's great balance; willynilly, it stood for his own notion of integrity—such as it was. He could not exist without it. He cannot exist now without it. There is no such thing as Atheist. The word is a misnomer, a no-fact. For he who says there is no

God has merely a particular God-symbol of his own. For the no-God idea is but a phase of the God-idea. The God-idea is perennial. The God is the Ego. It must therefore last as long as man lasts—and must change as man's thought changes. It must range in beauty and clarity and power as man's thoughts so range; and likewise, it must so range in cruelty, in hypocrisy, in humanity.

Therefore it is not wholly in derision that we view the men of the past as more or less futile and humorous and pathetic God-makers. Such view is far from the purpose of our Man-Search. We wish to search man in his prodigious and heart-rending follies. To find why he has broken his heart without just cause—why he has broken his heart for a phantasm. And, further, if we set forth man broadly to view, in his dramatic role of God-maker, it is but to look steadfastly into his ego that we may see, therein, in that selfsame creative power, the vast, unused power of man to create man in the image of integrity. It is to weigh and solidly judge his appearing power to create a new civilization in the image of his integrity. It is to balance his historic power to create *Gods* in the image of *Master*, against his evident collateral power to create *Man* in the image of *Man*. This is the very essence of the Man-Search. Hence is the God-Search the Man-Search, and the Man-Search the God-Search. They are one. And it is man, primordial and eternally youthful man, the ancient artistic and extravagant dreamer of the Gods, who is to become the modern sane dreamer of Man. Hence are we seemingly pitiless and iconoclastic; for, to the feudal imagination, with its profound and phantasmal fear, and of the reality of man, Democracy seems indeed pitiless and destructive. To the feudal mind, Democracy seems likewise a terrible phantasm. For the feudal harbors naught but phantasms and it can harbor naught else; that is its psychic quality. Hence, saturated with the traditions of caste, it cannot grasp the sublimity and clarity of the idea of human equality. Hence, with far-focused vision, it cannot short-focus upon those powers that are clearly natural to all men, nor perceive the reach and certitude of those powers.

Hence it is that the Feudal-God-Idea is extravagant, wasteful and futile. It is too unscientific. It costs too much in blood and sorrow, and the degradation, through folly, of man by man.

Thus the bond between man and God is at once beautiful and terrible: For the God-idea is the most powerful of ideas—the most searchingly potent: The most far-reaching in its action and reaction. And yet truly God has been a little thing to make so small a thing as man so much trouble. There is a grim and ghastly humor in it all. And yet he who is devoted to man, and loyal to man even in his follies, must feel toward man's many gods of many moods, the thrall of affection and pity—a tenderness toward the God-children and the men-children who created them in the garden and the nursery of the beauteous savory Earth: Under the stars, under the sun, within the shadows and the dusk, amid the moon-beams, on desert and river and lake, on mountain peak and in dell and dale, by the mighty sea, in the sombre forests: Where the man-child was—there was the God-child with him at his call. And the two communed, embosomed both, in the sweet amplitude of Life—and they talked to each other of Death; and what it all meant: these two children that went forth every day in the garden of the world: and what the two wished—they became: So sang they at times the song of Life—so danced they, at times, the dance of Death: These two, together.

Man-Search

By the power of what light within or without, has man hitherto customarily sought man? In what light has he expected to see him? In the light of selfish self? The light of the law of the jungle? The transfiguring light of abnormal ego? Has man with open eyes sought the neighbor, or with eyes astigmatic and pre-judging? With mind wide open in welcome for him, or held as a door suspiciously against him?

Has man really sought man? Has he gone forth fully intent upon finding? Has he sought him busily, determined as busily not to find? Has man with keen calculation avoided the real man? Has he held him at arm's length? Has he erected a barrier, a wall of feeling and thought, a wall of fear and doubt and distrust and cruelty, of utter selfishness and vanity and hypocrisy and benevolence and charity, and fiction of good will between himself and the neighbor?

If not, what does caste mean? What does master and man mean? What do wars mean? What does the so-called struggle for existence mean?

And what, then, do broken hearts mean? What means the warrior-man, what the priest, what the politician? What does the successful man signify for us, what the self-made man, what the parasite? What do rich and poor mean, what do lowly and exalted mean? What does the outcast mean?

What, then, do you and I mean? What do all men mean?

How, then, are we to interpret history? How then are we to interpret ourselves, if there has hitherto been a valid Man-Search? By what light then, within or without, are we to see ourselves, and interpret ourselves, and thus know the Man of the Past, and the man on the street?

Surely, there has been no valid Man-Search by the many, and there has been no sane, clear Man-Search by the few. There has been a man-hunt and a man-plea: feudal man, hunting feudal man and pleading for him; and in the hunting and pleading glimpses were caught here and there of what was deemed a super-man. All of which was moonshine and the dance of death therein; for the normal man was never sought. He was assumed to be negligible and not worth the seeking.

Yet there has always been a general and a special sense of mutual aid, of tolerance and dependence. For, somehow and in some way, men had to cling together, since they all feared Life. Leadership, therefore, was desired, was deemed requisite, and was paid for. The weak and simple, and the strong but simple, paid a price to warrior, politician, and priest for services rendered and to be rendered. The price was high. It bred ambition then, it breeds ambition now. It sets agoing violently the dream of power, of gluttony, of over-much of everything. It hardens men's minds so that they can behold suffering unmoved. It awakens a monster in the dream of possession. It has kept and keeps men apart, this terrible price. It evoked the dream of exploitation, this high price—this premium set by the multitudes upon the powers of might and cunning; this prize offered by the multitudes to those who should betray them in the name of glory.

The average man is not weak. He merely thinks he is. He thinks so from force of habit, because of the grip of tradition, because of his absurdly false education, because of a varied and curious self-deprecation, an over-valuation and an over-awe of externals, an over-confidence in the powers of might and cunning, and a total misunderstanding and under-valuation of his own natural powers. For the average man will not search to find in himself the normal man.

He need not pay to be exploited under the guise of leadership. He need not foster the predatory. He need not warn the parasite.

For he is getting now a daily education in the practical way of life. He is beginning to see something new and novel to him within the stage-setting of the social play. Its traditional hidden secrets are becoming open secrets.

To the millions of men object lessons are coming very thick and fast, and they are coming too plain to be misunderstood. They are brutal lessons. Disillusioning, and yet awakening.

You are going to the public school now. Going to the great free but costly school of real life. There they are curiously watching the veils, rising seemingly of themselves, one by one, in an impressive transformation scene, as the plain ways of crafty men are set forth so unmistakably that each average man may now see, therein, his own ways, sharply stated.

It is a new school and a good school, for it is a strictly modern and plain school which all the people are attending every day. They are learning the way the thing has been done; the magical way of doing treacherous things, the magical and glorified way of stealing, of lying, of murdering.

No man need now wear the dunce's cap.

Formerly the children, only, went to school. Now at last it is the turn of grown men also. The time has been long in coming, but it is here.

The average man needs the training. His great need is to see complicated things in a simple way, that their underlying simplicity may reveal itself to him, and he thus acquire the rudiments of the great and only art of plain-seeing, plain-feeling, plain-thinking, and plain-doing.

The average man may now affirm his manhood if he choose. Such thing was not deemed possible in the past, either by himself or by the exalted parasites which he harbored in his fantasy of fear. But it is possible, now.

To achieve this he must pay the new price. That price is none other than the immediate abandonment of his own private rascality, his own private superstitions, his own particular recklessness, his own special and general irresponsibility, his absurd and destructive unwillingness to think beyond himself, to feel beyond himself and his private prejudices. It is to these vices that he is and ever has been slave, not to any potentate, warrior or priest of the past, or any high financier, captain of industry or politician of the present. No man is, or ever was, or ever could be, slave to another man. The average man is now and ever has been slave to himself alone, and his enfranchisement, his freedom rests now, as ever, with himself alone.

The mighty have ever been but the mirages, symbols, the explanation of the average man; the little things mentioned are the origins of the mirage. The small everyday perfidies and stupidities of men are the realities that fertilize all the big rascalities and all the big stupidities because, forsooth, men do not see the neighbor with open eyes; because, they habitually see him by and in a false light.

Man may therefore now substitute the new price for the old, if he will. Has he the nerve? Can he, as yet, see straight enough, think straight enough, feel straight enough and act straight enough to accomplish the thing in himself. Or is he still intoxicated and maudlin with the old-time luxury of self, and thus an easy victim of the beguiler, high and low, eminent and obscure, rich and poor?—for the betrayer is of all men, and all things to all men.

It is a little thing, a simple thing; but it means self-control. Has he that self-control? Can he muster the resolve? Does he see himself clearly, or is he still in fact a weakling? If this latter were true, then would our man-search be ended, and man found. It would have been proven that he is too luxurious, too sentimental to be free.

And yet we, climbing to the towers, there looking far abroad to the horizon of mankind, descending to the level ground, prying familiarly, sharp and near, we are not yet satisfied, we are still searching. The searching that men have done in the past does not suffice us. It was not conclusive, clear. We are not satisfied with their light within or without. It was not the true light of man. The modern light is better: Still, it is not clear enough; but it is growing daily clearer. It is growing white, this modern light: Much like the sunlight. The old light was weaker—more like the moonlight and the starlight.

It is our dream to seen ancient and modern man set forth in outline, clearly defined; to have him accurately weighed in mind and heart, in thought and deed, and unequivocally known. To see the character of his thoughts very plainly shown: so plainly that he will know them as his own. That is our dream: it will surely take shape. It is now beginning to take shape in the world of men, for man now is being searched by man in earnest, in a new way. He is being examined high and low, rich and poor, eminent and obscure, present and past, by a new light within and without. He is being put under the microscope, his motives searched, his guiding thought searched, his acts searched, the near and far-reaching effects of his thoughts and acts searched. His attitude toward the neighbor is being carefully examined; and by what light within and without he confronts the neighbor, by and in what light he regards all men. The quality of this light is being carefully examined. We are much less impressed now, by what men say than was the man of the past. We prefer to scrutinize what they do. We prefer to assume as a working basis, what men do and have done toward their fellow men explains exactly what they think concerning man. And on this basis we will determine whether their thoughts are harmless or injurious to men. We are enquiring thus what "the survival of the fittest" means. And thus we examine the "standard" thoughts, the "classic" thoughts of men. We put them in contrast and in harmony with acts. We must know all. All must be opened up. All the dark corners must be explored. Not a cranny left unexplored. There must be no let-up, no hesitancy, no bashfulness, no timidity, no fear of man or God, no superstition concerning man or God—but one, single, fixed resolve to search all, to know all, to bring all into the open, to search man to the core, find that core, to ascertain its exact value, to cast aside that which is worthless, to cherish that which is of genuine value and worth, here and now, for the good of the man of today, and for the good of the man to come.

It is a serious business. It must be carefully and accurately done, relentlessly pushed to a conclusion, once and for all established, and man's real nature defined. We have had enough of mystery, of wonder and of Phantasm, let us now have the clear light. This is the new man-search, the real man-search, the new school. This is what the dawning of Democratic thinking and feeling means: that the people are to be bitten awake, and forced to do their own thinking, by the folly, the incompetence and the ignorant cruelty of the privileged few, that the people must sting themselves awake to a realization of their own folly, incompetence and ignorant cruelty. They must become aware, also, of the value of that good within them which has been theirs always, is now and ever shall be—of that very quality which makes them men, dependable and sound; of that, precisely, which they have hitherto quite stupidly denied and belittled; of that of which they are now, as of old, curiously ashamed, because they deem it almost jocularly small, simple, negligible—this splendid urging of creative good in them—their one sound, sane and lovable possession.

This is our dream. For there are modern dreams as well as ancient. Let us not forget that.

By the character of the dream, the dreamer is known. Let us not forget that either. Let us not be ashamed to dream: For that is all we do anyway.

There is much to dream about in our modern day! Fine new dreams. There is, for instance, a new man to dream about. There is quite certainly a new civilization to dream about. There is common sense to dream about —that new common sense which is, plainly enough, the beginning of practical Democracy.

And there is a new beauty to dream about. The beauty of a new day and its new doings. Its splendid new undertakings, its vast adventures. And there is kindness to dream about; the kindness of a new day and its clear new deeds as between man and man.

There is a new art of expression to be dreamed about. That new and splendid art to be of the real life of a wide-awake people, in which new, joyous and natural uses shall be satisfied, as simply, in terms of a new fitness, and a new propriety and warmth.

Let us not be ashamed. For to be not ashamed is in itself a new art for the people. And out of this new art will spring all the new arts. To be not ashamed is the very soul of inspiration: the beginning of the natural outburst of the song of man.

There is much to dream vividly about, plenty upon plenty, O men of today! The materials of inspiration are right with us and about us. It is for us to see them, for us to hear and feel them, to recognize the urge and the call and the need, and at once to do! For the new art will be the art of fittingly doing all things in accord with man's integrity and the beauty and the power of his spirit.

We do not dream enough, we moderns. We are to dream more; dream wisely, in a clean purposeful way.

We are to dream of the reality of man, of the reality of life, of a joyous life, a full and well-lived life for him; a life that counts—a man that counts. For if man, the real, living personality—any man—does not count, what counts?

How can a God count, when the average man does not really count?

We are thus to dream real and right dreams of human sunshine and gladness, with the joy of efficiently living and of efficiently doing, for why live if not to do? And why do if not to live? Dreams of health of body and mind; of radiant health, of health that shows in a lustrous eye. Dreams of the clean, sound, courageous and devoted heart. Dreams that count for us all—that really avail. Dreams of integrity; gentle, manly, spiritual integrity—livable, lovable, and delightfully valuable to all mankind, over all the earth.

So must we dream, naturally and intelligently of man. For he is worth dreaming about. He is filled with splendid native power.

It is such dreams that are apt to make a present and a future for us; something we can take hold of with our minds, something which shall give to our thoughts a definite aim, a clear purpose, a warm unifying inspiration and aspiration, with one clear, sane and ever in view: the liberation, development and utilization of what we are beginning to know as man's efficiency in all his faculties, all his capacities, all his uses. That is, the freeing of the real spirit in the real man. That is worthwhile.

Then will our dream spontaneously shape into a new civilization, a civilization that shall be true to man, and which, for that basic reason, shall be unending in purpose, inexhaustible in fertility—just as man himself is inexhaustible in his natural powers, his splendid powers.

That is a dream worthwhile.

That dream, we can achieve.

It is living in us all. It is altogether natural that we dream it. It is as completely natural, as the dream we now enact is completely a caricature and a barbarism.

Arouse, sleepers, our hour is at hand!

For the multitudes are the slumbering gods.

Remember the multitudes!

In them lies the power of creation, of sanction, of denial.

In them lies the all-powerful working will.

In them is the voice that says Yea!

The multitudes of earth are awakening, like seed wheat in the spring-time, they are pushing forth, from their ancient dream of the soil, the air, the forests, the seas, the mountains, the deserts. For the multitudes have been the earth-dreamers, and because of their faithful dream of the earth, they shall inherit the earth, as was said of old, by him who gave his life for the multitudes, by him who said: 'I am Life.'

Each man knows his heart.

Each man knows that he has the power of choice.

Each man knows that choice is everything.

Each man knows that to choose right is to choose well. It is simple.

Each man knows that to choose well is to do well.

Each man knows, to a living certainty, that to do well is the clear mission of man.

Each man knows that it is for this that he inhabits the earth.

Each man knows clearly, in his heart and his mind, that this is his sole reason for being. That thus, alone, can he justify his existence.

*   *   *   *

So dream the new dreams—dreamers all!!

Dream the dream of the awakening multitudes.

Help dream the dream of man and mankind.

This is the right road at our parting of the ways.

This is the first forward step on the new right road.

This is the law, without exception—the law of the life of the multitudes.

The law the world of men has searched for through the long ages.

The one law of self-preservation.

The splendid law of self-creation, of self-utterance, of self-efficiency of the multitudes of earth.

So shall we dream to see a people self-created in the image of its plain and clear integrity.

Then will human life cease to be the mirage and phantom it has been and the reality of civilization will surely emerge in the image of this new thought, this new wish, this new will, this new desire of the heart of the multitudes for the whole fair earth.

This is the law which the spirit of the All-Life is seeking to awaken to conscious recognition and acceptance in the spirit of all men today.

This is the Messianic law of the world's people, which, since the beginning, have dreamed to be truly free.

We shall arrive.

*   *   *   *

Now are we, earth-wide, awakening from the mystic dream of the past. Push on! All! Over all the earth! Push on! in the new Man-Search.

All ye dreamers dream on, work on, and the dream will come true. For it is a dream of thought, of action, of reality. It is indeed a dream of simple common sense, of simple common honesty, of simple common humanity; that is, of simple common kindness.

It is a dream to be dreamed by all in the open daylight, within the practical every-day working world of men and their thoughts and their doings.

The dream to be dreamed when we are all widest awake.

More than that: It will be the convincing sign, the proof, that we are all awake.

Then shall we cohere over the earth as one people, with one purpose— the good of all, the free spirit of each. That is the real Individualism. That is the real Collectivism. That is the real Democracy.

* * * *

It is now ours to invert the thought of the past. To set it right side up, right end to. We have the power because we are beginning to see straight, to feel straight, to think straight, to act straight. That was the only power needed.

* * * *

So let us dream this kindly and strong dream of dreams, supreme among all the dreams of all the peoples of the earth. We have seen something of man in his instability and folly. Let us seek to find and know him in his superb integrity, even though to find him we must walk through the valley of the shadow of death.

Man must now take an accounting of himself. In that accounting he will, for the first time, behold in himself the phantasm of the past, and for the first time will see likewise the real world of things and thoughts and men reflected within himself; and will understand it and himself.

It is simple.

That consciousness, that will, are becoming ours.

* * * *

Many were the prophets, poets, and teachers of yore who caught gleams and flashes of this truth. For this truth has been ever present. To see it is not new, but to see it clearly, to hold it steady, to put it to use is the modern power. Efficiently to utilize this power, the modern mind must completely rid itself of the ideals of warrior and priest, of trader, of parasite, and politician, that is to say of the hitherto exalted conceptions of what these, historically, have stood for as the elect of earth, namely, the right and the power of might and cunning, the sanctity of betrayal, the sacro-sanctity of exploitation. In place of these must be reared on high in the minds of men the conceptions of the inexhaustible power and right of man's integrity—the clearness, cleanness, sanctity, serenity and power of his free spirit, and this must be held universally true, not for one man, not for a few men, but for all men, for the multitudes who shall come thus into their heritage of the spirit and of the earth. This is what liberty means. This is what equality means. This is what fraternity means. These are not academic phrases. They are true word-symbols of man's reality: They stand for the intuitive and profound however dim perception by men, of the reality of what we are here calling Democracy. Truly there have been teachers and prophets. But the multitudes of the whole earth were not ready. It was still winter in their souls. The warning commotion of an Earth-springtime had not come. Hence there could have been no valid Man-Search by the multitudes; and until the multitudes should seek man, man could not effectively be found; for of what avail was it for one man, or a little coterie of men to find man? It is only what the mulitudes, what the peoples of the earth, broadly speaking, think and do and sanction, that counts, that ever did count or that ever will count: Witness the tragedy of the Christ!

Spirit

Throughout the history of men's thoughts, no conception has been so tragically obscuring and paralyzant as the notion of a Personal God.

It is against this adamantine wall that historic man, eminent and obscure, has broken his heart. (But not now for us in vain.)

It is this God, that has said: 'What is the use?'

It is this God that has said: 'This is no door! The wall alone is real!'

The personal God has been a twilight phantom by the door of truth. A phantom born of the darkened and pathetic soul of man to grow big therein and affright man, that he give it birth, and a name, and a place.

The phantom can not withstand the steadfast gaze of him who, seeking man, regards the gods as passing shows.

No god shall stand between us and man; for man is too precious that a god shall weigh against him in the balance.

All gods have failed to reflect justice on man. It remains for man to be just to himself.

This is of the philosophy of Democracy. It is to make short work of the great trifles we have called gods; and to stretch out to man the hand of welcome in the open world—our world—here—now—the round and kindly earth—our home. That fair earth upon which we must plant our feet, solid, secure, that the eye of Democracy, steadied, may focus clear, and plainly see; plainly recognize, and, with its high power of light-gathering, plainly accept the Spirit. For the gods are too gross—too material, too fatuous for this modern day of modern men and their quick needs, their earnest searching and desires, their unsatisfied seeking and yearning—their hope for that which shall fulfill their spirits, which shall ease the void in their hearts.

Let us burst our bands asunder. Let us brush aside all vain quibbles, and come forth at once to the perception that the mind is not in the body as we narrowly say, but that the body is in mind, and the body is mind. That the "power of mind over matter" is but a figure of speech. For there is no matter. But that the power of man's spirit is at one with the All-Spirit—and by this alone he lives. That man is first, last and all the time a spiritual being—that to consider him aught else is folly, and is to know him not.

When we fully, clearly, vividly recognize man as Spirit, then and not till then can we conceive of him sanely as a power and a personality in the great way of Life. Then, and not till then, can we know and actually grasp what Choice means, what Desire means, and what Will means. Then we shall understand that we are to control imagination, that it is not to control us—as it has led astray our forebears, in its immensity of instant creative power—its marvellous response to the wish and will—its instant answer to the heart's desire.

Knowing man as spirit, as free spirit, we shall begin to know what Democracy means—that its program involves not a work for gods to do, but for men to do. For no god is equal to the task. Man's freed spirit alone is equal to its undertaking, and its undertaking is worthy and alone worthy of his spirits.

Thus we put the free spirit of man above all the gods; for if in his illusion he made them all, what, in his rationality, can he not make? He can make happiness—and this no radiant god is a symbol, has been powerful enough to do, He can make the grotesque thing we now call man into real man—and this no conception of a god has availed to do.

A just conception of man, alone can make man.

Thus man must rise above all his gods.

He must proclaim his free spirit.

He must create anew in the power of that spirit.

This is what Democracy means.

Gods are for slaves—

Spirit is for Man—

Arouse then, Man! Shake off the nightmare of the gods—and the sensuous dream of the gods—and with feet emplanted on the solid earth, shake off that fear which is the heritage of the dream of gods.

For man is Creator. No conceivable god can exist without man's consent—without his permission.

For man is still in his spirit masterful.

His grandest mastership is to be the mastery of himself.

His highest proclamation to say: 'I am spirit, I choose aright!'

Man has been supine before his god—

He must now stand erect before man.

He shall no longer hide behind a god.

He must come forth.

Come forth into the open world.

Where all may see.

Cleansed of mind, cleansed of heart, he must appear.

The day when man can hide is now good as gone forever.

For Democracy has surely dawned within the spirit of the world-man.

That dawn shall brighten until there be no place obscure—

No veil of illusion shall hide a god or an unjust man.

This is fiat!

*   *   *   *

The time is up—we must begin.

*   *   *   *

That man has waited long to find his spirit in the All-Spirit—how melancholy.

But let us not repine.

We have no time.

We must begin.

We must begin to undo and to do.

We must begin to build anew.

To recreate.

To regenerate

To transfigure.

To uprear out of the sweet sane kindliness of our hearts a civilization in the image of the free, the altogether glorious spirit of man.

For man is power. No other word means really aught to him.

Yet solely in his spirit will he justly know what power truly means.

Power means creation.

Creation means bringing forth.

To bring forth man must call forth—Liberate.

He in his spirit must evoke its integrity. Then shall we say to Life the Worker: I know thee—for thou art of my Spirit—come forth, thou— come forth into my world—For I in the clarity and integrity of Spirit have chosen aright—Have chosen man as my fellow Spirit.

Then shall he say to the All-Spirit: Come forth thou, Spirit Sublime! Spirit of earth and air—come thou forth into my new world, the world of Life, its joy, its abundance, its everlasting sweetness. Come thou forth for I am Man the Welcomer!

Lo! I open the door to thee, the door of the truth in me. Lo! I part all veils for thee, that thou come in to my sanctuary.

Lo! I go out to thee to greet thee in the open—in a fair world, a world grown now fair in the power of my wish and will.

For I, willing, wishing in my spirit to be erect, have become man, and so becoming, have reached that wisdom wherein the neighbor-man rises to the level of mine eyes—and the world becomes a fair, fit world for him and for me—our home, our dwelling place.

It is enough!

The scales have fallen from mine eyes.

Risen to manhood I see man.

Awakened to my spirit, I see Spirit in all, by all and for all.

Awakened to my heart, I behold as a revelation what justice means— that justice of integrity which is begotten of my spirit, and whose new name shall be Kindness.

Awakened to my strength, I know now what work means—Its new name shall be Usefulness.

Awakened to my calm—I know now what gentleness means—its new name shall be Power.

So shall I name, with new names, as my spirit moves forth into my new world, and the new names shall stand for new thoughts, new deeds, for a new joy, a new peace, a new serenity, a new virility—a new and an everlasting certainty.

For I, of Earth, shall walk upon the Earth, even as my Spirit is of Spirit.

Thus shall the myriad things be plain.

And thus in new power shall I make the Great Way of the Life of Mankind—

For to my spirit alone befits Spirit.

This alone is worthy of man.

And this shall englory man.

Dusk of Gods: Dawn of Ego

It is man himself that we find precious.

It is the startling drama of his historic life that we find impressive as an object lesson explaining him. For that drama is the phantasm not only of what he has been and is, but as well, and even more impressively, the clear symbol of what he is to be and is becoming.

Therefore we treat man freely—without fear, without reproach, without self-reproach. We set him forth as he has set himself forth plastically in his acts. We portray him as he has portrayed himself. We picture him as he pictures himself. In passing, we peradventure tread on the toes of those egoists who today deny and seek to obscure man's natural powers and the wonder of his spirit.

For the wonder of man lies in this, that he is man. And to him who with broad view and sweeping vision sees man pictured forth in his great historic and natural setting the wonder increases with the thought that man, amid all the complexity of his self-created environment, never perceived himself therein as clearly as the creator thereof. Never saw in his own environment the explanation of himself. Never suspected that his civilizations, lying plainly before his eyes were clear testimonials or witnesses of himself.

It is the strangest of phenomena that man, living with himself, has not suspected himself; has not divined his real nature.

Thus has historic man been as subjective, as self-engrossed as is the modern man on the street.

So engrossed with self that he seems to have been unaware that he himself was present.

He neither saw himself, felt himself, nor heard himself, so completely dominated was he by the phantasms he had put forth out of himself, and believed in turn to be realities independent of himself.

This is the marvel of the man of the past as it is the marvel of the man of today, that he has no rational notion of himself, as man.

Man throughout his career has been deeply subjective, and is so today. Clearly he has been self-imprisoned; clearly he is so today.

He has been the historic dreamer, the visionary who dreamed not of himself as a spirituality nor of his powers as spiritual powers. Who dreamed out of himself, not of himself; whatever in viewing the splendor of his philosophies and his religions he may have believed to the contrary.

He has been rather the historic dramatist who imaged forth the action of his own soul, believing it, meanwhile, a play of portentous externals.

He has been the automatic philosopher responding in a trance to the pressure of the unseen, and pushing forth into the hallucination of abstraction that which was of the very essence of the Worker Life, working in response to the predisposing choice of his spirit.

He had been the ecstatic, painting upon the heavens an image of his emotions of hope and fear, yes, of supreme longing; suffusing the earth and all things thereon with the passionate coloring of his heart's intense desires. But withal he saw not the reality of earth, nor of the firmament. For he believed his heaven and his earth to be not of himself.

He has been the lowly earth-creeper—denying all of himself, abasing himself—attributing all power to all things and all men but himself. And yet behold, the earth-creeper as god-creator and adorer of that which he, like the one busy in sleep, made out of the tissue of that sleep—even as he believed himself awake, and that which he adored to be beyond his reach.

Behold him too a worker with his hands. See the marvels he has made with his hands. See how he has written of himself in enduring stone, records of himself, of his moods and his doings. How he made of himself pictures in stone. How he made of himself pictures in everything that he did with his hands. He saw before himself, saw with his own eyes these very pictures that he made with his hands—those hands that interpreted his soul, and yet he knew them not as likenesses of himself, he knew not how faithfully and objectively they portrayed him.

We know how well they portrayed him, but we do not know how faithfully our own civilization portrays us, what a startling likeness it is. We do not seem to know how vividly it is an object lesson explaining to us the free spirit. For we too, like the man of old, believe it all to be external to ourselves. And we call it our environment; we do not call it ourselves.

For we too are somnambulists, making things out of the urge of ourselves and calling meanwhile the urge, Fate, Destiny.

We too do wonderful things with our hands. And with our hands we have made marvels which are powerful and subtle extensions of our hands. But we know not what these marvels mean. For in them we have utterly failed to see ourselves pictured, have dismally failed to see them as explanations of ourselves and of the significance of man.

For we say we need perspective; we say one cannot see his own times, his own generation, the significance and the drift of it. Unaware are we that we make the perspective along with the rest, that it is all there. Easily enough seen when man emerging from his subjectivity, comes forth into the world and sees himself from the many points of view of the things he has created.

For man is the timid animal. A fearless fighter, a reckless gambler, a desperate adventurer, he has been a bashful thinker. Even in his loftiest flights he has not dared to go out of himself and look squarely at himself from without. He has been woefully afraid of the clear stillness of the great open world.

Fond has he been of the obscurity he has created, even as he has shrunk from the light in which he lived—imagining the delicate and diaphanous obscurity of his tenuous thinking to be the light.

At times man has awakened briefly, and then has closed his eyes again in sleep, and gone on with his dream-work. Even as his eyes were open seemingly, he saw only that which he projected forth. Thus he saw man not as man, but as what he in his dream believed man to be—that is he saw the neighbor as a vivid phantasm, pleasing or horrible—and knew not this phantasm as an explanation of himself and his power—an object lesson. Hence he could not explain himself by the neighbor, but thought the neighbor different.

Thus the lowly could not understand that the powerful and exalted were phantasms or subjective projections of themselves. They could not objectively see the exalted.

And thus equally, the exalted knew not that the lowly were but their own subjective images, creeping on the earth.

Nor does the modern intellectual man see the world of his day other than as he conceives it subjectively; for he is but an intellectual prisoner, in contradistinction to the unintellectual prisoner. He too does not go forth into the world to see what it is, to see what he is from the viewpoint of the world. He remains within and gazes upon dissolving views. He does not go forth into the world, there to seek an explanation of himself. How can he, for he believes that other men are different. This is his subjective preconception. He seeks not objective illumination.

Hence he talks foolishly about the world of men and about himself—knowing neither.

Therefore he utters dreamy things concerning man and man's god. Frivolous things concerning man's natural powers. Imbecile things concerning the struggle for existence. Idiotic things concerning the survival of the fittest, inhuman things concerning humanity, unjust things concerning justice, false things concerning truth, and unreal things concerning reality.

In other words, this shadow-man makes with his intellect but a magic play of shadows, having naught to do with the real man and the real way of life. For not knowing his projections to be shadows, he suspects not that these shadows explain him.

For the one thing the intellectual man seeks not is an explanation of himself and his futility. His feudal ego will not permit this. He does not wish to believe himself futile; he half believes this only in a world-engulfing vision of despair—a despair that is itself futile. And yet it is now become necessary and fitting that he perceive his futility in order that he may perceive a deeper and a real usefulness in himself, a usefulness that is surely there, a genuine usefulness to his fellow man—the thoroughgoing usefulness of seeing straight, thinking straight, and acting straight, in a straightening world.

We need real men because we have so many dreamers whom we deem real and who deem themselves real.

What we want to dispense with is that elaboration of getting at simple things, which passes under the name of intellectuality, or the other misnomer 'practicality.'

What we want is to get at simple things (which are the real things— the great, portentous things) simply, quickly and clearly.

We want focus!

We have too much apparatus.

We have too much harness, too many intellectual trappings.

We are overburdened and in our own way.

The light within now casts but a shadow without. Each man casts a long murky shadow spreading like a fan.

What we want is to discover that there is a great white light without— that in this light we belong.

When we step out into that light, we can see things clear and plain and we can see ourselves clear and plain—without the artifice of elaborate intellectuality. It is absurd for man to live within a walking library. This is not culture, it is folly. Things are too plain for that, man is too plain, injustice is too plain, so is unhappiness; and so is the great way out!—The Door!

Man has but to open the Door, and go through that portal of self OUT into the world. It will be for him a great new world indeed. The object lessons are all there, the explanations are all there. The clarity, the light is there; and in that clarity man will see himself newly pictured forth objectively and will behold the marvellous nature of his powers for creative good, which he has chosen hitherto to obscure.

Heretofore man has been the slave of his objectivity. He has gaged the world by his selfish ego, brutal or refined or superfined as the case may be.

Hereafter his spirit shall assume mastery—for spirit is objective—no matter what has been said to the contrary. Spirit alone is clear, direct, single.

Thus has man's ancient and long-lived world been a world of the subjective; and man therein has been ignorant of his ignorance, and thus prisoner of self.

His new world of Democracy shall be an objective world of vastly greater power. A world wherein man shall be free, conscious of himself, conscious of the neighbor, clearly aware of his responsibility to man: a world wherein his marvellous latent powers shall unfold, because he will release them. A world in which injustice would be an incongruity for he will see man clearly.

A world in which unhappiness would be an absurdity for rational man cannot create unhappiness.

A world in which man would not lie—for what would there be to lie about?

A world in which man would not steal, for why steal?

A world in which man would not betray—for why betray?

In which he would not kill, for why kill?

It is impossible that rational man, he of the free spirit, he of the clear eye, should do such gross self-contradictions.

It is only feudal man, subjective, self-engrossed, self-inverted, creator of phantasms and believer in their solidity to whose mind such horrors are welcome, who has for them a cultivated appetite.

That man in the twentieth century should remain feudal is one of the marvels of the history of his subjective and imprisoned mind, one of the phenomena of his fear, of his astounding timidity.

That he is beginning to emerge from his subjective state of fear, that he is beginning to suspect vaguely, dimly, furtively, that there is another world for man, the world of his freed spirit, that he is beginning to have vague sensations of justice, glimmerings of humanity, fitful flashes of insight into man's true powers, wandering impulses of self-reliance, misgivings concerning the evil he is doing and the follies he has considered sacred, is but to say that these are among the tremors of his awakening—

disturbances within the soul of feudal man of today, heir of feudal man of the past.

This however is not to deny or belittle the imaginative power of the man of the past. It is however to say that he did not understand the true nature of that power and how magically it victimized him, bewildered him, exalted and depressed him, rewarded and punished him, made a heaven and a hell for him, and populated for him an unseen world. Also it inspired him to deeds of valor, of hardihood, of adventure. It solaced him in the agony of his sorrow. It urged him on in his desire to know, even as it created within him all his passions, all his virtues. Remove imagination from the man of the past and there is no man of the past. What he could not grasp was that such enormous power should be his own. So he attributed it to divinity, which was what his imagination itself pictured to him, though he knew it not. When it did flicker forth before him, it but envenomed him with the lust for power and an intoxicating ambition to be himself a god of might, and subjugate his kind through force and cunning.

Thus from his subjectivity poured forth a gorgeous and marvellous stream of thought immeasurably varied, resplendent, sombre, delicate, majestic, pictorially sublime, playful, dainty, exquisite, fierce, portentous, towering, and bottomless.

But man knew not, except in glimpses that this power was himself, and that its superb workmanship explained himself—that in the very works of his imagination was to be found his explanation, if but he looked. But he as mass-man did not look. At times the few looked, and then in profoundest illusion. Had he but looked he would have been Life, the Great Worker, at work—the genius of his Choice. But man looked out not in, and in, not out; hence he saw not his imagination; it was always otherwhere. Hence his spirit and its power he knew not; for phantasms held him in too great a thrall; he but ascended to the heights of automatism.

Thus the man of the past stands forth a stupendous figure, sublime in his varied modes of subjectivity.

And just therein is sure prophecy that he, in us, as his heirs (perennial man) is to stand forth anew, sublime in objectivity, in the knowledge and sure grasp of his imagination and the clear consciousness of his spirit's power.

For man has been long in preparing. That preparation has been naught else than the great drama of his feudalism. That drama in which imagination created forth as phantasms, as veritable ghosts, through man as medium, the hosts of gods of earth and air—and the hosts of the egos of man.

Thus came forth from man his religions to be for us explanations of him. And likewise came forth his philosophies, his literatures, his poetries, his arts, all to be for us explanations of him, and powerfully, likewise to suggest to our own imagination that it peer carefully into his, and there find the key to our own hallucinations, and to body forth with that self-same imagination, henceforth controlled, the conception of a new world of clarity, wherein we are to recognize the quality and power of that very imagination itself, which, having first made man slave, will anon make him free. For the great and superbest quality of imagination is its power not so much to make pictures, as to illuminate facts.

Hence having once discovered imagination for what it is—man's direct response to the worker Life—the wondrous tie between himself and all that is in but seeming other than himself, it remains to utilize it for the creating forth of a new civilization, befitting man, thus so marvellously endowed.

For man surely is begotten, as we say, of Spirit. He is of spirit only, because there is naught else of which man can be. He is far greater in fact than his imagination, even, has ever yet bodied him forth to himself.

His actual powers are indeed beyond our present grasp. But of all his powers available now, the most useful is his power to banish the phantom of feudalism.

For him then to create by choice a true civilization formed in the image of his own free spirit by the power of his imagination, his will and his hands, must clearly be for him the joy of joys, the enterprise of enterprises, the most thrilling adventure of man—to create a new world.

And such is the imminent program of Democracy—for time flies—we must begin.

*   *   *   *

Thus if the civilizations of the Man of the Past explain him, that is, set forth the systematic working of his imagination, his choice, his will, and the work of his hands, so, in the same sense does our civilization explain us, and set forth the systematic working of our imagination, our choice, our will, and the work of our hands.

And if the phenomena or facts of his civilizations form as it were a closed circle about the Man of the Past from the vantage ground of any point, or all points in the periphery of which we may look straight into his soul, so it is with our civilization and ourselves.

If we take our moving standpoint in the phenomena or facts of modern civilization, we may clearly see modern man. Thus may we see ourselves, either by viewing our thoughts, going forth and reaching their conclusions in phenomena or facts; or by tracing back from the facts to their origin in our thought.

The result of such progress is startling in its revelation of our intense feudalism. It sets forth our world of phantasms; that we have not our feet upon the ground, that our eyesight is unsteady, our imagination violent, and our will weak because it seeks to accomplish its ends by force and cunning and not by the release of Life. It sets forth that we are unhappy because we cherish an inverted, and a truly sombre tragic notion of ourselves—even as we know it not.

Historic man has had his thousands of egos pushing out of him like buds upon a tree, and the Man of Today has his thousands of egos— attitudes of his spirit.

Out of the selfish ego spring the two great subjective phantasms—I and mine—and not I and not mine.

Therefore out of his same ego springs the desire to kill. Out of what else could it spring?

For the selfish ego itself is a cruel phantasm.

It is subjective man's inverted notion of himself.

Hence is man unhappy because of this inversion.

Because he cherishes this inverted notion of himself he says; I—I! And, so saying he talks as in a heavy sleep.

Thus it is man the phantasm that says I—I!

This is manifestly not the real ego.

The real ego of all the egos is spirit, not phantasm; and spirit is clear, luminous, universal, objective.

And the will of the phantasmal or feudal ego is not the real will of man.

The real will is of spirit—of its clarity, its luminosity, its universality in power. The true will operates not by force—which is weakness—but by its release of the power of Life, which is the true and the tireless power and process.

And the imagination of the phantasmal, the feudal ego is not the real imagination of man.

The real imagination is of spirit—of its lucidity, its clarity, its powerful and universal luminosity. It is the white light of the liberated democratic ego, rather than the phosphorescent gleaming of the submerged and feudal ego.

Hence the real imagination will body forth real things in a real world wherein men are real, clear, visible to each other.

Indeed, it will body forth the splendor and the peace of such a world.

*   *   *   *

Thus is the history of man a history of hallucination and inversion. Under the sway of hallucination he has lied, stolen, betrayed, and killed his kind because he knew them not, and this also is the story of the man of today.

Historic man had not his feet upon the ground; nor has the man on the street, today.

Man has lacked and now lacks firm footing on his earth. Thus unstable, he cannot see straight. When his feet shall touch the real earth, the shock will jar him awake and bring his mind to an objective focus.

Hence it is that man's religions have been unreal, unearthly, and unhuman. Man has sought beyond for a happines he confessed he could not create here on his earth—for he knew not his earth—he knew not the significance of HERE—hence he knew not how or where or when to look, and out of what to create.

Thus out of the squalor of his subjectivity he cast up phantom gods of purity. These he called ideals to distinguish them from his workaday illusions.

Now and then man turned his mind in upon itself and saw many wonders there; but he did not see the gods there for he had pushed them outside; nor did he see himself there—he should have looked outside for that.

*   *   *   *

Man pushes out his phantasms and then he draws them in. Out of his darkened soul he pushed a heaven and a hell, and now he is drawing them in again, drawing them into himself whence they came.

And man once pushed up a peasant and made of him a god in the heavens, making of him an interceder with a greater god, calling him the son thereof. Now he is pulling the son of god back into a peasant man again—drawing him to earth once more.

Truly is man a wonder and a magician, such a flock of things has he made to come out of himself with the waving wand of his imagination. Let him but wave the wand aright, and he will as magically come to know how and why he is a magician, and, so knowing, will cause new wonders to flow out of him and take shape as a civilization, in which there shall be such a new thing as joy in the life of the earth.

Foolish magician to lay such stress upon his reason, when that which he does transcends reason.

Modern man laughs at fairy tales; he says they are for children. Foolish man, for he himself is a fairy tale, the teller of it, and the child listening to it. It is a tale of goblins today. It may be a tale of sprites tomorrow.

Foolish magician to look upon himself as mere clay, because someone once said that he was of the dust of the earth. So is the fragrant flower of the dust of the earth—so is the forest tree—Truly of the dust of the earth, and what is this dust of earth that it becomes man and the flower and the tree?

One would suppose that modern man, having reason, would know what he is doing, but he does not; which would imply that he really has not reason, or that his reason is ineffectual, for he cannot see when and where and how he is now an ogre is devouring his kind.

Man has supposed that he can be only one thing at a time. Hence he has said, I am a practical man—thus mocking himself.

Once man the magician said that the Sun was God—then he said fire was the sun, and he must light a fire upon the rising of the sun. Then he said that unless first he lighted a fire the sun could not rise; that thus by his magic, he had made the sun his slave. Meanwhile the earth gently turned then as now, carrying the magician noiselessly round and about and along with it—while he lighted a fire that the sun, his god, his slave, might be compelled to rise. Man turns because he is on the earth. The earth does not turn because man is on it. Nor does the sun cease to go on its way because man does or does not light a fire—man's former view to the contrary.

Then man the magician discovered that the stars were larger than the sun. Then he said, I am but a speck, and powerless: forgetting that he had said but a short time before that if he did not light a fire the sun must surely die.

Truly man the magician discovered that although himself a speck he, in turn was made up of myriads of specks so small that he marvelled and said, behold I myself am a universe! and this that I have called matter is conscious like myself! But he went on killing his kind just the same as of old. He has not as yet changed his mind, concerning this.

Truly man is absurd; more fantastical and volatile than any fairy tale. He runs after sublimities, knowing not that he himself is sublime as he is absurd. And man is most erratic of all in the solemnity of his wisdom, for out of his wisdom he quaintly omits justice, and in his wisdom forgets man. For man, it seems, loves wisdom for its own sake—which is a luxurious folly. 'Twere better to esteem man for man's sake.

Nevertheless man also is a wonder, even in his folly, for naught else on earth or beyond the sun has such capacity for folly and such relish. Not satisfied with speech and his daily acts, he has put his follies in thousands of books, and, indeed, has institutionalized them that they might be sacredly perpetuated.

And yet man looms larger and larger and more potent even as we perceive his folly; for he, magician, has but to wave his wand and Presto!—The joy of life appears!

* * * *

It is man's magical imaginative power that has set up in him the ferment of unrest. Knowing not its nature, he suffered from its uncontrolled phantasies, its terrible pranks, the vast allegories that it made out of his simple desires and the passions it created; for he could not believe that he, mere man, could be possessor of such terrific and subtle power.

And yet he sighed for power, and even dreamed in solitude that he might perhaps enslave Earth and all the gods. This was his supreme allegory, his uttermost dream. It foreshadowed us and will come true with us; for we shall acquire that power, of which he dreamed, through liberation of those powers his earth and his supreme god and his ego stood for as symbols; that is, the powers of the worker, Life. For to the ancient sage the earth and the gods and his ego were but images, all unknown, of Life, The Worker—at work. Images he could not interpret, for he could not interpret himself as man, and, so failing, believed power to mean compulsion. Hence he could not see that his own true powers, when they were flowing, flowed without compulsion. Thus he could not interpret the results—could not see his spirit in them—could not see how he had forgotten man in the profound and sombre egoism of his dream of power. Hence he was a magician to create, but not a seer to interpret. It is for modern man therefore to become interpreter of past and present; to be seer of his own magical imagination; seer of his fellow man.

* * * *

Modern man now works with too heavy, harsh and literal an aspect of his mind. He uses his eyes too little, seeing with them too little. He has solemnly and cynically come to distrust his imagination, and believes he suppresses it, unaware that it is ceaselessly at work just the same, conjuring for him new and recrudescent phantasms, new hebetudes—gloomy and fatalistic as of yore—phantasms of toil, of industrialism, of commerce, of war, of poverty, of riches, of apathy, and of dominion—and yet evoking also glimmerings and gleamings—even as of old. For man's imagination can take all color and definition out of his life and make it sordid, dull, wearisome and inert. So man today is a magician as of yore; he bodies forth a world of strain and stress, and such a world is thus here with him—by the power and by the sole power of his choice.

It is now plainly time for modern man to see straight. The nature of his spirit which contains his power of choice is clear before him. So is the nature of the power of Life to work. The true nature and function of his will is, clearly to release the beneficence of that Worker Power by virtue of his choice. And the true magic of his imagination is to illuminate the world of men and thoughts and things as they now stand, to illuminate the true nature of man's responsibility to man, and to body forth as a picture great and clear, a New World of Democracy at whose threshold he now stands.

He has now seen spread before him the great world of Feudalism. He has seen the feudal thought-world pictured as an apparition standing beside the door of Democracy set within a phantasmal adamantine wall the feudal ego had upreared and had called Fate. He had heard the Phantom warning cry: What is the use?

It is for him to lay the ghost with its own cry. To open wide the Door. And, as a free man, a free spirit—enter his new world. There to be a truly practical man. Successful, at last, through the long brooding of the ages, successful in achieveing mastery of self through clarity of vision.

Ego

The universe and all therein may be expressed by the word Ego.

The ancient Jews questioned their God, Yahveh, asking, who art thou? And he said: I am.

And because this was the first and the last word that the god could say of himself, so is it the first and the last word that man can say of himself.

And man cannot logically say Ego without including All-Ego.

Nor can he speak of an All-Ego without including himself.

Ego is therefore the I AM of all things.

It is for this reason that there can be no dividing line between what we call physical and what we call spiritual.

Man has found no line that he could cross and say, here it is!

For, go where he will, search where he will—there he finds consciousness.

He speaks bravely of matter, but can find no such thing.

He speaks weakly of Life, for he fears.

And yet Life is I AM.

Life sings its song: It is the song of Ego.

Man sings the song of death—the song of fear, the song of distrust—for he knows not Ego. He will not believe that Ego is I AM—and that there is but one I AM, universal, and himself.

No, man has not believed in Integrity—hence his anguish.

Man has not believed in himself—hence his sorrow.

For man knows not Ego. He talks of the gods, and he talks of the great. He talks of the rich and he talks of the poor; But he speaks not of Ego, because he knows not Ego.

Man teaches the child to fear—knowing not what he does—for he knows not Ego.

Man sends the child to school: to learn what?—fictions. For the school knows not Ego.

Man takes the child to church: to learn what?—fictions. For the church knows not Ego.

School and Church speak not one word of Integrity—as though it were not the primal law—the only law—the I AM.

Hence are School and Church phantom; for Ego is real: and the spirit of man is Ego.

What pathos in man's self-inversion, his self-eclipse, that he should set up phantom for reality, shadow for light, and fear his own phantom—and break his heart for it. And, like a ghost walk with his back to reality, as though reality were not Ego.

And man talks, and talks, and talks; meanwhile kills he the first born and the last born alike.

Madman, to be a grafter! For where there is graft, there must be ghosts and sorrow, for you and yours, and perplexity, and disease and poverty and huge ghostly riches.

It cannot be otherwise.

Madman, to betray!

Madman, to steal!

Madman, to kill his young!

These are your phantoms.

Integrity, alone, is real.

Man has grafted through the ages.

He must now stop.

It is the way out.

It is the solution.

It is fantastic to suggest as a social basis any law but the law of Integrity—the law of Ego.

Man has thought otherwise through the ages, and has paid the price.

Man still thinks otherwise and is still paying the price.

Hence his Song of Death and his Dance of Death.

Hence his Phantom by the Door.

Hence the wall which he calls Fate.

Hence the Crucifixion, now, as of old.

For it is graft, graft, graft!

O, man on the street, can you not see, can you not hear? Can you not see the Dance of Death and hear the Song of Death, when they are so plain and the cause of them is so plain and near to you and of you!

Why walk, or pretend to walk, in a trance, O, man on the street, knowing not Ego?— or denying Ego?

Why be so absurd, or so malignant, as to say you are sensible and practical?

You are now at the parting of your ways. O, man on the street, whoever you are and whatever your name may be, high or low, rich or poor, eminent or obscure.

Your time has come.

The cock is crowing the shrillest dawn that the world has known.

You must declare yourself!

For you are found out—one and all.

You must declare for Integrity or against it.

You must declare for social efficiency or against it.

You must declare for an art and science of civilization or against it.

When you cease to graft your thoughts turn in splendor to your fellow men.

The rest is easy because it is clear and straight.

It merely means work.

And, to create, to construct, to build, to put forth out of himself, is man's natural work.

It is the free and full expression of Ego.

A new world will open.

The world of Ego and its dream of power.

The world of Integrity of man and his works.

Then will awaken in you, Poetry, long sleeping; and you will vision forth!

Then will you do things right because you will seek, with unswerving attention and reflection, how to do things right.

Then will the artist in you and the scientist in you awaken and be strong, whoever you are.

Then will you go forth into the great open world.

Then will you hear Life sing its Songs of Songs

To you!

Then shall you wish and will.

And you shall become, because of your wishing and willing.

Then will the wall you have called Fate

Tremble and dissolve.

Then will the Phantom by the Door

Hover and go.

Then will you know the use

For you will know man

The Ego.

The dawn is breaking.

NOW BEGIN!

A SELECTION FROM
THE AUTOBIOGRAPY OF AN IDEA

In the very last months of his life, the dying Sullivan roused himself to the production of two final works, each of which he intended as a memorial to vital aspects of his life's work. One of these, *A System of Architectural Ornament According with a Theory of Man's Powers* (published by the American Institute of Architects in 1924 and recently re-issued by the Prairie School Press, Park Forest, Ill.), consists of a series of plates illustrating, with brief text, the elements of design for which he was famous. The other, *The Autobiography of an Idea,* was an attempt to explain how his basic insights and convictions grew out of the circumstances of his life—and withstood them. Both volumes were finished and published in the year of his death, 1924. Mortal exhaustion is evident in many pages of the *Autobiography*—but least so, perhaps, in the following chapter where he eloquently restates his faith.

Face to Face

If with open mind one reads and observes industriously and long; if in so doing one covers a wide field and so covering reflects in terms of realism, he is likely, soon or late, to be brought to a sudden consciousness that Man is an unknown quantity and his existence unsuspected.

One will be equally amazed to note that the philosophers, the theologians, of all times turned their backs upon Man; that, from the depths of introspection, fixing their gaze in all directions save the real one, they have uniformly evolved a phantasm, or a series of phantoms, and have declared such to be man in his reality—and such reality to be depraved. A small feature, however, was overlooked by them in the neglect to observe that their man, in his depravity, had created the gods. Their insistent view of man—a further product of their phantasy—lay in the dogma, protean in form, that man is creature.

Meanwhile the real man was always at their elbow, or moving in groups or multitudes about them, or even looking them in the eyes and holding converse with them. But they did not see him; he was too near, too com-monplace—too transparent. The gods were far away and could be under-stood.

The mighty man of war also turned his back. Yet the wise man, the warrior and the priest differed in no valid sense from the multitude en-folding them as in a genesis; for man in his state of depravity as creature, created these also, as his demigods.

Thus man, not knowing himself, and none else knowing him, lived as a mirage, within a world of mirage which he fancied real. It was real for him; for such is the habit of man's imagination in playing tricks with him in his credulity.

The careful reader and observer again may be astonished to note that to the multitudes imagination, as such, is unknown—that the multitudes are unconscious of this power within themselves. Hence the reader, the observer, who is not so completely unconscious of himself, becomes aware of the imposing phenomenon that the huge and varied superstructures of the civilizations of all times have rested for support on so tenuous a foundation as the fabric of the radiant dream of the multitudes. That in such dream he will clearly see Imagination playing its clandestine role. The mass imagination of the multitudes is thus seen to be the prime impell-ing and sustaining power in the origins and growth of the civilizations. Let the mass imagination withdraw its consent, withhold its nourishing ac-quiescence and faith, then the civilization founded thereon begins to wither at the top, emaciates, atrophies and dies. One will further note that such changes in the mass imagination, in the mass dream, are of highly varied origins; but once under way, are beyond recall.

One also minutely notes that the tricks of imagination are universal and beyond numbering in variety, permeating all phases of the social fabric. Hence man's vagaries and follies and cruelties are beyond computa-tion; yet all these betrayals and cajolings and trickeries flow from the same single source, namely the individual, unconscious that his imagina-tion is incessantly at work. Because he is not acquainted with its nature, and unaware that he is its puppet, his waking hours are a continuing dream of inverted Self.

It is the mass dream of inverted self, populous with fears overt and secret, that forms the continuous but gossamer thread upon which are strung as phantom beads all civilizations from the remotest past of record to that of the present day and hour. As we follow back upon this thread—one end of which is delicately attached to our own inverted secret thoughts, we find it unchanging from end to end, regardless of environment; the civilizations it passes through and upholds on its way are but local manifestations and exhibits.

This intense and continuing preoccupation with inverted self makes it clear why man has turned his back on man, and why man is still unknown to himself—and unsuspected.

So long as imagination slyly tricked him into self deprecation, self debasement, and the slavery of the creature conviction, or into the opposite, megalomania, with its unquenchable thirst for blood, for plunder, and dominion; or with siren song beguiled him through the portals of a closed world of abstraction, he could not know himself, and the neighbor must remain a stranger to be feared, despised, or placated.

Indeed, until we come as pioneers, to seek out and know imagination as such, to view it clearly defined as an erratic and dangerous power, to be controlled; until we have observed with realistic clarity its multifarious doings from black magic upward to mighty deeds of hand and head and heart, we shall remain remote from man's reality, and from the splendor of his native powers.

One who has made the rough pilgrimage through the jungled infirmities of philosophy, of theology, and through the wilderness of turbid dreamwords uttered by the practical man who deals in cold, hard facts; one who as pioneer worked his troubled way through the undergrowth of culture with its acceptances, its preconceptions and precious finalities; one who, led on by a faith unfaltering, at last arrives at the rendezvous with Life, here testifies the natural man as sound to the core and kindly, yet innocent of himself as the seat of genius, as container of limitless creative powers of beneficence.

Solely on the strength of this faith was begun the story of a child-dream of power.

*   *   *

Wherefore we may now inquire: What are these powers, and what is the reality we affirm to be man?

He is none other than ourselves divested of our wrappings. If we in imagination divest ourselves of our wrappings we may see that he is ourselves. If we remove our blinders we shall see more clearly. If we look out between the bars of our self-imprisonment, we may note him nearby, walking familiarly in the Garden of Life. Undoubtedly he is ourselves, he is our youth, he is our spirit, he is that within us which has yearned for frank utterance—how long—and still yearns.

It is appalling to think he is ourselves; to wake from our dreams and see him. Yet will it not be inspiriting to find him at our elbow—no longer a stranger—no longer to be feared? To know that he is like us all? To feel the widening sense, as we regard him, that he stands not only as our explanation, but as our self-revelation. True, he is not at all what we had supposed and what we have affirmed. Yet will he be grimly recognized as he comes into view—to our amaze, for he is precisely that which we have denied.

We may be shocked at first, retreat, and disclaim; for denial of the power of life is our habit of old. We have other habits of old woven into weird grotesqueries. These are among our wrappings.

* * *

Inasmuch as man has been affirmed herein as sound and kindly, let us examine him. Rest assured we shall find naught in him that is not truly in ourselves and was not there in latency at birth.

To begin: He is a *Worker* and a *Wanderer* in varied ways. With his bodily powers he may go here and there, he may move objects about, he may change the order of things. Here at the onset we find a portentous power—the power to change situations; he can make *new situations*. With his ten fingers he can do wonderful things, make things he needs, make accessory things to extend his muscular powers. Thus he *manipulates*— he further changes situations. He changes his own situations, he creates an environment of his own. One sees here the Adventurer, the Craftsman, the Doer—ever growing in power. Thus man's first collective power within himself is the power to aspire, to work—to wander—to go from place to place near and far—to return to his home.

Now comes into view that power we call *Curiosity*—and coupled with it the power to *inquire*. Man's power to inquire we call a mental power, to distinguish it from his somatic power. It may have had a beginning, it can have no end. The result of inquiry we call knowledge; its high objective we call science. The objective of science is more knowledge, more power; more inquiry, more power.

Now, if to the power to do we added the power to inquire, Man, the worker, grows visibly more compact in power, more potent to change situations and to make new situations for himself. The situation may be a deep gorge in a wilderness; the new situation shows a bridge spanning the chasm in one great leap. Thus it is that man himself, as it were, leaps the chasm, through the adventurous co-ordination of his power to inquire and his power to do. And thus the natural man ever enlarges his range of beneficence. His life experiences are real. He reverses the dictum I think: Therefore I am. It becomes in him, *I am: Therefore I inquire and do!*

It is this affirmative I AM that is man's reality.

Wherefore warrior, philosopher and priest turned their backs. This "I am" they could not see, could not suspect, even as it stood at their elbow regarding them with ordinary human eyes. For it had been settled long ago on abundant evidence that man is creature and depraved.

In the history of mankind there are recorded two great INVERSIONS. The first, set forth by the Nazarene to the effect that love is a greater power and more real than vengeance. The second, proclaimed the earth to be a sphere revolving in its course around the sun. These affirmations were made in the face of all evidence sacred to the contrary. Who could feel the earth revolving? Who could fail to see the sun rise and set? What but blood could satisfy, or an eye for an eye?

Hence man's powers were not seen as himself, nor himself as his powers. Such recognition would involve a reversal and inversion both of sacred lore and common sense.

In reactive consequence of age-long self-repression and self-beguilement the world of mankind is now preparing its way for a Third Inversion. The world of heart and head is becoming dimly sentient that man in his power is Free spirit—Creator. The long dream of inverted self is nearing its end. Emerging from the heritage of mystical unconsciousness and phantasy, the world of mankind is stirring. Man's deeds are about to become conscious deeds in the open. The beauty, the passion, the glory of the past shall merge into a new beauty, a new passion, a new glory as man approaches man, and recognizing him, rejoices in him and with him, as born in power.

Never in man's time has there been such sound warrant for an attitude of Optimism as in our own, the very present day. Yet to him who in myopic fear looks but at the troubled surface, there appears equal warrant in the phantasy of Pessimism. What a price man shall have paid for freedom! For freedom from the thrall of his parlous imagaination! For freedom from the strangle hold of his own phantasmal self!

* * *

He who has lived, alive, during the past fifty years has viewed an extraordinary drama. He who starting young, shall live through the coming fifty years will move within the action and scene shifting of a greater drama.

The gravitation of world thought and dream is shifting. Out of the serial collapses of age-long feudalism is arising a new view of man. For man's powers in certitude, approach the infinite. They unfold their intimate complexity to our view as an equally amazing solidarity, as we hold, steadfast, to the realistic concept of man as free spirit—as creator—even as the vast complexity in the outworking of the feudal thought simplifies into a basic concept of self-delusion and self-fear.

*   *   *

Our portrayal is not yet wholly clear. Let us go on. There lies another power in man. That power is MORAL: Its name is CHOICE! Within this one word, Choice, lies the story of man's world. It stands for the secret poise within him. It reveals as a flashlight all his imagings, his phantasies, his wilful thoughts, his deeds, from the greatest to the least, even in this gliding hour we call today. *This one word, Choice, stands for the sole and single power; it is the name of the mystery that lies behind the veil of all human appearances.* A word that dissolves the enigma of men's deeds. A word, a light that not only illuminates all his obvious works, all the inner springs and motives of his civilizations, but a light whose rays reach within the sanctuary of the secret thought of each and all, thus revealing the man of the past and the man of today, starkly in personal status as a social factor of beneficence or woe. Need we know man's thoughts? View his works, his deeds; they tell his choice.

Implicit in true freedom of spirit lies a proud and virile will. Such glorious power of free will to choose, envisages beneficent social responsibility as manifest and welcome. Here now stands in full light Man erect and conscious as a moral power. The will to choose aright lifts him to the peak of social vision whence he may forecast new and true situations.

*   *   *

The Free Spirit is the spirit of Joy. It delights to create in beauty. It is unafraid, it knows not fear. It declares the Earth to be its home, and the fragrance of Earth to be its inspiration. It is strong, it is mighty in beneficence. It views its powers with emotions of adventure. Humility it knows not. It dreams a civilization like unto itself. It would create such a world for mankind. It has the strength. It sees the strength of the fertile earth, the strength of the mounains, the valleys, the far spreading plains, the vast seas, the rivers and the rivulets, the great sky as a wondrous dome, the sun in its rising, its zenith, and its setting, and the night. It glories in these powers of earth and sky as in its own. It affirms itself integral with them all. It sees Life at work everywhere—Life, the mysterious, the companionable, the ineffable, the immensest and gentlest of powers, clothing the earth in a pattern of radiant sublimity, of tenderness, of fairy delicacy—ceaselessly at work. Thus the free spirit feels itself to be likewise clothed as with a flowing shoulder-garment, symbol of power akin to the fluent mystery and fecundity of Life. Thus it moves on the open with vision clear. Thus is man the wonder-worker bound up in friendship with the wonder-worker—Life.

Now the real man begins to shape within our vision.

Consider his primary powers: He, the *worker*, the *inquirer*, the *chooser*. And to these the wealth of his emotions—also powers. Think how manifold they are, how colorful; how with them he may dramatize his works, his thoughts, his choosings; how he may beautify his choice. Think of his power to *receive;* to receive through the channels of his senses, to receive through his mystic power of sympathy which brings understanding to illumine Knowledge. Think of what eyesight means as a power, the sense of touch, the power to hear, to listen; and the power of contemplation. Add these to his cumulating interblending power; then think again of his enlarging power to act. Deep down within him lies that power we call Imagination, the power instantly or slowly to picture forth, the power to act in advance of action; the power that knows no limitations, no boundaries, that renders vivid both giving and receiving; the inscrutable dynamic power that energizes all other powers. Think of man as Imagination! Then think of him as Will! Now enrich the story of his prior-mentioned powers with the flow of imagination and the steadiness of will. Think anew of his power to act; of the quantity and quality of this power.

Now thing of the freedom such power brings!

Think of the power we call Vision; that inner sight which encompasses the larger meanings of its outer world, which sees humanity in the broad, which beholds the powers without itself, which unifies its inner and its outer world, which sees far beyond where the eye leaves off seeing, and as sympathetic insight finds its goal in the real.

Now see Man go forth to work, inspired by his vision of the outer world, himself made eager by the passion to live and worthily to do!

See him go forth in certitude as seer, as prophet, as evangelist, proclaiming his faith—in certitude as worker, to build a new home.

See him, as poet, as troubadour, as he goes forth, singing the new song, the refreshing song—calling in carols: Awake! ye dreamers all, lift up your heads, and be your hearts lifted up that Life in splendor may come in: Ye who dream in the shadows and are sore perplexed.

Thus the multitudes vibrate, as they dream—at the sound of their dream.

It is the richness of the soul-life of the multitudes that inspires and at times appalls the observer. For the multitudes are compact of human beings—a vast ceaseless flow of individuals, each a dreamer, each latent in power, the mass moving noiselessly through time—slowly changing in its constancy of renewal.

*　　*　　*　　*

Thus though Man now appears before us in glamor as a maze of powers, we have not yet made his image clear in full, and in diversity.

While it is plain, when all wrappings are removed, we shall find all men to be alike in native possesion of essential powers, we are at once confronted by this paradox: That all men obviously are different; that no two are alike. In plain words we find each human being unique. When we say unique, we mean *the only one*. Thus each one is the only one. If we have mused long upon the immense fecundity and industry of Life, the paradox vanishes: The only one and the all coalesce. The individual and the mass become *one*, in a new phase of power whose stupendous potency of creative art in civilization stuns the sense of possibility.

Now opens to our view the Democratic Vista!

Now see unfold the power of the *only one* in multiple, and the *One* become a vast complex of unique powers inspired of its free spirit and its power of beneficence—its works now solidly founded on the full emergence of courage—the evanishment of fear!

*　　*　　*

Alas, the world has never known a sound social fabric, a fabric sound and clean to the core and kindly. For it has ever turned its back on Man. Through time immemorial it has, in overt and secret fear of self, been impotent to recognize the only one, the unique. Hence wars and more wars, pestilence, famine, and desolation; the rise and crumbling of immense fabrics.

The feudal concept of self-preservation is poisoned at the core by the virulent assumption of master and man, of potentate and slave, of external and internal suppression of the life urge of the only one—of its faith in human sacrifice as a means of salvation.

The *only one* is Ego—the I am—the unique—the most precious of man's powers, their source and summation in diversity. Without Ego, which is Life, man vanishes. Ego signifies Identity. It is the free spirit. It is not a tenant, it is the all in all. It is present everywhere throughout man's wondrous being. It is what we call the spiritual, a term now becoming interchangeable with the physical. It is the sign and symbol of man's immense Integrity—the I am that I am. To it the Earth, the world of humanity, the multitudes, the universe—become an Egocosm.

Thus to the eye of the earnest watcher, the dual man of legend and of present mythical belief fades, incorporeal as a ghost. Departing it leads the ghostly feudal scapegoat with its burden of sin.

It is man's manifest integrity that reveals him valid—sound to the core. It is this spiritual integrity that defines him human, that points true to his high moral power—the power of valid choice.

This new vision of man is the true vision of man.

Toward this new truth, this inversion, the world of mankind slowly turning, vaguely conscious, strives to articulate that which is as yet too deep, too remote, too new for its words. But it is not too deep, too remote or too new for its aspirations.

*   *   *

Thus in portrayal stands *Man the Reality:* Container of self-powers: A moving center of radiant energy: Awaiting his time to create anew in his proper image.

Are then the multitudes infertile? Is genius rare? Has our traditional education and culture left us wholly blind? Have we forgotten the children—Egos at our elbow? The springtide of genius there! Shall we continue to destroy? What is our *Choice?* How have we exercised it? How shall we exercise it? Is our moral power asleep? Are we without faith in our own?

Whence, then, this story of a child's dream of power?

What shall *our* dream be?

Our dream shall be of a civilization founded upon ideas thrillingly sane, a civilization, a social fabric squarely resting on man's quality of virtue as a human being; created by man, the real, in the image of his fruitful powers of beneficence; created in the likeness of his aspirant emotions, in response to the power and glory of his true imagination, the power of his intelligence, his ability to inquire, to do, to make new situations befitting his needs. A civilization that shall reflect man sound to the core and kindly in the exercise of his will to choose aright. A civilization that shall be the living voice, the spring song, the saga of the power of his Ego to banish fear and fate, and in the courage of adventure and of mastership to shape his destiny.

Such dream is the vigorous daylight dream of man's abounding power, that he may establish in beauty and in joy, on the earth, a dwelling place devoid of fear. That in the so doing he shall establish an anchorage within his universe, in courage, in the mighty spirit of adventure, of masterful craftsmanship, as he rises to the heights of the new art of all arts— the art of upbuilding for the race a new, a stable home.

* * *

Plainly the outworking of so sublime a conception as that of rearing the fabric of a worthwhile civilization upon the basic truth of man's reality as a sure foundation, implies the inversion of a host of fixed ideas consecrated by the wisdom of the ages. The time has come to place the wisdom of the ages in the balance of inquiry; to ascertain, when weighed, wherein it may be found wanting in the human sense. One sure test is sanity, for to be unkind is to be dangerously unbalanced.

It is also time to test out the folly of the ages, the multifarious corruption involved in abstract and concrete irresponsibility, the abuse of power, the abuse of the useful, the successive collapses and ruin, the ever present sense of instability, the all-prevading fear, the lack of anchorage.

So testing, we shall find that alike the wisdom and folly of the ages rest in utter insecurity upon a false concept of the nature of man. For both wisdom and folly have committed and still commit the double folly of turning away from man in contempt.

Glancing at our modern civilization we find on the surface crust essentialy the same idea at work that has prevailed throughout the past. Yet if we search beneath the surface we discern a new power of the multitudes everywhere at work. It is the power of a changing dream, of a changing choice; of Life urging upward to the open the free spirit of man—so long self-suppressed under the dead weight of the consecrated wisdom of the ages and its follies.

* * * *

The fabricating of a virile, a proud and kindly civilization, rich in its faith in man, is surely to constitute the absorbing interest of the coming generations. It will begin to take on its functional form out of the resolve of choice, and the liberation of those instincts within us which are akin to the dreams of childhood, and which, continuing on through the children and the children of the children, shall be a guide evermore. For who shall say the child is not the unsullied well spring of power!

The chief business now is to pave the way for the child, that it may grow wholesome, proud and stalwart in its native powers.

So doing we shall uncover to our view the amazing world of instinct in the child whence arises genius with its swift grasp of the real.

The great creative art of upbuilding a chosen and stable civilization with its unique culture, implies orderly concentration and organization of man's powers toward this sole end, consciously applied in each and every one of his socially constructive activities in the clear light of his understanding that the actualities of good and evil are resident in man's choice—and not elsewhere. Thus will arise a new *Morale* in its might!

And let it be well understood that such creative energy cannot arise from a welter of pallid abstractions as a soil, nor can it thrive within the tyranny of any cut and dried system of economics or politics. It must and will arise out of the heart, to be nurtured in common honesty by the intelligence, and by that sense of artistry which does not interfere with the growth of a living thing but encourages it to seek and find its own befitting form. Thus the living idea of man, the free spirit, master of his powers, shall find its form-image in a civilization which shall set forth the highest craftsmanship, the artistry of living joyously in stable equilibrium.

Thus widens the Democratic Vista!

* * *

The historic Feudal thought, sought and found its form in a series of civilizations resting upon a denial of man by the multitudes themselves, who sought cohesion in mutual fear of life, and out of the culture of fear they created their tyrants. Their unsafe anchorage lay in the idea of force, in its convincing outward show of domination, splendor and glory.

In terror of the unknown, in appeal for mediation, the multitudes passed their immense unconscious power to those they raised aloft—gods or men, and as value received they created and accepted the status of servitude. Those thus raised aloft became enormously parasitic, capping and sapping the strength of the multitudes. As the latter grew in self-sacrifice and poverty, they become luxurious in that they gave their all in the name of glory that their children, the great, might flourish. They staggered beneath the weight of the mighty they upheld aloft and who came to know them not—other than as beasts to toil or fight. Thus has the feudal superpower ever undermined its own foundation, ever, in recurring cycle, collapsing and renewing—renewing and collapsing. Times, places, names, local colors, mechanisms, countenances, change. The idea, the thought, the fear, persists through the ages.

* * *

For us the chief impress of the self-revealing story of mankind lies in the perception that all sanctioning power comes from below. From the vast human plenum we have called the multitudes, it arises gently, massively, step by step, stage by stage, height upon height; all of which but signifies the peoples' dreams of glory taking shape vicariously in their times and places. The spectacular and imposing groups and summits of the feudal superstructure have no other base, no other sanction. Like towering cumulus clouds they float upon thin air.

As there are truths that lie within truths, so are there dreams that lie within dreams. The most ancient of dreams lies indeed within the feudal dream. This dream is none other than the dream of the reality of man.

As truths one by one appear above the surface, ever more powerful, farther reaching as they come from greater depths of life, so the great deep dream of man's free spirit has been moving upward through the feudal dream. The flair of his powers is now sensing in the thought of the man of today.

* * *

With the great inversion of the Earth and the Sun, brought definitely about by so small an object as a telescope which man in his curiosity invented—created—to extend his power of eyesight and the daring thought —the dream—it stood for; with this shock of inversion definitely began the greatest of man's adventures upon his Earth.

We in present sense and in retrospect call it the MODERN.

The feudal flow poured on, the germ of the modern growing in embryo apace and inexterminable. Inquiry upon inquiry followed; invention upon invention, discovery upon discovery; and wars and more wars, tremors, and the downfall of mighty superstitions; cunning and betrayal raged in abuses of delegated power, institutions rocked, dogma came forth in the open, knife and torch in hand the feudal flow went on in stealth, the modern power grew and ramified; there was calm and there was turbulence; onward flowed the feudal stream with its new arrangements, its new collapses, its new horrors, its new deaths, its new resurrections, as the power of man's self-determination, the assertion of his free spirit, none too articulate as yet, none too sane, clarified in growing strength, its inventions seized upon, its uses turned to abuse, yet goading the feudal power into titanic writhings, fears and dreads, desperations, ruses and stratagems, wars and more wars—the dread phantom of awakening multitudes—the resolve to foster hate.

Yet man the worker, the inquirer, ever pushed onward in hope. Came the printing press, the mariner's compass, the power of steam, railroads, great ships, the discovery and development of new vast hidden riches of earth, the harnessing of the mystical power of electricity, the land telegraph, the ocean cable, the telephone, the growth of libraries, the daily papers, the public schools, the technical schools, the automobile, vast systems of transportation of all kinds, the radio, the aeroplane, the mastery of the air, the mastery of the seas, the mastery of the earth, the increasing mastery of ideas. The immense growth in power of constructive imagination and of the will to do. And all to what end? What may tomorrow and tomorrow bring forth out of blood-stained yesterday and the flowing yesterdays since History's dawn?

The great drama we herein have called the Modern, unique in the story of mankind, beginning with a small telescope, advancing to the radio, to the measurement of the stars, to the searching out of the utterly minute in Life's infinitude of variety, to enormous strides in developments of utility, we may say is in character so eye-opening as to constitute the first act in the drama of the universal education of mankind through a series of imposing object lessons, changing situations, shifting scenes. Also, in that act begins the lifting of veils revealing object lessons coming closer up, and closer, from beneath the surface of feudal repression, and of the savage inertia of superstitions born of the habit of fear, and of unawareness, of dread of the reality of man; object lessons—ever object lessons—crowding upon us.

Among the most startling of these object lessons we are coming to apperceive the significance of choice—its dire or its joyous man-made results. Slowly in consequence comes forth from the hitherto invisible, and shapes before us, a presence no gesture can debar, no noise of words deter—the sublime, the warning, the prophetic image of man as Moral Power.

Thus clarifies in the dawning light of our modern day the fuller meaning, the effulgence of the Democratic Vista; the super-power of Democratic Man.

Moral Power, in the intensity of its choice, in the full exercise of its purpose to create a world of sanity, of beauty and of joy, alone can cause to dissolve and fade into thin air as though it had never been, the baleful feudal superstition of dominion and blood-sacrifice.

This moral power residing in the multitudes and awakening to voice, is what Democracy means.

To envisage Democracy as a mechanical, political system merely, to place faith in it as such, or in any abstraction, is to foster an hallucination, to join in the Dance of Death; to confuse the hand of Esau with the voice of Jacob. The lifting of the eyelids of the World is what Democracy means.

*   *   *

The implications of the Democratic Idea branch into endless ramification of science, of art, of all industrial and social activities of human well-being, through which shall flow the wholesome sap of its urge of self-preservation through beneficence, drawn up from roots running ever deeper and spreading ever finer within the rich soil of human kindness and intelligence. For kindness is the sanest of powers, and by its fruits shall Democracy be known. It is of the antitheses that Feudalism has prepared the way for kindness. Kindness, seemingly so weak, is in fact the name of a great adventure which mankind thus far has lacked the courage, the intelligence, the grit to undertake. Its manly, its heroic aspect has been unknown, by reasons of inverted notions of reality. This form of myopia is of the feudal view.

In place of myopic ideas, democratic modern thought uses clear vision. Clear vision leads to straight thinking, sound thinking to sane action, sane action to beneficent results that shall endure.

In this sense of sound thinking and clean action all sciences, all arts, all activities, become sentimentally, emotionally, dramatically, and constructively imbued with the stirring, the self-propelling impulse of the democratic idea. Therefore they will all hold in common a thought whose inexhaustible power will shape a common end which shall signify in the solidity of its logic fruitful peace and joy on earth, as equally the romance of good will toward men.

*   *   *

Now that we have a clarifying idea of the nature of man and his powers; now that we behold in him that which lies deepest and surest in ourselves, we may suggest the nature of a democratic education.

These things it shall do:

It shall regard the child body, the child mind, the child heart, as a trust.

It shall watch for the first symptom of surviving feudal fear and dissolve it with gentle ridicule while it teaches prudence and the obvious consequences of acts. No child that can toddle bravely is too young to know what choice means, when presented objectively and humanly. Thus it shall teach the nature of choice at the beginning.

It shall allow the child to dream, to give vent to its wondrous imagination, its deep creative instinct, its romance.

It shall recognize that every child is the seat of genius; for genius is the highest form of play with Life's forces.

It shall allow the precious being to grow in its wholesome atmosphere of activities, giving only that cultivation which a careful gardener gives— the children shall be the garden.

It shall utilize the fact that the child mind, in its own way, can grasp an understanding of things and ideas, supposed now in our pride of feudal thought to be beyond its reach.

It shall recognize that the child, undisturbed, feels in its own way the sense of power within it, and about it. That by intuition the child is mystic—close to nature's heart, close to the strength of Earth.

The child thus warded will be a wholesome, happy child. It will forecast the pathway to its maturity.

As from tender age the child grows into robust demonstrative vigor, and ebullition of wanton spirits, the technic of warding will pass by degrees into the technic of training or discipline—bodily, mentally, emotionally; the imagination, the intellect, organized to work together; the process of co-ordination stressed. The idea of the child's natural powers will be suggested a little at a time and shown objectively.

The child by this time is passing out of its reveries; life is glowing, very real, very tangible. So shall its awakening powers be trained in the glowing real, the tangible, the three R's, made glowing and real to it as a part of its world. It is here the difference between welcome work and a task comes into play; the difference between a manikin and a teacher.

Now arrives the stage of pre-adolescence, unromantic urge of hastening vegetative growth; the period of the literal, the bovine, disturbed at times by prophetic reverie. This is the time for literal instruction.

Now comes the stage of adolescence, when the whole being tends to deliquesce into instability, vague idealisms, emotions hitherto unknown or despised, bashfulness, false pride, false courage, introspection, impulsiveness, inhibitions, awkward consciousness of self, yet with an eye clairvoyant to that beauty which it seeks, a stirring in the soul of glory, of adventure, of romance. The plastic age of impressionability, of enthusiasms. Also the Danger Age; the age of extreme susceptibility under cover of indifference in self-protection: The age when thoughts and musings are most secret. The age that makes or breaks.

This is the crisis where democratic education, recognizing it as such, shall attain to its first main objective in fixing sound character, in alert intensive training of the native power to feel straight, to think straight, to act straight, to encourage pride in well-doing, to make so clear the moral nature of choice that the individual may visualize the responsibilities involved in the consequences of choice. To train the imagination in constructive foresight, in the feeling for real things, in the uses of sentiment, of emotion, in the physical and the spiritual joy of living; to stabilize the gregarious into the social sense; to set forth the dignity of the ego and all egos.

This is the time to put on the heavy work, to utilize to the full this suddenly evolving power, the recrudescent power of instinct, to direct this power into worth-while channels, to prepare adolescents to become worthwhile adults, free in spirit, clean in pride, with footing on the solid earth, with social vision clear and true.

The later technical trainings shall be imbued of the same spirit. The varied kinds shall all be set forth as Specialized yet Unified social activities. Science shall be thus understood and utilized, the fine arts shall be thus understood and utilized, the industrial arts, the arts of applied science, and most urgently the science and art of education, all shall thus be understood and utilized as social functions, ministering to the all-inclusive art of creating out of the cruel feudal chaos of cross purposes, a civilization, in equilibrium, for free men conscious of their powers, and with these powers under moral control.

Such civilization shall endure, and even grow in culture, for it shall have a valid moral foundation, understandable to all. It will possess a vigor hitherto undreamed of, a versatility, a virtuosity, a plasticity as yet unknown, for all work will be done with a living purpose, and the powers of mankind shall be utilized to the full, hence there shall be no waste.

No dream, no aspiration, no prophecy can be saner.

Man shall find his anchorage in self-recognition.

Thus broadens and deepens to our comprehension the power and the glory of the Democratic Vista!

Invocation to the Winter God

The following (and final) selection is from *Kindergarten Chats, XLVII*. It is a highly characteristic example of a kind of prose poetry that Sullivan was easily seduced into writing: characteristic both in its literary vices and in its frequent capacity to engage the reader's sympathy by a force of feeling that triumphs over the obsolete rhetoric.

I would be alone, here; alone with that Mighty Spirit which fathers all the seasons, and whose breath is the breath of life and likewise the breath of death.

I would fain talk with the God of this leaden sky, of the leaden snow, of the sombre, silent trees, of this freezing air.

I would fain immerse my spirit in his spirit.

I would fain question God, here, in this wilderness; for my soul is become such a wilderness—a solemn, wintry wilderness in which no voice is heard:

Lord of this vast o'erhanging sky, Lord of the wintry heart, Lord of every sombre tree and pallid snowflake! Why hast thou let a winter fall upon my soul? Why are the seeds of my spirit dormant? Why are the fair flowers of my fancy moribund? Why are the well springs of my heart congealed? Why do they no longer ripple and murmur in sunshine and gladness?

Spirit Sublime! Why hast thou let a winter fall upon the hearts of my countrymen?

Have I not lived for my art?—an art grown up in praise of thee.

Must I then die for it?

And, dying, leave nought behind else a few precarious, scattered seeds, overlaid with the snow—when my heart was so filled with fertility, in thine honor, and in response to thine everlasting glory and power.

Must I repeat the ancient cry: Oh, for a daysman between thee and me!

Mysterious Power, why dost thou bring agony to them that bring forth in thy name?

Why art thou silent as birth, silent as the tomb, when the heart cries out to thee in its extremity of sorrow?

Inscrutable Presence! Why hast thou caused me to know sorrow, 'less it be that my soul shall be pregnant of Sorrow—and give birth from Sorrow?

All-bearing Spirit! Why dost thou suppress my spirit? Why is it locked up and sealed, in winter's ice; as thou dost lock up the violet and the wind-flower in winter's tomb; as the lily and the gentian are rigid and still, under the snow; as all life, here, is so silent under the silent snow?

Do they dream of thee, as my soul dreams of thee in this silence of winter? Or are they, thy children of the woods and fields, soulless, and dreamless under the pallid coverlet of white petals fallen from the sombre garden of the clouds?

The strength of thy spirit is the strength of thy winter which, as a white breath, breathes over the broad earth; for it, also, is the breath of thy spirit. But in my winter is no strength; no spirit; no breath.

For thou are Lord of Death. For Death, also, is the breath of thy spirit. For thou art all in all.

But what is Man! What shall he know of Death, other than to see his shadow, to see his smile!

So little is man, in his understanding, that he knows not whether Death be the child of Life, or Life the child of death.

But thou, Inscrutable Spirit—in thy unfathomable purpose, why leavest thou man to his sorrow as thou leavest him in his joys? Thou disturbest him not in his living death!

Man may see thee, thou seekest not man—but leavest man helpless before the inscrutable mystery of his own soul.

Why dost thou not seek man?

Why dost thou not cross the chasm of his isolation?

Canst thou not cross?

Why dost thou leave man a riddle to himself?

Why dost thou leave man helpless and perplexed before the mysteries of thy works:

Helpless and torpid in the winter of his soul—the emptiness of his mind?

Why hast thou made the soul of man an endless marvel to himself, yet but a speck among the myriad works of thy hand?

Why hast thou sent a night to darken the mind of man, that he has set up gold for god in thy stead?

Why hast thou filled man's eyes with ugliness, that he ignores the endless, radiant beauty of thy works?

Why has thou estopped man's ears, that he hears not, day by day, the beauty of thy voice, the ceaseless melodies thereof?

Why hast thou let man so go astray that he praises thee with lip-praise, not with heart-praise, and the pæans of his spirit, the adoration of his mind, the works of his hand; meanwhile praises he himself with over-praise.

Why abidest thou, in the winter, here silent and grim, imperturbable, passionless, voiceless?

Dost thou speak, and I hear not?

Dost thou call me, and I am unaware?

Unspeakable mystery! Where art thou? What are thou, that thou dost affright and fascinate me here? That I cry out, and the wintry silence alone answers me— that the chill and the torpor alone answer me— that no man, no thing answers me; that mine own soul answers me not! That thou dost answer me not!

Alas! there is no answer; save the merciless and sombre gloom—the falling snow!

So, must I go my way.

So, must I seek my way alone—if way there be.

So, must my soul abide its wintertime.

So, must the tiny, hidden seed of hope await its day.

For man is unto man alone!

God hears him not, God sees him not in his winter—in the fatal winter of his soul—nor does God see him in his springtime—in the springtime of his soul—nor in the summer thereof, nor in the autumn—God sees not man.

Man surely is alone—and so must he be his own and only god— his only god; aside from Thee!